Edited and with an introduction by
Virginia Wright Wexman

Film and Authorship

Rutgers
University
Press
New Brunswick,
New Jersey,
and London

Library of Congress Cataloging-in-Publication Data

Film and authorship / edited and with an introduction by Virginia Wright Wexman.
p.   cm. — (Rutgers depth of field series)
Includes bibliographical references and index.
ISBN 0-8135-3192-6 (alk. paper) — ISBN 0-8135-3193-4 (pbk. : alk. paper).
1. Auteur theory (Motion pictures).   I. Wexman, Virginia Wright.   II. Series.

PN1995.9.A837 F55   2003
791.43'0233'01—dc21   2002024832

British Cataloging-in-Publication data for this book is available from the British Library.

Manufactured in the United States of America

For My Students

Contents

Film and Authorship

Virginia Wright Wexman

Introduction

> *Question:* What's your role, your function, in directing
> a Warhol film?
> *Answer:* I don't know. I'm trying to figure it out.
> —From an interview with Andy Warhol

In a certain sense, the above quotation can be thought of as describing the project of cinema studies during the 1960s, the early years of its establishment in the Academy. Attempts to understand what directors do and how to discuss this work was driven largely by the idea that directors—even many of the directors who worked within the factory-like conditions of the Hollywood industry—should be thought of as the authors of the films they helm. The project of defining just how the principles of authorship should be applied to film analysis occupied much scholarly attention during this period and has continued to drive an array of projects of both a scholarly and popular nature. Books and articles on directors are still being written. Courses on directors are taught. Directors are honored by film festivals. The assumption that directors hold the keys to a film's quality is accepted as a given in most movie reviews. And the Hollywood industry has become increasingly concerned with marketing directors as salable commodities.

Even film theorists continue to speak of directors, though they frequently reformulate the role of these figures by positing them as the source of an unconscious process of textual writing. This directorial function is often disguised under the obfuscatory designation "the film" (as in "the film implies . . .") or masked by such latently passive constructions as "preferred readings," "against the grain readings," and "cultural work." Such locutions set aside the question of how an inert object—a roll of celluloid—could elicit a meaningful aesthetic or ideological response in the absence of a human agent (or agents) assumed to have produced it. Even if we accept the poststructuralist conception of an omnipresent textuality and a fragmented subjectivity that is constantly in flux, we are still left with the presumption of some form of agency which is implicitly understood as having brought a work into existence. Such an agency, however defined, is eminently worthy of examination.

The neglect of authorship that characterized the early years of *ciné*-structuralism during the seventies and eighties led some of those committed to feminist or multicultural agendas to indulge in dark speculations about why this issue had dissolved into a vast sea of textuality just at the moment when the previously marginalized voices of women and people of color were beginning to be heard. Such concerns have led a number of scholars to continue to explore aspects of authorship. Cognizant of the poststructuralist critique of the originary genius, their analyses are more clearly defined, carefully nuanced, and tightly focused than in the past. Some scholars, interested in cognitive approaches, have investigated the ways in which directors function as conscious craftspeople. Others have examined the ways in which authorial discourses within and among filmic texts govern the ways in which they are read. The legal context of copyright ownership and authorial rights have formed yet another area of interest. Many feminists have pursued a psychoanalytic line, examining the ways in which the fantasy lives of female directors are represented in their films. Queer theorists have analyzed motifs of gender and sexuality in the productions of gay film and media artists. Another flourishing line of research examines the contexts in which minority directors have worked and the ways in which these filmmakers have defined and addressed their audiences. The present volume brings some of this work together in order to suggest the rich veins of inquiry that can be tapped when the issue of authorship is openly addressed.

———

Historically, the most influential work on film authors has taken place in the pages of select journals and cultural institutions in France, England, and the United States. The most significant of these is the Parisian publication *Cahiers du Cinéma*. The young critics who clustered around *Cahiers* during the 1950s attacked the prevailing Tradition of Quality in French cinema, a practice based on literate scripts and adaptations of works by established writers. In its place they called for a cinema marked by visual artistry. Drawing inspiration from Alexandre Astruc's 1948 article "The Birth of a New Avant-Garde: The Camera-Pen" and from Jean Epstein's 1921 coinage of the designation *auteur* to refer to a film director, they championed moviemakers who managed to produce visually distinctive films under the constraints of the Hollywood studio system. Articulated most famously in François Truffaut's 1954 article "A Certain Tendency in the French Cinema," the approach was dubbed *la politique des auteurs,* or the policy of looking at films in terms of authors. The thematic preoccupations of auteurs were revealed in what the *Cahiers* critics referred to as *mise-en-scène,* a term designating a film's overall style. Glimpses of an auteur's distinctive mise-en-scène typically appeared within the conventional forms of Hollywood productions only at certain privileged moments; thus critics were encouraged to master the entire body of a director's output (or *oeuvre*) so that a pattern of these privileged moments of personal vision could be discerned. Eric Rohmer, the journal's editor, called this method *"la critique des beautés"* (the appreciation of moments of beauty).

Many of the young *Cahiers* critics were headed for careers as directors themselves; they included such well-known figures of French New Wave cinema as Rohmer, Truffaut, Jean-Luc Godard, Jacques Rivette, and Claude Chabrol. These young Turks acquired an education in the history of world cinema largely through their patronage of the Paris *Cinémathèque,* whose proprietor Henri Langlois had amassed an immense film archive. Armed with this background, they lavished praise on Hollywood directors like Samuel Fuller, Nicholas Ray, Vincente Minnelli, Anthony Mann, Douglas Sirk, and Alfred Hitchcock, as well as on European filmmakers like Max Ophuls, Robert Bresson, and Roberto Rossellini. The stature of these figures was affirmed by the journal's tradition of publishing extended interviews with them. In contrast to the careful detail and reverential tone of these pieces, the critical writing in *Cahiers* tended toward the oracular and the iconoclastic. One member of the group, Luc Mollet, famously declared that "morality is a question of tracking shots"; another, Fereydoun Hoveyda, began an article, "The subject of *Party Girl* is idiotic. So what?"

The *Cahiers* vision of directors as inspired creative geniuses grew out of a view of artists that had come to the fore in the early nineteenth century, so the group's approach subsequently came to be known as "Romantic auteurism." The purpose of the *Cahiers* critics was to elevate the films of a few directors to the status of high art. This introduction of popular cinema into a privileged aesthetic realm came after a decade of debate over what was then called mass culture, a phenomenon commonly dismissed with terms such as "entertainment" and "escapism." Such designations had the effect of excluding movies and other popular diversions from being considered genuine art forms. Arguments of this nature had been advanced most notably by members of the prestigious and influential Frankfurt school. The auteurists countered this discourse by treating gifted directors as transcendent figures who expressed timeless truths and who therefore merited serious critical scrutiny.

The Romantic auteurist approach was brought to America by Andrew Sarris, whose contribution helped consolidate the impact of the movement. Sarris's writings in the journal *Film Culture* during the early 1960s were published in his book *The American Cinema* in 1968. There he ranked two hundred directors, with an emphasis on Hollywood filmmakers, including brief appreciations of each; the top echelon consisted of Charlie Chaplin, Robert Flaherty, John Ford, D. W. Griffith, Howard Hawks, Alfred Hitchcock, Buster Keaton, Fritz Lang, Ernst Lubitsch, F. W. Murnau, Max Ophuls, Jean Renoir, Josef von Sternberg, and Orson Welles. Sarris's suggestive comments on the visual techniques of a range of cinematic auteurs, combined with his awe-inspiring command of the whole of film history, made his work widely admired, especially among the new generation of cinephiles then coming of age in the youth culture spawned in American universities during the late 1960s and early 1970s. A 2001 festschrift entitled *Citizen Sarris*, edited by *Variety* critic Emmanuel Levy and featuring contributions by many of the nation's leading film reviewers and filmmakers, including Leonard Maltin, Richard Schickel, and John Sayles, re-emphasized in the twenty-first century how enduring Sarris's influence has been.

The *Cahiers* initiative also inspired a group of young British film lovers at Oxford University including Robin Wood, Ian Cameron, and Victor Perkins. The group's journal, *Movie,* which began publication in 1962, was devoted to lengthy auteurist analyses of Hollywood cinema and interviews with filmmakers. Steeped in the then-dominant New Criticism with its emphasis on close readings of literary texts, the *Movie* group provided auteurism with a solid grounding by producing detailed appreciations of selected films by favored Hollywood directors. Ian Cameron wrote, "We believe our method is likely to produce criticism which is closer, not just to objective description of the film itself, but to the spectator's experience of the film" (Caughie 52).[1]

During the late 1960s and early 1970s the British Film Institute's Educational Division gave birth to a more theoretically ambitious form of auteurism known as "auteur-structuralism" to distinguish it from Romantic auteurism. Drawing on the work of linguist Ferdinand de Saussure on language and anthropologist Claude Levi-Strauss on myth, this approach identified the style of a given director with a series of structuring oppositions that recurred throughout his or her oeuvre. The scientific model behind such readings allowed the auteur-structuralist critics to practice a descriptive mode of analysis that moved them beyond the impressionistic declarations of value that characterized Romantic auteurism. Peter Wollen's essay on John Ford and Geoffrey Nowell-Smith's book on Luchino Visconti were the most widely admired examples of this method. Wollen saw Ford's cinema as one preoccupied with the contrasts between such opposing terms as garden/wilderness, settler/nomad, book/gun, plowshare/sabre, East/West, civilized/savage, and European/Indian. He argued that the director's development could be measured in terms of the ways in which these oppositions shifted. For example, in an early Ford work like *Stagecoach* (1939), the civilization/savage pair could be equated with European/Indian; but by the time Ford made *Cheyenne Autumn* in 1962, the terms had been reversed: Indian now appeared in the civilized part of the chart, while European was equated with savagery.

Meanwhile, *Cahiers* itself underwent a transformation. By the late 1960s most of the critics who had made the journal internationally famous had left. But a new set of voices took their place, led by editors Jean-Louis Commolli, Jean Narboni, and Jean-Pierre Oudart. Deeply affected by the Utopian ideals that characterized the international youth culture during these years, especially the sentiments fueling the mass student uprisings in France during May 1968, the new *Cahiers* editors were both more intellectual and more political than their predecessors. Where the earlier group had produced brief ripostes, the new critics wrote dense theoretical tracts and extended readings of selected films. Adapting the theories of French intellectuals like Louis Althusser (on Marxism) and Jacques Lacan (on psychoanalysis), they emerged with an approach to Hollywood cinema that sought to reconcile its commercialism with their own radicalism. After creating a series of categories into which they could place all cinematic works, they focused their attention on their "E" category. The "E" category was made up of films which, though conventional and even conservative on the surface, contained a submerged radical discourse. The *Cahiers* critics attributed this discourse to the stylistic "writing" (or *écriture*) of the films' directors. The past, however, was not entirely left behind; the directors whose works were placed in the "E" category remained much the same group as those singled out by the original auteur critics.

The new generation of *Cahiers* theorists conducted a series of impressively original and persuasive analyses of "E" category films, including most famously an essay on Ford's *Young Mr. Lincoln*. In the *Cahiers* reading of this film, the director emerged as a subversive force who wove a subtle tapestry of sexually-charged motifs throughout the cinematic text. These motifs cast the hero as an atavistic figure who transcends politics and thereby (presumably) undercut the reactionary politics embedded in the script. Another prominent French critic, Raymond Bellour, added his own twist to this approach by producing a series of interpretive essays on Alfred Hitchcock's oeuvre analyzing what Bellour termed the "enunciative presence" of the director within the films. This presence makes itself felt through both Hitchcock's customary cameo appearances and his revealing use of point-of-view editing techniques.

The model underlying such readings conceptualized authorship as an unconscious process. In place of the knowing transcendent genius enshrined by the Romantic auteurists, the new generation of French critics theorized the auteur as a force-field of libidinous energies whose presence could subvert the surface meanings of a given filmic text. Such energies had social as well as psychic determinants and were highly unstable. Influenced by Barthes's "The Death of the Author," the new *Cahiers* critics viewed textual meaning as emanating not from self-conscious authors, but from readers and spectators. To construct these meanings, one could rely only on the text itself—language—rather than a deliberative being who communicated with a clear intention in mind. Barthes describes the author as a "scriptor" rather than a creator. "The modern *scriptor* is born simultaneously with the text," he states; "he is in no way equipped with a being preceding or exceeding the writing, is not the subject with the book as predicate; there is no other time than that of the enunciation, and every text is eternally written *here and now* . . . the hand, cut off from any voice, borne by a pure gesture of inscription (and not of expression), traces a field without origin—or which, at least, has no other origin but language itself, language which ceaselessly calls into question all origins" (*Image-Music-Text* 145–46). Foucault's complementary formulation in his essay "What Is an Author?" characterized the figure of the originary author inspired by a mystical spark of creativity as a historical phenomenon, not an eternal verité. Foucault asserted that authors have come to be associated with certain categories of privileged texts because the presence of such figures supports a culture in which individual expression has become an ideological cornerstone.

The new *Cahiers* project that this theoretical agenda represented was subsequently adopted as the program of *Screen*, a journal sponsored in part by the British Film Institute and edited by a group that included Ben Brewster, Ed Buscombe, Pam Cook, Christine Gledhill, Stephen Heath,

Claire Johnston, Colin MacCabe, Laura Mulvey, Geoffrey Nowell-Smith, Sam Rohdie, Paul Willemen, and Peter Wollen. All were committed to the new critical agenda that the *Cahiers* critics had proposed. At the same time, *Screen* perpetuated the auteurist tradition by publishing interviews with directors like Douglas Sirk and Pier Paolo Pasolini as well as special issues on Jean-Marie Straub, Nagisa Oshima, and Jean-Luc Godard (himself a member of the original group around *Cahiers*). Arguably the most influential work to come out of the new British initiative was Mulvey's 1975 essay "Visual Pleasure and Narrative Cinema," which mapped a Lacanian reading method onto a feminist political agenda. Mulvey argues that all narrative films are built around an opposition between a voyeuristic male gaze and a woman's body exhibited for its pleasure. The threat of castration inherent in this psychoanalytic scenario invariably leads to one of two textual strategies: a sadistically-oriented filmmaker like Hitchcock typically punishes the woman, while a fetishist like von Sternberg either adds decorative clutter to the female form or dismembers it by means of repeated cuts to close-ups of body parts. Mulvey's essay occasioned innumerable follow-up commentaries and analyses of an endless number of films using the schema she had proposed.

———

It now appears that Andy Warhol's confusion was prescient, for as recent theoretical critiques have made clear, authorship is not a simple concept. Are directors to be thought of as social agents, psychic scribes, or spectator-induced fictions? Are they conscious craftspeople, bundles of libidinous energies, or cultural conduits? Do they express their preoccupations though stylistic motifs, narrational strategies, idiosyncratic character types, self-reflexive cameos, or structuring oppositions? How do they function in relation to the industrial, sociopolitical, and legal contexts in which they work? One can speak of "biographical authors," a designation that has spawned an enduring publishing industry in the form of books and articles documenting filmmakers' lives. A closely related concept is that of the "biographical legend": as theorized by Boris Tomashevsky, this approach focuses on discourses circulated about authors which affect the reception of their works. Yet another conceptual framework is that of the "implied author," the governing presence behind a work that is understood by spectators as the source of textual effects, an idea put forward by Wayne Booth and others.

Many of the most widely recognized approaches to authorship have been developed with traditional art forms in mind. When confronted with filmic or televisual works, critics are faced with special difficulties. Such texts are typically produced by groups, not individuals. Many are generated as part of gargantuan business enterprises in which the value of financial as well as aesthetic contributions must be weighed. Further, the technological resources that are mobilized in movie production raise the problem of distinguishing artists from technicians. In addition, films readily lend themselves to conceptualizations casting them as mechanical reproductions of a pre-existing reality rather than as humanly crafted expressions of the imagination. Moreover, as Walter Benjamin has pointed out, a film—unlike traditional forms of visual art, such as painting—exists not as a unique original object, but as a series of copies created from a negative functioning as a matrix. Finally, in contrast to high art forms such as poetry and painting, most films and television productions are intended to appeal to mass audiences who may lack the specialized educational backgrounds that could enable them to appreciate subtleties of style and imagery.

Even in the case of members of moviemaking teams who hold an unequivocal status as artists rather than businesspeople or technicians, the allocation of authorship credit remains a contested issue. Despite the designation of the spaces in which Hollywood films are created as studios, most such spaces are more nearly comparable to factories. (John Ford, for example, once complained to his boss Darryl F. Zanuck that he felt himself to be "a piece-goods worker in the Hollywood sweatshops."[2]) Many commentators accept this characterization of Hollywood, arguing that movies made there during the heyday of the old-style studio era should be regarded as collective endeavors and analyzed accordingly. Others believe that one or another of the participants in the studio-based filmmaking process deserves greater recognition as a decisive authorial force that may, at times, determine a given movie's success. The Hollywood industry awards its Oscars for best picture to a film's producer. In *The Hollywood Screenwriters*, Richard Corliss pleads the cause of writers as the most important authors of many American feature films. Industry references to productions as "star vehicles" suggests the central position actors occupy in the creation of large numbers of films as, from a different perspective, do the star-centered textual reading strategies practiced by many members of the gay community. Other members of a movie's creative team have also been put forward as significant authors: for example, editors (Verna Fields, *Jaws;* Walter Murch, *The Conversation*), cinematographers (Gabriel Figueroa, *María Candelaria;* James Wong Howe, *The Sweet Smell of Success*), and production designers (Natacha Rambova,

Salome; William Cameron Menzies, *Gone With the Wind*). In most cases, however, directors are taken to be the crucial creative force involved in the filmmaking process, even in Hollywood cinema, because directors manage a movie's production and thus exercise the most control over its overall style.

Authorship is a historical phenomenon. Moreover, as Foucault and many other scholars have pointed out, the impulse to personalize artistic creation is closely related to the importance of individualism within Western culture and has become a concept anchoring modern understandings of aesthetic value. As Pierre Bourdieu has put the matter, in today's world "art is what is created by artists." Societies that are historically and culturally removed from this value system typically lack such a notion of the aesthetic, upholding instead traditions of craft, protocol, and the sacred, which celebrate collective enterprise and social custom rather than individual endeavor and cultural innovation. Even in Western society, authorship is a fragmentary and fleeting convention. Further, the meaning of the term "author" has varied over time. During the medieval period, for instance, *auctors* (as authors were then called) were thought to derive their authority from the wisdom of the past and ultimately from God. The modern concept of originary authorship emerged in the early nineteenth century with the Romantic notion of the creative genius nurtured by an inner spark of inspiration; as we have seen, the auteurists drew on this formulation to position Hollywood directors as part of the pantheon of high culture.

Film directors, like other authors, have not always existed. As Helen Kritch Chinoy has shown, in the nineteenth century theater the directorial role emerged to fill the gap that was created when plays were no longer able to draw on a reliable store of common traditions to encode their meanings. In this absence, the unifying hand of a director could bring together the diverse elements of a stage production into a unique— and personal—statement. Once the role of the director had been consecrated in the world of theater, a model existed for filmmakers, who eventually assumed a position of far greater authorial power than they had ever known in the theatrical context. Yet the model of the director-author imposed itself in the motion picture world only gradually and still operates unevenly, carrying different valences in different cinema cultures.

In America, D. W. Griffith was able, at the beginning of the twentieth century, to assert his authority over a filmmaking process that had previously been dominated by cameramen because he could claim to have played a crucial role in the development of stylistic strategies out of which cinematic narrative was born. In the wake of Griffith's success and the efforts of many others, directors as a group gained considerable power and prestige during the silent era. However, they were increasingly opposed by the Hollywood studios, and by the 1930s their authority had waned. Toward the end of the decade, though, the directors improved their situation by uniting to form the Directors Guild of America, which fought for directorial control over all phases of the filmmaking process. The DGA also promoted the ideal of directors as Romantic artists by taking control of credit allocation, insisting in virtually every case that only one director could sign each film and thereby aligning directorial signatures with the mythology of the solitary genius. Today the stock of Hollywood directors is high. The turn to independent production in the 1950s gave all top-ranked film artists—and especially directors—more power to pick and choose projects and to control them from beginning to end. Moreover, by the 1970s the popularity of the international art cinema, which featured highly individualistic directorial stylists like Ingmar Bergman, Akria Kurosawa, and Michelangelo Antonioni, had given rise to a competing crop of European-edged American talents like Robert Altman, Francis Ford Coppola, and Martin Scorsese.

In the filmmaking traditions of other nations, directorial control has rarely been a subject of serious debate. The cinema cultures of Europe and Japan have generally looked to the model of authorship in the older arts for guidance; for the most part these industries have placed directors in leadership positions, positioning their productions as the expressions of filmmaker-artists. The creative freedom enjoyed by such directors has resulted in a tradition of art cinema which flourished from the 1910s on. During the 1920s names like F. W. Murnau and Ernst Lubitsch became widely known throughout the world. Hollywood has put its own spin on the European tradition of authorial control by touting its productions as entertainment that can provide audiences with an experience of uncomplicated pleasure, implicitly characterizing the art cinema from abroad as a difficult and demanding form produced by ambitious artists rather than crowd-pleasing entertainers. Tellingly, such discourses have the effect of marginalizing foreign films in the marketplace.

Despite its enviable tradition of directorial autonomy, international cinema has been increasingly plagued by its tangled relationship to nationalist agendas. Foreign filmmakers have historically been the beneficiaries of government policies designed to promote patriotism at home and a favorable national image abroad, typically through generous subsidies and protectionist legislation designed to limit the incursions of Hollywood into the local marketplace. Yet few of the moviemakers so favored have enjoyed unproblematic relations with their home cultures. Directors like Sayajit Ray, along with the major figures of the New German and Fifth Generation Chinese cinema, have aimed their output at the international film festival circuit, exporting auteur names and images of exotic cultures to a global audience while largely bypassing the public in their home countries. Other filmmakers, especially in Third World nations, have attempted to speak to local peasant or proletarian culture from positions of bourgeois privilege. Some have used state funds to create a cinema critical of the status quo. Many directors have responded to the growing trend toward international coproductions by creating films in which touristic motifs coexist in a pastiche with nationalist agendas, creating a hybrid "glocal" cinema. Often denigrated with labels like "Europuddings" and "National Geographic Cinema," such films employ a polyphonous rhetoric that allows their authors to speak to both a global art house market and a local constituency.

The avant-garde cinema, with its artisanal modes of production, its intensely individualistic conventions of stylistic expression, and its association with museums, universities and other bastions of high culture, has drawn freely on the model of authorship associated with the traditional arts. Like lyric poems or abstract expressionist paintings, most such productions announce themselves as personal expressions of the filmmaker's innermost feelings. This tendency, however, is not universal among the avant-garde directors. The art world's unceasing quest for innovation and iconoclastic breakthroughs has given rise to contrarian independent filmmakers as well, such as the impassive Andy Warhol.

The phenomenon of television presents yet another set of issues. As Horace Newcomb and Robert S. Alley argue in *The Producer's Medium*, in the United States television producers, who are often also the chief writers of the shows they oversee, call the shots. Directors, by contrast, are typically called in only to oversee individual episodes of series in which the visual style must remain consistent; hence they wield little power over the look of programs they helm: "the television producer is the creative center who shapes, through choices big and small, works of television that speak of personal values and decisions" (12). Even in the realm of publicly funded television, which lacks the formulaic straightjackets and commercial interruptions which shape the structures of American network programming, tv auteurs are frequently frustrated in their attempts to assert the rights of authorship by an intransigent hierarchy of executives often blind to their goals and needs.

In both cinema and television an honored tradition of collective authorship has long flourished. Though the Hollywood studios—capitalist institutions par excellence—have produced the most widely-known examples of such collaborative art, more Utopian agendas drive other group-centered endeavors. In the United States left-leaning documentary filmmakers such as Chicago's Kartemquin group have thrived. On the international scene similar Marxist-inflected collaborative practices have emerged as well, frequently having been inspired by the work and writings of Bertolt Brecht and Jean-Luc Godard. In Latin America, the *Ciné Liberation* group formulated the concept of a "Third Cinema," opposed to both Hollywood (the "First Cinema") and the auteur films of the European tradition (the "Second Cinema"). In place of these models, the *Ciné Liberation* espoused a collective practice that even included audiences. The monumental documentary *Hour of the Furnaces*, co-directed by Fernando Solanas and Octavio Getino in Argentina in 1968, was created out of this conviction. After the first of the three parts was publicly screened, the audience's suggestions were incorporated in the second and third parts.

Most recently, poststructuralist understandings of creative endeavor as diffuse and culturally conditioned have resulted in a body of films that downplay authorial originality by foregrounding intertextuality. Such productions present their makers not as originary artists but as transmitters of cultural knowledge. They may feature images and storylines that constitute homages to past filmmakers, a strategy practiced by directors like Brian de Palma, Jean-Luc Godard, Sally Potter, Wim Wenders, Rainer Werner Fassbinder, and Robert Altman. Even shot-by-shot remakes of admired films have been produced, including Gus Van Sant's *Psycho* and Jill Godmilow's *What Faroki Taught*. By thus deconstructing authorial omnipotence, the directors of such works are willingly relinquishing a position of power that has evolved over centuries. Paradoxically, these anti-authorial gestures have emerged as popular discourses of authorship have achieved unprecedented currency.

―――――

All new work on film authorship owes a great debt to the superb anthology on this topic published by the British Film Institute in 1981. The volume's editor, John Caughie, pulled together an impressive array of scholarship on the subject and interwove this material with thoughtful and informative introductions. Now, more than twenty years later, however, new scholarship has been produced, and there is reason for scholars in the field of media studies to focus again on the topic of authorship. *Theories of Authorship*, published at the height of the era of high theory, emphasized structuralist and poststructuralist treatments of the subject. Because Caughie's anthology remains in print, I have avoided reproducing work that appears there. Instead, the present collection offers examples of the broad array of approaches that have emerged since that time. Caughie identified three areas that, while offering productive research possibilities, were then underrepresented by scholarship of value: the relationship between authors and institutions, the historical context of authorship, and the ways in which authorship functions in avant-garde cinema and documentary filmmaking. All of these emerging areas are covered in this volume.

Any collection of this sort must begin with an example of the landmark work done by Andrew Sarris. Sarris's essay, "The Auteur Theory Revisited," written for *American Film* in 1976, looks back at his groundbreaking 1968 book *The American Cinema* and its seminal introduction, which had originally appeared in *Film Culture* in 1962. Here Sarris recapitulates the guiding principles of the politique des auteurs, which he had adapted from *Cahiers du Cinéma*. "For the hard-core *auteurist*," he writes, "the hitherto despised Hollywood movies could be judged as high art." The essay defends this approach against attacks by critics like *New Yorker* writer Pauline Kael, novelist Gore Vidal, and art historian Lawrence Alloway, who argued that auteurism denigrated the contributions of screenwriters and inappropriately classified movies as high art rather than popular culture.

Colin MacCabe's essay, "The Revenge of the Author," revises Sarris's transcendental formulation by redefining authorship as a negotiation between directors and their audiences. MacCabe conceives of audiences as either actual or hypothetical; they consist, in the first instance, of the filmmaker's various collaborators. Speaking as someone immersed in the high theoretical explorations of the group involved with *Screen* as well as a participant in the actual activity of moviemaking by virtue of his position as the former head of production for the British Film Institute, MacCabe uses the model of director-audience interaction to reconcile the concept of dispersed subjectivity posited by poststructuralism with the material realities of the production process. In his view, the author should be seen as "a contradictory movement within a collectivity rather than a homogeneous, autonomous, and totalizing subject." MacCabe thus offers a more tentative and provisional view of authorship than that proffered by the auteurists.

David Bordwell's essay, "Authorship and Narration in Art Cinema," focuses not on the production process but on the films themselves. He traces the ways in which codes of authorship function in the modernist international art cinema that came to the fore in the 1960s. Bordwell argues that this art cinema constitutes a distinct mode defining itself against Hollywood filmmaking in part by foregrounding its authors, who typically both write and direct. Audiences and critics rely on ideas about these guiding presences to enable them to read the loose narratives and ambiguities that characterize such films. "To [the] personalization of creation, the director as artist," Bordwell states, "there corresponded certain narrational aspects which critics could highlight."

The ways in which gender-related fantasy scenarios affect the cinematic practices of female directors is the subject of Kaja Silverman's essay, "The Female Authorial Voice." Like Bordwell, Silverman is concerned with the ways in which audiences read filmic texts, but she relates this process to the spectator's identification with the libidinal economy of gendered authors. Working from a Lacanian theoretical framework, she argues that women filmmakers harbor gender-related fantasies that may be represented in their works in the form of what she terms "nodal points" or "authorial spoors": sounds, images, scenes, places, or actions to which a given director's oeuvre repeatedly returns.

Judith Mayne is similarly concerned with the ways in which audiences are encouraged to read signs of an author's sexual identity through filmic texts. Mayne's essay, "A Parallax View of Lesbian Authorship," focuses on the films and videos of lesbian directors, arguing that such works challenge conventional assumptions about gender paradigms. Many media works produced by lesbians showcase irreconcilable conceptions of sexual identity which are held in tension as a way of both acknowledging and critiquing the status quo. Mayne writes, "the lesbian author is defined as complicit in and resistant to the sexual fictions of patriarchal culture, and . . . lesbian irony holds competing definitions of lesbianism up to each other, while refusing to collapse one into the other."

The anthology's second section focuses on the institutional contexts in which authorship functions. Thomas Schatz's essay on Hollywood studio filmmaking, which begins the section, argues that an emphasis on auteurs obscures the shaping role of what André Bazin called "the genius of the system." Producers and executives like Darryl Zanuck, Hal Wallis,

David Selznick, and Irving Thalberg, who coordinated the distinctive styles of their respective studios, deserve much of the credit for productions like *The Bride of Frankenstein* and *The Story of Louis Pasteur;* but, Schatz argues, in the final analysis, it was the system itself, with its atmosphere of struggle and negotiation, that ultimately made such films work. "What's remarkable about Hollywood," he writes, "is that such varied and contradictory forces were held in equilibrium for so long."

Timothy Corrigan's essay, "The Commerce of Auteurism," updates Schatz's examination of Hollywood filmmaking by analyzing the ways in which the American movie industry in the post–studio era has learned to market the names of directors to the public, "address[ing] the potential cult status of an auteur." Despite their differences as filmmakers, Corrigan argues, all directors who participate in this culture "have had to give up their authority as authors and begin to communicate as simply figures within the commerce of that image." Using the career of Francis Ford Coppola as his main example, Corrigan shows how Coppola has used interviews, in particular, to advance an image of himself as alternately controlling the industry in which he works and being swallowed up by it.

The issues that face directors functioning outside of the Hollywood industry are taken up in Marvin D'Lugo's essay, "Transnational Film Authors." D'Lugo argues that such directors, in particular those currently working in Latin America, must manage any number of conflicting agendas, including those of the funding entities on which they rely, the nations they represent, and, not least, their own. Increasingly in recent years, these divergent imperatives have included a mandate to appeal to an international market. Directors who find themselves caught in this web of contradictory demands have frequently resolved their dilemma by designing multivocal filmic texts that can speak to audiences around the world through universalized formulas like melodrama, while simultaneously containing submerged discourses that are readable by a regional constituency in what D'Lugo terms "a dialectic of the global and the local."

Chon Noriega's essay, "'Our Own Institutions': the Geopolitics of Chicano Professionalism," builds on D'Lugo's discussion by documenting the ways in which independent Chicano film and videomakers in the United States must strike a balance between their own political aims and the realities of a financing context that includes granting agencies and public television. To clarify their goals in the midst of an atmosphere of frustration and compromise, these directors have drawn sustenance from transnational initiatives, especially those involving their interaction with Latin American filmmakers at international festivals. "Chicano cinema both juxtaposed and straddled two locations, America and América," Noriega states, "not so much as a matter of an either/or choice (even though it was presented and debated as such), but rather as an attempt to define tightly-coupled oppositional terms—nationalism and assimilation; revolution and reform—so that the one would inevitably produce the other."

The final essay in this section, Marjut Salokannel's "Cinema in Search of Its Authors," addresses the interaction between media artists and the law. The contrasting understandings of authorship embedded in the distinction between the European doctrine of authors' rights and the Anglo-American principles of copyright and works for hire have significant ramifications for the ways in which media artists can function. These opposing juridical regimes also reflect the ways in which their respective cultures conceptualize media products in relation to traditional models of art. "In the civil law doctrine [of continental Europe]," Salokannel writes, "the subject of protection is the person creating the work, the author, and what is protected is the author's specific economic manifestations, whereas in the copyright system [of the United States] the work is protected as marketable merchandise having only economic relevance to its creators."

The book's final section consists of case studies of directorial figures whose careers exemplify specific problems in relation to the larger issue of film authorship. Tom Gunning's essay, "D. W. Griffith: Historical Figure, Film Director, and Ideological Shadow," documents the ways in which Griffith struggled in the early days of moviemaking to establish both his own reputation and the preeminence of the role of the director. Griffith positioned himself as the author responsible for the artistic merit of the productions he directed at the Biograph Company by publicizing his achievement as the primary creator of the filmic narrative system that came to be known as the classical Hollywood style. "As the narrator system highlighted the filmic narrator with new clarity," Gunning states, "it also allowed the emergence of the concept of the film director as author." Gunning further argues that such a claim to authorship was a function of larger developments in the film industry itself. "The integrative and dominant role of the director at Biograph was not the result of the force of Griffith's personality," he writes, "but the product of an industrywide redefinition of the film commodity through a new emphasis on film as a fictional dramatic medium."

Cecil B. DeMille, also working to establish a career in filmmaking in these early days, grappled with quite a different set of problems. Coming from a legendary theatrical family and having worked for the distinguished Broadway producer David Belasco, DeMille brought considerable cultural capital with him to the profession of filmmaking, as Sumiko Higashi's essay, "Cecil B. DeMille and Highbrow Culture," shows. Using the DeMille name and the names of other high-culture figures such as opera star Geraldine Farrar, the young Cecil attempted to recreate the image of movies—and especially his own movies—in the minds of American audiences as high art during the mid-to-late 'teens. But he had difficulty specifying what his role should be. After experimenting with a number of different job titles, he ultimately assumed that of director. Subsequently, with the help of former Belasco set designer Wilfred Buckland, DeMille devised a heavily chiaroscuroed system of illumination he called "Rembrandt lighting," which he used to distinguish his early productions from those of others and align his practice with the traditions of high art. By means of this strategy he was able to fashion a place for himself as an artist in the minds of the American public.

The independent African-American auteur Oscar Micheaux operated in a milieu far removed from the studio settings of mainstream moviemakers, functioning as kind of a one-man band who wrote, directed, distributed, and marketed his films virtually singlehandedly. The essay by Pearl Bowser and Louise Spence, "Writing Himself into History: Oscar Micheaux," describes the way in which, during the course of his career, Micheaux created a persona that served as a model of self-help heroism for his black audiences. Micheaux accomplished this feat of self-creation in the face of the many inconsistencies that surrounded the project by fashioning a legend about his life and by inserting authorial surrogates within his films to elaborate it. Micheaux developed this biographical legend despite the many contradictions it posed in an attempt to articulate a vision of himself that would serve both his self-expressive and entrepreneurial aspirations.

Finally, David James's essay, "The Filmmaker as Poet: Stan Brakhage," examines the career of a figure who, perhaps more than any other, translated the Romantic conception of authorship into filmmaking. Profoundly influenced by the examples set by the pioneering avant-gardist Maya Deren and the modernist poet Charles Olson, Brakhage created deeply personal, often abstract films that eschewed the formulaic distractions of narrative to focus on the inner life of their maker. "The installation of the filmmaker as a *poet*," James writes, "had . . . both theoretical and practical components. It involved a conceptualization of the film artist as an individual author, a Romantic creator—a conceptualization made possible by manufacturing a tradition of such out of previous film history; and it necessitated a working organization, a mode of production and distribution, alternative to the technology, labor practices, and institutional insertion of Hollywood."

Like most films, this book has many authors. I am grateful for the cooperation of all of those whose essays are included here; several reworked previously published materials to fit the format of this anthology. A conversation with Ben Brewster was invaluable in clarifying for me some aspects of the history of scholarly work on film authorship—though I suspect Ben would not be unhappy if I were to stipulate that he should not be held responsible for any remaining inaccuracies or distortions in my treatment of this topic. My research assistants for this project, Jennifer Rupert and Jeff Gore, have been tremendously helpful, as have my editors Charles and Mirella Affron and Robert Lyons, as well as Leslie Mitchner, the editor at Rutgers. The continued patience and support of all of these authorial collaborators is greatly appreciated. Grants from UIC's Institute for the Humanities allowed me time off to develop this volume as well as funds for travel and to support research assistants. I must also extend special thanks to my husband John Huntington, whose contributions to this project, as to all others I have engaged in, are incalculable. Finally, I want to acknowledge the invaluable enrichment I have received from interactions with my students over the years; this book is dedicated to them.

NOTES

1. All references in the text refer to citations in the bibliography at the end of this volume.

2. Dan Ford, *Pappy: The Life of John Ford* (Englewood Cliffs, N.J.: Prentice-Hall, 1979), 211.

Theoretical
Statements

Andrew Sarris

The Auteur Theory Revisited

One would think that after so many years of furious controversy there would be no need for another article on the auteur theory. Yet all sorts of scholarly books and articles continue to disseminate an astounding amount of misinformation on the origin and evolution of auteurism. What to do? Having been officially credited or blamed for bringing the words *auteur, auteurism,* and *auteurist* into the English language, I seem to be stuck with these tar-baby terms for the rest of my life. My own previous writings on the subject have been compiled in *The Primal Screen,* a little-read volume that came out in 1973. "Notes on the Auteur Theory in 1962" first appeared in *Film Culture,* "Notes on the Auteur Theory in 1970" followed in *Film Comment,* and so now in 1977 a pattern of periodicity seems to justify my current endeavor. Also, auteurism seems to have become a scapegoat for just about every cultural affliction associated with the cinema.

For example, Gore Vidal (in the April *American Film*) associates auteurism with the deification of directors over writers in the movie-making process. Speaking of Renoir's "great heist" of *The Southerner,* Vidal explains: "Renoir was a man who had great trouble speaking English, much less writing it, and the script was written by William Faulkner. According to Zachary Scott, who acted in it, Faulkner really liked the script and would have been pleased to have had the credit. But Renoir so muddled the business that the credit finally read: 'Screenplay by Jean Renoir.'"

Unfortunately, Vidal neglects to mention that *The Southerner* was adapted from a novel entitled *Hold Autumn in Your Hand* by George Sessions Perry, the forgotten man in the anti-Renoir, pro-Faulkner anecdote. Who was George Sessions Perry? I have no idea, and neither, apparently, does Vidal. He is (or was) a veteran of the vast army of virtually anonymous authors who have supplied so many of the stories on the screen. Vidal's

From *American Film* 2, no. 9 (July/August 1977). Reprinted by permission of the American Film Institute.

anecdote implies that Faulkner thought up the story of *The Southerner* all by himself, and Renoir then stole the script and "muddled" it, whatever that means. The anecdote loses something if Faulkner is revealed as the middleman in the screenwriting process. Until Vidal is prepared to research how much Faulkner's script owes to Perry's novel, the indictment of Renoir as a plagiarist must be thrown out for lack of evidence. Besides, Renoir's reputation does not rest excessively on *The Southerner* any more than Faulkner's reputation rests on his screenplays, credited or uncredited.

Both Renoir and Faulkner must be evaluated in terms of the total context of their careers. This is one of the basic assumptions of auteurism, one that we have always taken for granted in literature, music, and the fine arts, but one that came very late to cinema because of the lack of archival facilities. Hence, film history existed long before there were qualified historians to appraise it. It might be said that the early auteurists discovered so many lost and forgotten treasures in the cinemathèques[1] that a theory of history was thrust upon them. They then suggested thematic and stylistic hypotheses which they sought to establish with the proof of a pattern of achievement. But movies were still alive and kicking, and individual careers were still evolving. Some auteurists had placed their bets on Hawks and Hitchcock, others on Renoir and Rossellini. Violent debates ensued between the partisans of Mizoguchi and Kurosawa, Dreyer and Bergman, Antonioni and Fellini, Walsh and Losey. No auteurist completely agreed with any other.

"The auteur theory itself," I wrote back in 1962, "is a pattern theory in constant flux." Despite all my disclaimers, qualifications, and reservations, however, a composite image of the auteurist emerged in anti-auteurist writings. Auteurists were invariably male (at least according to Pauline Kael).[2] They never bathed because it took time away from their viewing of old movies. They shared a preposterous passion for Jerry Lewis. They preferred trash to art. They encouraged the younger generation not to read books.

Vidal himself seeks to establish a dialectical confrontation between the word and the image: "Movies are stories; only writers can tell stories. So the wrong people are making the movies." It might be argued by the defenders of directors that movies are stories told primarily through pictures, or, at least, movies *should* be stories told primarily through pictures. Vidal has an answer for that, too: "We do need the cameraman, the editor. But above all we need the script."

Vidal's position is not particularly audacious for Hollywood. One can imagine the ghosts of the old Hollywood moguls nodding in agreement with Vidal's summary dismissal of directors. All you need to make a good movie is a good story. Everybody on the Bel Air circuit knows *that*. A few years ago *Esquire* published a screenplay entitled *Two-Lane Blacktop* with a come-on across the cover to the effect that this was going to be the best movie of the year. When the critics and public failed to concur with *Esquire*'s prediction, the magazine sheepishly shifted the blame to director Monte Hellman, accusing him of being an auteur. Actually, *Two-Lane Blacktop* was not a bad movie. Choking on the exhaust fumes of the more vulgar and more violent *Easy Rider,* it never caught on at the box office with its subtly modernist malaise, and a brilliant performance by Warren Oates was wasted. This is one of the problems in resolving arguments between auteurists and anti-auteurists: The two sides can never agree entirely on what is good and what is bad. In opposition to the horror stories of Gore Vidal and Rex Reed, there is even a small cult for the movie version of *Myra Breckenridge*.[3]

If one were to examine the pertinent texts of the fifties, the sixties, or the seventies, one would be hard put to find a single generalization in auteurist criticism sweeping enough to justify the simplistic attacks made against it. For one thing, auteurism did not evolve in a vacuum. In the beginning, particularly, its preoccupation with visual structure and personal style was largely a reaction against the sloganized vocabulary of social significance and socialist realism. The open-minded and open-hearted French attitude toward myth and genre enable a new generation of American critics to rediscover and reclaim the American cinema. Suddenly there was credit to parcel out for Hollywood's long-despised output, whereas before the auteurists there was only blame. After years on the front lines, my own attitude to the auteurist controversy may have been summed up in the defiant words sung by the late Edith Piaf: "*Non, non, je ne regrette rien.*"

Still, if I had to do it all over again, I would reformulate the auteur theory with a greater emphasis on the tantalizing mystery of style than on the romantic agony of the artists. Why, I wondered back in the mid-fifties, had so many Hollywood movies endured as classics despite the generalized contempt of the highbrows? The auteur theory turned out to be a very workable hypothesis for this task of historical reevaluation. But I was never all that interested in the clinical "personalities" of directors, and I have never considered the interview as one of the indispensable weapons in my critical arsenal.

The interview is an autonomous art form like any other, and it follows that directors who give good interviews do not necessarily make good movies, and directors who give bad interviews do not necessarily make bad movies. I am, if anything, anti-interview in that I believe that a director's formal utterances (his films) tell us more about his artistic personality than do his informal utterances (his conversations).

That is why I was far more strongly influenced by the cinémathèque-oriented critics on *Cahiers du Cinéma*[4] before 1960 than the tape-recorder interviewers on *Cahiers du Cinéma* after 1960. It is not a question simply of Truffaut, Godard, Chabrol, Rohmer, Rivette, Valcroze, and others validating their pre-1960 critiques with their post-1960 filmmaking. I doubt that Gore Vidal has any notion of what Truffaut was writing about back in 1954 when Truffaut first articulated *la politique des auteurs* as an attack on the tradition of quality in the French cinema.[5] Godard's translated criticism has merely mystified even his most determined American admirers. Having published twelve editions of *Cahiers du Cinéma in English* between 1965 and 1967, I can testify that many of my French-speaking acquaintances in America were frequently unable to decipher the cryptic pronouncements of *Cahiers*.

Indeed, few people seem to be aware that my original article on the auteur theory was largely an examination of André Bazin's critique of la politique des auteurs.[6] Vidal lumps together all French film critics into one monolithic auteurist block as if *Cahier*ism was a national vice. Yet *Cahiers* never sold more than fifteen thousand copies of any monthly issue, and its opinions were violently opposed by other specialized French film publications, most notably and most persistently by *Positif,* which made a point of preferring Huston to Hitchcock, and Fellini to Rossellini. For every Bazin in French film criticism there were a dozen French Bosley Crowthers[7] and Siegfried Kracauers.[8] One did not have to be an auteurist or a *Cahier*ist to adore Jerry Lewis.[9] He happened to be a very catholic French taste. In fact, the most prominent of the Lewis lovers were on the staff of *Positif.*

Similarly, the auteurists of the fifties and sixties did not introduce the cult of the director. Dwight MacDonald[10] and John Grierson[11] were writing very knowledgeably about Hollywood directors back in the early thirties. The great majority of film histories around the world have been organized in terms of the collected works of individual directors. If, as Vidal implies, all that auteurism represents is an emphasis on directors, this so-called theory should be banished for its banality.

A great deal of confusion has been caused by the assumption that auteurism was inseparably linked with the personal tastes of individual critics. Since I was one of the first two American auteurists (along with the late Eugene Archer), I must bear a large part of the blame for this confusion. Let me state at this point, albeit belatedly, that auteurism and Sarrisism are not identical. Both, I hope, have been evolving over the past quarter of a century on a widening front of scholarly activity. Along the way, certain tendencies have clustered around auteurism to form a basis for discussion. Among these tendencies have been the antimontage writings of André Bazin,[12] the many French meditations on mise-en-scène, Lawrence Alloway's celebrations of pop art,[13] and Peter Wollen's valiant efforts to reconcile auteurism with semiotics.[14] Some of these formulations conflicted with others to such an extent that alleged auteurists were often at one another's throats. I have written extensively on many of these internal conflicts, and I have no desire to rehash them now. What I propose instead is a report on the theoretical fallout from the polemical explosions of the past. An attempt will be made to add historical perspective to auteurism, and to emerge with a usable residue of critical theory for 1977.

Bazin's most striking contribution to film aesthetics was the restoration of interest in the integrity of the visual field. If he did not actually demolish the montage theories of Eisenstein, Pudovkin, Kuleshov, and Vertov,[15] he did succeed in reducing these theories from imperatives to options. Bazin's writings were never systematic enough or comprehensive enough to establish new imperatives, and there is little indication that he ever wished to establish a new orthodoxy to replace the old. But he did change the way many critics looked at motion pictures. No longer was the ambiguity of the individual image disdained for the dialectical conflict between successive images. Examining both the deep focus shots in *Citizen Kane* and the slow pans in *Open City,* Bazin managed to link these two otherwise dissimilar films in the very ingenious concept of optical realism.

When Bazin's writings first began to filter across the Atlantic in the mid-fifties, the American cinema was in the midst of a formal crisis with wide screens. Most American reviewers either ignored the width altogether or dealt with it in isolation from the script. Wide-screen color canvases like *East of Eden* and *Rebel without a Cause* were reviewed in America as if they were small-screen, black-and-white Philco Television Playhouse productions like *Marty.* I recall Claude Chabrol's attack on my review of *East of Eden* as *"ennuyeux."* He was right to the extent that my critique did not do justice to the film's emotional sweep encompassed in tilted, distended compositions.

American movies are often discriminated against in America because the ear takes precedence over the eye. By contrast, the French were able to provide a detailed visual analysis of American movies precisely because they were undistracted by the dialogue. To an American ear *Rebel Without a Cause* is still gravely flawed by its undigested clinical dialogue. But one would have to be blind to fail to realize that Ray has transcended the tedious social worker rhetoric of the film with a succession of striking initiatory ceremonies all filmed with profound splendor. And it is to our everlasting disgrace that the French understood James Dean on a mythic level long before we did. Similarly, they understood how deeply Alfred Hitchcock's *Vertigo* had influenced Alain Resnais and Alain Robbe-Grillet's *Last Year at Marienbad.* While the New York critics were honoring Stanley Kramer's *The Defiant Ones,* the *Cahiers* critics were cheering Orson Welles's *Touch of Evil.* Obviously, their eyes were quicker than our ears.

Although in the long run they could not have the last word on the American cinema, they gave many of us the first glimpse of this elusive entity. American film criticism has not been the same since. There was a time when movies were judged almost entirely in terms of an absolute fidelity to social reality. Good intentions alone were too often considered the paving stones to heaven. By establishing the notion of individual creation in even the Hollywood cinema, the French shifted the critical emphasis away from the nature of content to the director's attitude toward content.

This attitude was expressed through a somewhat mystical process called mise-en-scène, defined perhaps most eloquently by French critic-director Alexandre Astruc:

> But Mizoguchi knows well that, after all, it is not very important for his film to turn out well; he is more concerned with knowing whether the strongest bonds between himself and his characters are those of tenderness or contempt. He is like the viewer who sees the reflection of pleasure on the features of the one he watches, even though he also knows quite well that it is not this reflection alone which he is seeking but perhaps quite simply the tedious confirmation of something he has always known but cannot refrain from verifying. So I consider mise-en-scène as a means of transforming the world into a spectacle

given primarily to oneself—yet what artist does not know instinctively that what is seen is less important than the way of seeing, or of a certain way of needing to see or be seen.

As I wrote some years ago, I would suggest a definition of mise-en-scène that includes all the means available to a director to express his attitude toward his subject. This takes in cutting, camera movement, pacing, the direction of players and their placement in the decor, the angle and distance of the camera, and even the content of the shot. Mise-en-scène as an attitude tends to accept the cinema as it is and enjoy it for what it is—a sensuous conglomeration of all the other arts.

Bazin, Astruc, and Roger Leehardt caused a ferment in film aesthetics by demystifying so-called "pure" cinema. There was no such entity, they insisted. We could now discuss hitherto verboten subjects as adaptations without placing surgical masks over our faces. What were once considered germs from the other arts were now treated as vitamins. Hence, whereas Agee worried that Olivier's film treatment of *Henry V* was not truly cinematic, Bazin applauded Olivier for honoring cinema by honoring theater.

The French critics tended to brush aside the distinctions between cinema as a medium and cinema as an art form. "The cinema is everything," Godard declared. And he meant it. Every scrap of film was grist for his sensibility. The cinema was no longer a holy temple to which only certain sanctified works were admitted. Cinema was to be found on every movie screen in the world, and Hollywood movies were no less cinematic than anything else. There was still room for disagreement in this new critical climate, but the disputes were couched in terms more relative than absolute.

About the time that auteurism was swimming across the English Channel to London's moviemanes and across the Atlantic to New York's film cultists, pop art exploded all across the cultural landscape, and nothing has seemed the same since. The two movements converged uneasily in the sixties in such multifaceted artifacts as Richard Lester's *A Hard Day's Night* with the Beatles, John Boorman's *Having a Wild Weekend* with the Dave Clark Five, Jean-Luc Godard's *One Plus One* with the Rolling Stones, the experimental kinetics of Frank Zappa, and the personal appearances on film of Bob Dylan.

Lawrence Alloway, who had coined the term "pop art," proposed "a criticism of movies as a pop art which can have a critical currency beyond that of footnotes and preposterous learning." Alloway thereby came into conflict with the scholarly tendencies of auteurism. The terms in which he defined the cinema—whether as "the index of a Baudelairean art of modern life" with "modernity" defined by Baudelaire as "that which is ephemeral, fugitive, contingent upon the occasion" or as "the art synthesis proposed by Wagner, the total work to which all arts contribute"—were terms that pertained more to sociological criticism than to auteurist criticism. For the hard-core auteurists, the hitherto despised Hollywood movies could be judged as high art. For Alloway, high art had been supplanted by pop art, and new forms of judgment were required. Alloway's stress on the topicality and expendability of movies as consumer products was not without a certain ironic condescension toward the medium. By contrast, most auteurists tended to view movies as sacred relics of a spiritual medium. Their tone was reverent and, hence, vulnerable. Their only excuse (and mine) was that they thought that they were writing only for other believers.

No one to my knowledge has ever commented on the Kierkegaard quotation from *Either/Or* with which I introduced my 1962 auteur article:

> I call these sketches shadowgraphs, partly by the designation to remind you at once that they derive from the darker side of life, partly because like other shadowgraphs they are not directly visible. When I take a shadowgraph in my hand, it makes no impression on me, and gives me no clear conception of it. Only when I hold it up opposite the wall, and now look not directly at it, but at that which appears on the wall, am I able to see it. So also with the picture which does not become perceptible until I see through the external. This external is perhaps quite unobtrusive but not until I look through it do I discover that inner picture which I desire to show you, an inner picture too delicately drawn to be outwardly visible, woven as it is of the tenderest moods of the soul.

Kierkegaard's "inner picture" eventually found its way into my essay as "interior meaning," a term that gave me a great deal of trouble at the time, but one that has since come to define what all serious film criticism seeks to discover. Auteurism has less to do with the way movies are made than with the way they are elucidated and evaluated. It is more a critical instrument than a creative inspiration. Peter Wollen has suggested the hypothetical nature of the enterprise, and I will go along with that. The cinema is a deep, dark mystery that we auteurists are attempting to solve. It is a labyrinth with a treacherous resemblance to reality. I suppose that the difference between auteurists and structuralists is the difference between knowing all the questions before finding the answers, and knowing all the answers before formulating the questions.

At this late date I am prepared to concede that auteurism is and always has been more a tendency than a theory, more a mystique than a methodology, more an editorial policy than an aesthetic procedure. Contrary to anti-auteurist legends, auteurist critics around the world are an unruly lot. For the most part, they do not describe themselves as auteurists. They are content to describe the stylistic and thematic epiphanies of their favorite auteurs.

NOTES

1. A cinémathèque is a movie theater devoted to revival programming.

2. Pauline Kael was a film critic who wrote a widely circulated attack on Sarris and auteurism.

3. Gore Vidal wrote the novel and screenplay for the film *Myra Breckenridge;* Rex Reed, a popular movie reviewer, starred in it.

4. *Cahiers du Cinéma* is the Paris-based journal in which the principles of auteurism were first set forth.

5. The Tradition of Quality was a filmmaking practice prevalent in France after world War II that relied on adaptation of highly regarded literary properties and/or scripts by respected writers.

6. André Bazin was an older member of the group that surrounded *Cahiers du Cinéma*. His opinions were often at odds with those of his younger colleagues. In particular, Bazin stood for a kind of realist aesthetic realized through long takes and deep focus photography which emphasized the ambiguous nature of reality. This position was opposed to the more stylistically showy point of view shots and heavy editing admired by the younger members of the *Cahiers* group.

7. Bosley Crowther was a longtime first-string film critic of the *New York Times*. He had little sympathy for auteurism.

8. Siegfried Kracauer, a member of the Frankfurt School of German expatriate cultural theorists, espoused the theory that film should be judged according to its capacity to capture physical reality, a principle of evaluation diametrically opposed to the auteurists' emphasis on stylistic bravado.

9. The auteurists' admiration of Jerry Lewis's films was a frequently cited criticism of their approach.

10. Dwight MacDonald was a movie reviewer and commentator on popular culture whose work was widely disseminated in the middle years of the twentieth century.

11. The Scottish-born John Grierson was a pioneering producer and theorist of documentary films.

12. See note 6.

13. Art critic Lawrence Alloway proposed that popular cinema be judged according to the criteria applied to pop art, which had embraced an aesthetic of mass production and commercialization.

14. Peter Wollen, who now teaches at UCLA, was an early member of the British auteurist group. He attempted to reconcile the auteur approach with subsequent theoretical developments inspired by the science of semiotics, which treated film as a language.

15. These Russian theorists and filmmakers espoused the idea that editing held the key to cinematic artistry.

Colin MacCabe

The Revenge of the Author

This essay is an attempt to bring into alignment two major and contradictory areas of my own experience. I have had few intellectual experiences that so deeply marked me as the introduction to the work of Barthes in the late 1960s. Barthes's emphasis on the sociality of writing and the transindividuality of its codes has been a major and continuing gain in our understanding of literature and its functioning. At the same time, I have always been uneasy about the attempt to abolish notions of authorship entirely, and this uneasiness grew when, in the mid-eighties, I became actively involved in the making of films. The most general concern of the cast and crew of a film, not to mention the producer, is that the director know what film he is making, that there be an author on the set.

There is no more elegant statement of Barthes's opposition to the concept of the author than his extraordinarily influential essay titled "The Death of the Author," which summarised many of the most powerful theses of *S/Z*. Barthes's concern, in both the brief essay and the major study, was to stress the reality of the textual: the contradictory series of relations that a text enters into with the writings that precede it. The project may seem to have something in common with the New Critical attack on the author, but its aims are very different. New Criticism sought to liberate the text's meaning from the unfortunate contingencies of an author's time and place. Barthes's attempt is to liberate the text from meaning altogether. The author becomes for Barthes the privileged social instance of this meaning. The massive investment in the author which we witness in contemporary culture is for Barthes an investment in meaning, an attempt to stabilise the fragmentation of identity. Without the author as the crucial function that grounds and identifies the text, we could begin to emphasise how the text obliterates all grounds, all identities: "Writing is that neutral composite oblique space where our

From *The Eloquence of the Vulgar* (London: British Film Institute, 1999). Reprinted by permission of the author.

subject slips away, the negative where all identity is lost, starting with the very identity of the body writing."[1]

Barthes emphasises the priority of language in writing and derides any aesthetic based on expression. All one is able to analyse in a text is a mixture, more accurately a montage of writings, and the writer's only activity thus becomes that of editor—regulating the mix of the writings. It is at the moment we grasp the nature of the textual that we can also understand that the determination of the multiple writings making up the text is to be focused on the reader and not the writer: "The reader is the space on which all the quotations that make up a writing are inscribed without any of them being lost; a text's unity lies not in its origin but in its destination." But Barthes goes farther than any orthodox kind of reception theory: "This destination cannot any longer be personal: the reader is without history, biography, psychology; he is simply that someone who holds together in single field all the traces by which the written text is constituted."[2]

Where are we to locate this etiolated ghost of a reader liberated from identity? How, historically, are we to place a reader without history, biography, psychology, and how can we socially situate his, her, or (as the lack of determination obviously includes gender) its emergence? The answer is to be found in considering modernism as a response to educational and social developments that posed readership as a major problem. It is Derrida who has stressed a constant fear of writing in terms of the inability of an author to control the reader's construction of reading. Derrida's concern has been to indicate how this lack of control is general to all situations of language use. What Derrida does not stress, however, is the historicity of this problem, the particular way in which technological advances pose this problem in specific forms to which there are specific responses. The advent of printing radically altered the relations of writer and reader, and our familiar category of author can be read in relation to that new technology. Whereas before printing all reading involved the prior transmission of an individual text, printing suddenly produced an audience which with the author is not, even in the attenuated relation of an individual copying, directly related.

If we look back to the Renaissance, we find that the etymologically prior meanings of the word "author" stress the notion of both cause and authority without any special reference to written texts but it is in relation to the new technology of printing and the associated new legal relations that our own concept of author is elaborated.[3] Once tied to the printed text, the national author of the vernacular languages replaced the classical authorities—and replaced them by virtue of his or her individual power. There are few clearer examples of this process than Milton. It is rarely stressed that in beginning his famous attack on Parliament's attempt to regulate printing Milton explicitly excludes "that part which preserves justly every man's copy to himselfe,"[4] for its ordinance of June 14, 1643 was the first properly to recognise copyright. But Milton's interest in copyright and his minute concern with the exact details of his printed text make clear how the new category of author relates to legal and technological changes.[5]

Most important, however, is the new relation to the audience which is thus figured. The dialogue implied in both the popular dramatic forms and the circulated manuscripts is replaced by a literal petrifying of meanings. Milton's first published poem, one of the prefatory poems to Shakespeare's Second Folio, uses the metaphor of readers turned into marble monuments to Shakespeare's "unvalu'd book." The audience may not be universal, may be fit though few, but it is certainly not an audience actively engaged in dialogue with the text. The act of composition is the poet's alone. Milton's blindness and the image of his solitary composition is almost an essential part of his literary definition. But the solitary author gains, in complementary definition, the possibility of a national audience.

When this concept is given a Romantic turn, the author ceases to authorise a national vernacular, but the new definition in terms of the solitary imagination and a local speech continues to presuppose, in its very definition, a potential national audience, although an audience now seen as at odds with the dominant social definitions. What brings the categories of both author and national audience under attack is the universal literacy of the nineteenth century, the production for the first time of a literate population. As the capitalist economy responded to this new market with the production of those mass-circulation newspapers that herald the beginning of our recognisably modern culture, we entered a new historical epoch of communication in which any author's claim to address his or her national audience became hopelessly problematic. Mass literacy spelled an end to any such possibility. There is now no conception of the national audience not threatened by a vaster audience that will not listen; the traditional elite strategies that defined the audience by those who were excluded are irredeemably ruined by those who will simply not pay attention. This historical situation is one of the crucial determinations of modernism, when all universal claims for art seem fatally compromised. Barthes's fundamental aesthetic is borrowed from the modernist reaction to this problem—a writing for an ideal and unspecified reader, for that reader who, in Nietzsche's memorable phrase is "far off," that ideal Joycean reader who devotes an entire life to the perusal of a single text.

There seems to me to be a historical explanation of why we get such a powerful resurgence of the modern aesthetic in France, and it is to be found in the delayed but very powerful impact of the consumer society there in the decade from the mid-fifties to the mid-sixties. The fascination with and distaste for mass culture which runs through work as diverse as that of Barthes, the Situationists, and Godard indicates the extent to which the dissolution of the relations that supported traditional culture were widely felt and perceived. The paradox of modernism is that it fully lives the crisis of the audience while postulating an ideal audience in the future; it fully explores the slippage of significations which become so pressing as a securely imagined audience disappears while holding out the promise of a future in which this signification will be held together. The form of this future ideal audience has been conceived across a range of possibilities throughout the twentieth century. After 1968 in France, however, the favoured solution was the alliance of avant-garde art and revolutionary politics which had marked post-Revolutionary Russia and pre-Nazi Germany and which theorised the audience in terms of a political mandate authorised by a future revolutionary society.

Barthes's classless, genderless, completely indeterminate reader is yet another version of the solution to the modernist dilemma, but it preserves the crucial relation of author and reader bequeathed by the national literary tradition. Indeed, that preservation can be seen in the way that Derrida's project (closely related to Barthes's) was so eagerly seized in the United States as a way of preserving the traditional literary canon against radical curricular reform. Foucault in a famous and almost contemporary article signals this danger. Speaking of the concept of *écriture* and its emphasis on the codes of writing, he warns that the concept "has merely transposed the empirical characteristics of an author to a transcendental anonymity" and that it thus "sustains the privileges of the author."[6]

It is the case, however, that Foucault shares Barthes's commitment to those aspects of literary modernism which concentrate on the difficulty of the author's position. Beckett's "What matter who's speaking, someone said, what matter who's speaking" acts as a kind of epigraph for the essay.[7] Despite Foucault's emphasis on the need to look beyond literature if we are to understand the functioning of the author and despite his concern to trace the history of authorship, the entire article is still written with an emphasis on the untenability of the traditional Romantic valuation of the author as the originator of discourse. In Foucault there is no consideration of the new forms of education and entertainment which have rendered that position untenable but, in the same moment, have opened up new possibilities.

It is significant that when Foucault does mention he has limited his discussion to the author of the written word that he catalogues his omission in terms of painting and music—arts whose development is contemporary with, and indeed dependent on, the evolution I have sketched within national cultures. Foucault offers no discussion at all of the cinema, which not only displaced the dominance of the written word but also introduced radical new relations between texts and audiences. This omission is in some way all the more surprising since a mere decade earlier *Cahiers du Cinéma* had half elaborated a new concept of the author in relation to cinema. I say "half elaborated" because the *Cahiers* critics (François Truffaut, Eric Rohmer, Jean-Luc Godard, and Jacques Rivette) never saw their task in theoretical terms. Their concerns were polemical and specific. Above all they were concerned with the importance of the script for the construction of a film. They saw the weakness of the French cinema in terms of its overvaluation of the written element in film, which failed to take account of the mise-en-scène which was accomplished by emphasising the role of the metteur-en-scène, the director. This emphasis went hand in hand with the second task: the redescription of the huge archive of Hollywood cinema by selecting from its thousands of films a series of corpuses that could be identified through the consistent use of mise-en-scène, the consistency being provided by those directors (John Ford, Raoul Walsh, Howard Hawks—the names are now familiar) who could be called "authors."

The project is thus curiously at variance with the literary use of the term "author." For Barthes, the author is the figure used to obscure the specificity of the textual. For *Cahiers,* the author, while sharing the Romantic features of creativity, inferiority, etc., was the figure used to emphasise the specificity of the codes that went to make up the cinema. It is exactly that mix that makes for the interest and pleasure of those articles, and no one was more elegant than Truffaut in his juxtapositions:

> You can refute Hawks in the name of Ray (or vice versa) or admit them both, but to anyone who would reject them both I make so bold as to say this: *Stop going to the cinema, don't watch any more films, you*

will never know the meaning of inspiration, of a viewfinder, of poetic intuition, a frame, a shot, an idea, a good film, the cinema.

The emphasis of this sentence, which I re-emphasise, is the necessity of understanding film in terms of the relation between the fundamental articulations of the cinema (viewfinder, frame, shot) and the fundamental themes of great art (inspiration, poetic intuition, idea). The scandal of *Cahiers*, however, is that it insisted on the relevance of themes of great art to a form whose address to the audience neglected all the qualifications of education, class, and nationality which the various national cultures of Europe had been so concerned to stress. This position is interesting because it is a theory of the author produced both in relation to the materiality of the form and also—and this is crucial—from the point of view of the audience.[8]

The attempts, in the late sixties and seventies, to develop this concern with the materiality of the form and to analyse further the cinematic codes that *Cahiers* had been the first to bring into discursive focus, ran into inevitable epistemological and political impasses because they sought to undertake the development without any recourse to the category of the author. The difficulties are clear in the pages of *Screen*, which most consistently tried to carry out this theoretical project. The logic of the codes revealed in analysis was not located in any originating consciousness but was immanent to the text itself. The emphasis on the textuality of meaning, independent of the conditions of either production or reception, brought great gains but, like Barthes's project of the late sixties (to which it was very closely allied), it rested on very precarious epistemological ground, constantly veering between freezing the text outside any but the most general pragmatic constraints (provided by psychoanalysis) and collapsing it into a total relativism and subjectivism where the reading inhered in the reader.

Parenthetically one might remark that it is not clear even from close reading of the *Screen* of this period that the category of author was ever abandoned according to the theoretical programme. Perhaps the most powerful single piece from that period, Stephen Heath's exemplary analysis of Orson Welles's *Touch of Evil*, unites formal and narrative determination in the attempt by the detective Quinlan (Welles) to keep control of his cane.[9] When we consider the significance of the signifier cane in Welles's own biography, then it is obvious that Heath's text as we have it is radically incomplete, needing elaboration in terms of Welles's own life and his relation to the institutions of cinema. *Screen*'s aim of producing readings independent of their grounding within specific determinates of meaning was always suspect. If there was great importance in emphasising the potential polysemy of any text, its potential for infinitisation, and if there was fundamental significance in analysing the transindividual codes from which any text was composed, it is still the case that texts are continuously determined in their meanings. The question is how we are to understand those determinations without producing, on the one hand, an author autonomously creating meanings in a sphere anterior to their specific articulation and, on the other, an audience imposing whatever meaning it chooses on a text.

It may be helpful in answering this problem to consider from a theoretical perspective the process of filmmaking. However one is to understand the collectivities at work in the production of a written text, it is obvious at a very simple level in the production of films that it is directly counterintuitive to talk of one responsible author. Even a very cheap feature film involves thirty to forty people working together over a period of some six months, and the mass of copyright law and trade union practice which has grown up around film has largely as its goal the ever more precise specification of "creativity," the delineation of areas (design, lighting, makeup, costume) where an individual or individuals can be named in relation to a particular element of the final artifact. The experience of production relations within a film makes clear how one can award an authorial primacy to the director without adopting any of the idealist presuppositions about origin or homogeneity which seem to arise unbidden in one's path. If we are to talk of an audience for a film, then, at least in the first instance, that audience cannot be theorised in relation to the empirical audience or to the readings that audience produces. So varied are the possibilities of such readings and so infinite the determinations that enter into such a calculation that it is an impossible task. Indeed, were it possible to calculate the readings produced by any specific film, then the Department of Reader Response would be the most important section of any film studio, and Hollywood would be a less anxious place with much greater security of tenure.

Any future audience can be approached only through the first audience for the film—the cast and crew who produced it. It is the director's skill in making others work together to produce a film, which is of necessity invisible at the outset, that determines the extent to which the film will be successfully realised. It is the collective determination to make visible something that has not been seen before that marks the successful production of a film, and it is insofar as the producers of the film are also its first audience that we can indicate the dialectic that places the author not outside the text but within the process of its production. It might be said further that such an analysis provides an ethic that is certainly important and may be crucial in differentiating among the numerous productions of the new popular forms of capitalist culture. I venture to suggest that those elements in popular culture which genuinely mark important areas of desire and reflection are those where the producers have been concerned in the first place to make something for themselves. Where the determination is simply to produce a work for a predefined audience from which the producers exclude themselves, one will be dealing with that meretricious and toxic repetition that is the downside of the new forms of mechanical and electronic production. A further generalisation would be that genuine creativity in popular culture is constantly to be located in relation to emergent and not yet fully defined audiences.

The process of filmmaking indicates not only how the moment of creation integrally entails the figuring of the audience but also how that audience is figured in relation to a reality that thus achieves social effectivity. This is a solution to the problem of realism which avoids the trap of representation (which elides the effectivity of the textual) and the snare of endless textuality (which endlessly defers the text's relation to the real). The repositioning of the reader or viewer by the work of art in relation to a social reality is thereby altered by the repositioning that allows the traditional heuristic and oppositional claims of realism without its traditional epistemology.[10]

Considerations of this order enable us to conceptualise the author as a contradictory movement within a collectivity rather than as a homogeneous, autonomous, and totalising subject. If the process of filmmaking allows us an obvious way of seeing the author in a plurality of positions, it should not be taken as an empirical formula for the studying of authors. If one were to take a specific film and attempt to constitute the author in relation to this first audience, one would be faced by a multiplication of the determinations on that audience to a level that makes any exhaustive analysis not simply technically but theoretically impossible. The usefulness of the film analogy, and the usefulness of the *Cahiers* critics who deliberately adopted a position similar to that of experienced technicians, is that it indicates the multiplicity of positions in which we must locate the author. It should not be thought, however, that the theoretical task is to specify the determinations that would limit the possible meanings of the texts in relation to possible positions in which it could be produced and received. Such a dream of scientific rigour discounts that our own position as reader is always present in any such calculation and that the very fact of a future allows for positions as yet unaccounted for. It should be stressed at this point that infinity once again becomes a real term in the analysis.

The difference between this conception of infinity, however, and Barthes's, is that whereas Barthes's is located in some atemporal and idealist account of meaning, this infinity is rooted in a historical and materialist account of significations. Marx so dominates our thinking about materialism that it may seem at first that any conception of infinite determinations is hostile to materialism. For over two millennia, however, it was the commitment to an infinity of worlds that distinguished materialist thought from the variety of religious views to which it was opposed. Indeed, it may well be that Marx's own unwillingness to produce the philosophy of dialectical materialism derived from his understanding of the centrality of infinity to any materialist philosophy.

If we are to understand the implications of these considerations for any practice of criticism, there is no doubt that the only place to start is with the most important example we have of materialist criticism: Walter Benjamin's fragments, *Charles Baudelaire: A Lyric Poet in the Era of High Capitalism.*[11] In a stunning tour de force Benjamin commences with an analysis of Baudelaire's physiognomy and its resemblance to that of a professional conspirator and then weaves in and out of the social and literary text as he moves from the taverns, where the political conspirators gather, to the question of the wine tax and how the tax relates to the poem on the ragpicker. He reintegrates the question of wine into the social spectacle of Paris—as the drunk family weaves its way home—and into its political economy: the *vin de la barrière* produced by the wine tax absorbs several social pressures that might otherwise threaten the government. Benjamin's method is to start with the doxa of nineteenth-century life and to work through until connections begin to reveal themselves. Eschewing any theory of mediations, he uses montage to imbricate the literary and social text. There is no question of judging this method in terms of cause and effect within a social totality (all of which categories in this context become idealist): the crucial causal relation is between the analyst and the past and is a truly dialectical one in which the proofs of reading develop in the analysis. Such methods are extremely alien to academic thought, and it is not surprising that the academic Theodor Adorno was so repelled by this text. In that most discouraging of letters which he sends to Benjamin in November 1938, he takes almost personal exception to "that particular type of concreteness and its behavioristic overtones" and warns Benjamin that "materialist determination of cultural traits is only possible if it is mediated through the *total social process.*"[12] But to imagine that the social process can be totalised is to misunderstand the living relation of the present, which determines that the past can be totalised only for now. It has no totality in itself but rather an infinite number of possibilities vis-à-vis a future it cannot know but which will bring it to life.

Benjamin saw quite clearly that the notion of "totality" and its associated concept of mediation were attractive because they were an attempt to fetishise the past into a controllable finitude and to avoid the risks of scholarly engagement in the present. His reply to Adorno stresses the personal basis of his own study and his need to keep the contradictions of his personal concerns in tension with "the experiences which all of us shared in the past 15 years." He distinguished sharply between this productive contradiction and a "mere loyalty to dialectical materialism." Indeed, so deep and productive is the opposition between the personal and the social that Benjamin refers to it as "an antagonism of which I would not even in my dreams wish to be relieved." And he goes on to state that "the overcoming of this antagonism consititutes the problem of my study."[13] It seems to me that his disagreement with Adorno was to dominate his thoughts for the short period of life that remained. The major text of that period is the fulgurant and elliptical paragraphs which compose the theses on the philosophy of history. I now find it impossible to read those paragraphs except as a prolonged and mediated reply to the *bêtise* of Adorno's letter. The constant opposition between the historicist and the historical materialist is fully comprehensible only if we read the text, in large measure, as an expression of the opposition between Adorno and himself. Every line of that remarkable text repays study, but for current purposes I want merely to quote the first half of the sixteenth thesis:

> An historical materialist cannot do without the notion of a present which is not a transition, but in which time stands still and has come to a stop. For this notion defines the present in which he himself is writing history. Historicism gives the "eternal" image of the past; historical materialism supplies a unique experience with the past.

Benjamin here makes clear the extent to which the critic enters into a full relation with the past in which his or her present reveals the past as it is for us. The crucial problem here is how we are to understand that "us." How does the critic's (and notice that the term must here be considered interchangeable with "historian") personal constitution relate to any wider social collectivity? Where Adorno relies on concepts of totality and mediation to constitute a fixed social past, Benjamin in the theses relentlessly uses the concept of "class struggle" to locate us in a mobile social present. The virtue of the concept is that it emphasises contradiction and division; its weakness is that it is very doubtful that any current definition of class, either Marxist or sociological, will not limit its contents to a reductive notion of the economic. The rhetorical function this concept plays in the theses cannot be sustained when it is given any substantial investigation. Benjamin would find himself limited to another form of the Adorno criticism from those who would demand "political correctness" in the present rather than "the total social process" in the past.

To elaborate Benjamin it would be necessary to build some notion of a social unconscious into the notion of class struggle. It is interesting that in early drafts of the "Arcades" project Benjamin had relied on Jung, for it is Jung, of course, who does propose a transindividual unconscious. Unfortunately Jung's concept of the collective unconscious is so historically unspecific that it is completely unequal to the task proposed. But the references to both Jung and Georg Simmel are not to be condemned from the pious position of the orthodox Adorno. They indicate a dimension that must be added to notions of class struggle which would radically transform that notion.

Without presuming on the content of such a transformation, one can indicate some of the effects of introducing the unconscious into the investigation of the past. The historical critic, the critical historian, brings to the past the currency of his or her own epoch; the effort to make the past speak must inevitably draw on resources of which the critic is unaware and which appear only in the construction of the past. The risks are considerable and there can be no question of guarantees. Adorno recalled Benjamin's remarking that each idea of the "Arcades" project had to be wrested away from a realm in which madness reigns, a realm in which the distinction between the nonsensically individual and the significantly collective disappears.[14] In this respect a critical work shares significant similarities with the creative work it analyses. The author finds him- or herself in their audience.

NOTES

There was one massive contradiction in film theory of the seventies. On the one hand there was the elaboration of theories—linguistic, psychoanalytical and Marxist—which challenged the primacy of the conscious subject. On the other, the auteur theory (which depended on just such a notion of the primacy of the conscious subject) was unavoidable: in its weak form, simply as a necessary descriptive grid for the archive; in its strong form, still a crucial evaluative term. The essay presented here tried to use my experience as a producer to elaborate an account of the role of the director which would square these particular theoretical circles. Two conferences in the United States, one organised by Fredric Jameson at Duke University in 1987 and the other by David Simpson at the University of Colorado in 1988, allowed me to organise my thoughts.

1. Roland Barthes, "The Death of the Author," in *Image-Music-Text: Essays,* selected and trans. by Stephen Heath (New York: Hill and Wang, 1977), 142.

2. Ibid., 148.

3. See Raymond Williams, *Marxism and Literature* (Oxford University Press, 1977), 192.

4. *Complete Prose Works of John Milton,* ed. Don Wolfe, 8 vols. (New Haven: Yale University Press, 1953–82), vol. 2, 491.

5. See, for example, Mindele Treip, *Milton's Punctuation and Changing English Usage. 1582–1676* (London: Methuen, 1970).

6. Michel Foucault, "What Is an Author?" in *Language, Counter-Memory, Practice: Selected Essays and Interviews,* ed. Donald F. Bouchard, trans. Bouchard and Sherry Simon (Oxford: Basil Blackwell, 1978), 120.

7. Ibid., 93.

8. François Truffaut, "A Wonderful Certainty," in *Cahiers du cinéma, the 1950s: New Realism, Hollywood, New Wave,* ed. Jim Hillier (Cambridge, Mass.: Harvard University Press, 1985), 108.

9. Stephen Heath, "Film and System: Terms of Analysis," *Screen* 16 (1975), no. 1, 7–77; no. 2, 91–113.

10. For details of this argument, see my "Realism: Balzac and Barthes," in Colin MacCabe, *Theoretical Essays: Film, Linguistics, Literature* (Manchester: Manchester University Press, 1985), 130–50.

11. Walter Benjamin, *Charles Baudelaire: A Lyric Poet in the Era of High Capitalism,* trans. Harry Zohn (London: New Left Books, 1973).

12. Adorno to Benjamin in Ernst Bloch, Georg Lukács, Bertolt Brecht, Walter Benjamin, Theodor Adorno, *Aesthetics and Politics* (London: New Left Books, 1976), 129.

13. Benjamin to Adorno, in *Aesthetics and Politics,* 136.

14. Adorno to Benjamin, in *Aesthetics and Politics,* 127.

David Bordwell

Authorship and Narration
in Art Cinema

The predominance of classical Hollywood films, and consequently classical narration, is a historical fact, but film history is not a monolith. Under various circumstances, there have appeared alternative modes of narration, the most prominent one of which I shall consider in what follows. As a start, ostensive definition might be best. *L'Eclisse, The Green Room, Rocco and His Brothers, Repulsion, Scenes from a Marriage, Accident, Teorema, Ma nuit chez Maude, Rome Open City, Love and Anarchy:* whatever you think of these films, they form a class that filmmakers and film viewers distinguish from *Rio Bravo* on the one hand and *Mothlight* on the other. Not all films shown in "art theaters" utilize distinct narrational procedures, but many do. Within a machinery of production, distribution, and consumption—the "international art cinema," as it is generally known—there exists a body of films which appeal to norms of syuzhet[1] and style which I shall call art-cinema narration.

We could characterize this mode by saying that the syuzhet here is not as redundant as in the classical film; that there are permanent and suppressed gaps; that exposition is delayed and distributed to a greater degree; that the narration tends to be less generically motivated; and several other things. Such an atomistic list, while informative, would not get at the underlying principles that enable the viewer to comprehend the film. A number of interlocking schemata explain the various narrational strategies, and their instantiation in syuzhet and style, characteristic of this mode of filmmaking.

One of these broad schemata is that of overt narrational "commentary." In applying this schema, the viewer looks for those moments in which the narrational act interrupts the transmission of fabula[2] information and highlights its own role. Stylistic devices that gain prominence with respect to classical norms—an unusual angle, a stressed bit of cutting, a striking camera movement, an unrealistic shift in lighting or setting, a disjunction on the sound track, or any other breakdown of objective realism which is not motivated as subjectivity—can be taken as the narration's commentary. The marked self-consciousness of art-cinema narration creates both a coherent fabula world and an intermittently present but highly noticeable external authority through which we gain access to it.

Thanks to the intrusive commentary, the self-conscious points in the classical text (the beginning and ending of a scene, of the film) become foregrounded in the art film. The credits of *Persona* and *Blow-Up* can tease us with fragmentary, indecipherable images that announce the power of the author to control what we know. The narrator can begin a scene in a fashion that cuts us adrift or can linger on a scene after its causally significant action has been completed. In particular, the "open" ending characteristic of the art cinema can be seen as proceeding from a narration which will not divulge the outcome of the causal chain. V. F. Perkins objects to the ending of *La Notte* on the grounds that "the 'real ending' is knowable but has been withheld. . . . The story is abandoned when it has served the director's purpose but before it has satisfied the spectator's requirements."[3] To complain about the arbitrary suppression of the story's outcome is to reject one convention of the art film. A banal remark of the 1960s, that such films make you leave the theater thinking, is not far from the mark: the ambiguity, the play of alternative schemata, must not be halted. Thus the unexpected freeze frame becomes the most explicit figure of narrative irresolution. Furthermore, the pensive ending acknowledges the narration as not simply powerful but humble; the narration knows that life is more complex than art can ever be, and—a new twist of the realistic screw—the only way to respect this complexity is to leave causes dangling and questions unanswered. Like many art films, *La Notte* bares the device of the unresolved ending when a woman at the party asks the writer Giovanni how a certain story should end. He answers: "In so many ways."

Art-film narration goes beyond such codified moments of overt intervention. At any point in the film we must be ready to engage with the shaping process of an overt narration. A scene may end in medias res; gaps are created that are not explicable by reference to character psychology; retardation may result from the withholding of information or from overloaded passages that require unpacking later. Lacking the "dialogue hooks" of classical construction, the film will exploit more connotative, symbolic linkages between episodes. Scenes will not obey the Hollywood pattern of exposition, pickup of old line of action, and start of new line. Irony may burst out: in *The Loneliness of the Long-Distance Runner,* Richardson cuts between a borstal choir singing "Jerusalem" and a captured boy being beaten. More generally, the canonic story schema we bring to the film may be disarrayed. There may be little or no exposition of prior fabula events, and even what is occurring at the moment may require subsequent rethinking (Sternberg's "rise and fall of first impressions"). Exposition will tend to be delayed and widely distributed; often we will learn the most important causal factors only at the film's end. Like classical narration, art-film narration poses questions that guide us in fitting material into an ongoing structure. But these questions do not simply involve causal links among fabula events, such as "What became of Sean Regan?" (*The Big Sleep*) or "Will Stanley seduce Roy's husband?" (*In This Our Life*). In the art film, the very construction of the narration becomes the object of spectator hypotheses: how is the story being told? why tell the story in this way?

Obvious examples of such manipulation are disjunctions in temporal order. One common strategy is to use flashbacks in ways that only gradually reveal a prior event, so as to tantalize the viewer with reminders of his or her limited knowledge. *The Conformist* is a good example. Such a flashback is also usefully equivocal; it might be attributable to the character's spasms of memory rather than to the narration's overt suppressiveness. A more striking device is the flashforward—the syuzhet's representation of a "future" fabula action. The flashforward is unthinkable in the classical narrative cinema, which seeks to retard the ending, emphasize communicativeness, and play down self-consciousness. But in the art film, the flashforward flaunts the narration's range of knowledge (no character can know the future), the narration's recognition of the viewer (the flashforward is addressed to us, not to the characters), and the narration's limited communicativeness (telling a little while withholding a lot).

What the flashback and flashforward do in time can also take place in space. Odd ("arty") camera angles or camera movements independent of the action can register the presence of self-conscious narration. The "invisible witness" canonized by Hollywood precept becomes overt. In *La Notte,* for example, the bored wife Lidia leaves a party with the roué Roberto. As they drive in his car down a rainy street, they talk and laugh animatedly. But we never hear the conversation, and we see only bits of it, because the camera remains obstinately outside the closed car, tracking along with it as it passes through pools of light. The narration has "chosen" to "de-dramatize" the most vivacious interpersonal exchange in the film. Such procedures tend to set an omniscient narration's range of knowledge in opposition to the character's; effects of irony and anticipation are especially prominent. In the *La Notte* example, the camera position deflating the scene foreshadows the sombre turn the action will take when Roberto soon tries to seduce Lidia. Unlike the classical film, however, which usually makes the profilmic event only moderately self-conscious, art-cinema narration often signals that the profilmic event is also a construct. This can be accomplished by means of unmotivated elements in the mise-en-scène, such as the sourceless strips of pink and blue light sliding through Fassbinder's *Lola*. Alternatively, stylized treatment of situations, settings, or props, or of an era or milieu, can seem to proceed from the narration. In *Senso* and *1900*, events are presented with an operatic opulence that invites us to consider the profilmic event itself as the narration's restaging of history.

The result is that a highly self-conscious narration weaves through the film, stressing the act of presenting this fabula, in just this way. Deviations from classical norms can be grasped as commentary upon the story action. More generally, the degree of deviation from the canonic story becomes a trace of the narrational process. Syuzhet and style constantly remind us of an invisible intermediary that structures what we see. Marie-Claire Ropars's discussion of écriture—the tendency of directors like Resnais and Duras to bar direct access to a profilmic reality—emphasizes the general tendency of the art film to flaunt narrational procedures.[4] When these flauntings are repeated systematically, convention asks us to unify them as proceeding from an "author."

In most films, there is no good reason to identify the narrational process with a fictive narrator. In the art cinema, however, the overt self-consciousness of the narration is often paralleled by an extratextual emphasis on the filmmaker as source. Within the art cinema's mode of production and reception, the concept of the *author* has a formal function it did not possess in the Hollywood studio system. Film journalism and criticism promote authors, as do film festivals, retrospectives, and academic film study. Directors' statements of intent guide comprehension of the film, while a body of work linked by an authorial signature encourages viewers to read each film as a chapter of an oeuvre. Thus the institutional "author" is available as a source of the formal operation of the film. Sometimes the film asks to be taken as autobiography, the filmmaker's confession (e.g., *8½*, *The 400 Blows*, many of Fassbinder's works).

More broadly, the author becomes the real-world parallel to the narrational presence "who" communicates (what is the filmmaker *saying*?) and "who" expresses (what is the artist's personal vision?).

The consistency of an authorial signature across an oeuvre constitutes an economically exploitable trademark. The signature depends partly on institutional processes (e.g., advertising a film as "Fellini's *Orchestra Rehearsal*") and partly upon recognizably recurring devices from one film to another. One could distinguish filmmakers by motifs (Buñuel's cripples, Fellini's parades, Bergman's theater performances) and by camera technique (Truffaut's pan-and-zoom, Ophuls's sinuous tracks, Chabrol's high angles, Antonioni's long shots). The trademark signature can depend upon narrational qualities as well. There are the "baroque" narrators in the films of Cocteau, Ophuls, Visconti, Welles, Fellini, and Ken Russell—narrators who stress a spectacular concatenation of music and mise-en-scène. More "realist" narrators can be found in the films of Rossellini, Olmi, Forman, and others. The art cinema has made a place for satiric narration (e.g., Buñuel's) and for pastiche (e.g., the many homages to Hitchcock). The author-as-narrator can be explicit, as in *Le plaisir* or *The Immortal Story*; or the narrator can simply be the presence that accompanies the story action with a discreet but insistent obbligato of visual and sonic commentary. The popularity of R. W. Fassbinder in recent years may owe something to his ability to change narrational personae from film to film so that there is a "realist" Fassbinder, a "literary" Fassbinder, a "pastiche" Fassbinder, a "frenzied" Fassbinder, and so on.

The authorial trademark requires that the spectator see this film as fitting into a body of work. From this it is only a short step to explicit allusion and citation. A film may "quote," as Resnais does when he includes classic footage in *Mon oncle d'Amérique*; it may be "dedicated," as *La sirène du Mississipi* is dedicated to Renoir; or it may cite, as when Antoine Doinel steals a production still from *Monika*. The film can allude to classical genre conventions (Fassbinder recalling the Universal melodrama, Demy the MGM musical). The art film often rests upon a cinephilia as intense as Hollywood's: full understanding of one film requires a knowledge of and a fascination with other films. At its limit, this tendency is seen in those numerous art films about filmmaking: *8½, Day for Night, Everything for Sale, Beware of a Holy Whore, Identification of a Woman, The Clowns,* and many more. A film-within-a-film structure realistically motivates references to other works; it allows unexpected shifts between levels of fictionality; it can occasionally trigger parody of the art cinema itself. In *La Ricotta*, Pasolini's episode of *RoGoPaG*, Orson Welles plays a director filming the Christ story; he is pestered by a journalist who asks him about his vision of life and his opinion of Italian society. Antonioni's *Lady without the Camellias* portrays a vacuous starlet who marries a scriptwriter. He immediately forbids her to play in any of the cheap romances that were her forte and instead puts her in a biopic of Jeanne d'Arc: "An art film, something that will sell abroad!"

A cinema of ambiguity required machinery to interpret it. During the 1960s, film criticism took up a task it has for the most part clung to ever since. Now a critic was expected to explain what a film meant—to fill in the gaps, explicate the symbols, paraphrase the filmmaker's statement. The *Cahiers du Cinéma* critics unashamedly interpreted works, sometimes in pseudophilosophical or pseudoreligious terms. In Britain, *Movie* subjected films to a detailed explication in the tradition of Oxbridge "practical criticism." Journals like *Sight and Sound, Film Culture, New York Film Bulletin, Moviegoer, Brighton Film Review, Artsept, Positif, Image et son, Jeune cinéma, Film Quarterly*, and their counterparts all over Europe ran analytical and interpretive essays as well as interviews from an auteurist standpoint. Publishers began to bring out monographs on art-cinema directors and surveys of the art cinema as a whole, such as Parker Tyler's *Classics of the Foreign Film* (1962), Penelope Houston's *The Contemporary Cinema* (1963), John Russell Taylor's *Cinema Eye, Cinema Ear* (1964), and Gilles Jacobs's *Le cinéma moderne* (1964). The onus of interpretation fell even upon journalist-reviewers. Some (e.g., John Simon) took it up gladly, while others—Pauline Kael and Dwight MacDonald are notable instances—somewhat nervously mocked their duty by welcoming films that did not require hyper-intellectual exegesis. The role of critical discourse in comprehending the art film was confessed by Bergman in *Not to Speak about all These Women* (1964), wherein a shot of a man running down a corridor waving fireworks is interrupted by a title warning critics not to interpret the fireworks symbolically.

So strong an intellectual presence was the 1960s art cinema that it shaped conceptions of what a good film was. Because the film was to be understood as a "personal statement" by the filmmaker, the art cinema effectively reinforced the old opposition between Hollywood (industry, collective creation, entertainment) and Europe (freedom from commerce, the creative genius, art). In 1965, Arthur Knight compared the Hollywood product with the European approach:

Art is not manufactured by committees. Art comes from an individual who has something that he must express, and who works out what is for him the most forceful or affecting manner of expressing it. And this, specifically, is the quality that people respond to in European pictures—the reason why we hear so often that foreign films are "more artistic" than our own. There is in them the urgency of individual expression, an independence of vision, the coherence of a single-minded statement.[5]

To this personalization of creation, the director as artist, there corresponded certain narrational aspects which critics could highlight. It is in this context that the auteur approach to criticism can be understood historically. The art cinema accustomed critics to looking for personal expression in films, and no one doubted that it could be found in the works of Antonioni, Bergman, et al. Auteur critics went further and applied art-cinema schemata to classical Hollywood films. The critic did not usually bother to explain how individual expression seeped into the Hollywood commodity.[6] More commonly, the critic concentrated on describing and interpreting selected films; as Jim Hillier put it in 1975: "The strategy was to talk about Hawks, Preminger, etc. as artists like Buñuel and Resnais."[7] Scenes in Ray, Minnelli, or Hitchcock could be taken as informed by subjective realism or authorial commentary. (The house in *Bigger Than Life* imprisons the protagonist; a camera angle in *The Birds* expresses the narrator's judgment.) V. F. Perkins could interpret a shot in *Carmen Jones* as if it were by Antonioni: "A metal strut at the center of the widescreen divides the image so as to isolate and confine each character within a separate visual cage. . . . [This shot] begins as a graphic expression of Joe's personality. It shows us his world as he wishes to see it—a world of order and stability."[8] Sirk's objects and decor could be justified as symbols of characters' mental states or as the narrator's ironic asides to the audience. The style of a Hawks or Walsh, on the other hand, was conceived of as avoiding authorial address or expressive realism; these were the "objective" directors. And there was always the possibility of complexity and ambiguity, as in the work of Hitchcock, Preminger, and the American Lang. Ironically, the "rereading" of Hollywood, which has been so central to film theory in recent years, has its roots in the schemata of European "artistic" filmmaking.

NOTES

1. The syuzhet (or plot) consists of the architetonics of the film's presentation of the story.

2. The fabula (or story) embodies the action as a chronological, cause-and-effect chain of events occurring within a given duration and spatial field.

3. V. F. Perkins, *Film as Film* (Middlesex, England: Penguin Books, 1972), 80.

4. Marie-Claire Ropars-Wuilleumier, "Fonction du montage dans la constitution du récit au cinéma," *Revue des sciences humaines* 141 (January–March 1971): 51.

5. In Michael F. Mayer, *Foreign Films on American Screens* (New York: Arco, 1965), vii.

6. V. F. Perkins eventually provided a plausible account in *Film as Film*, 158–186.

7. "The Return of *Movie*," *Movie* 20 (Spring 1975): 17.

8. Perkins, *Film as Film*, 80.

Kaja Silverman

The Female Authorial Voice

In 1968, Roland Barthes proclaimed the death of the author as individual and originating force behind the literary text.[1] Within film studies, however, this very male author still seemed to be at least vaguely alive as late as 1973, when Ed Buscombe made a qualified argument on behalf of authorial intention,[2] and "he" made a spectacular comeback in the late seventies in the work of Raymond Bellour.[3] In 1978, Sandy Flitterman offered an argument which would have seemed inconceivable to the Barthes of "The Death of the Author"—the argument that Hitchcock's "assertion of his presence as producer of the look"[4] works not to center his films ideologically, but rather to subvert the operations of dominant cinematic meaning.[5]

The author has also continued to haunt the edges of film theory, feminist cinema, political cinema, and the avant-garde as the possibility of a resistant and oppositional agency, at times in a less masculine guise. I think, in all four respects, of the "Laura Speaking" section of Laura Mulvey and Peter Wollen's *Riddles of the Sphinx*, which presents the spectator not only with the moving images of one of the film's two directors, but also with the recorded sounds of her voice talking about what she hoped to effect through the thirteen 360-degree pans ("When we were planning the central section of this film, about a mother and a child, we decided to use the voice of the Sphinx as an imaginary narrator. . . .").[6] This is a far more flamboyant authorial inscription than anything to be found in Hitchcock's films, and one which raises the specter of intentionality even more palpably than do any of his cameo appearances.

However, it is not my wish to reinstate the film author as a punctual source or transcendent meaning. The purpose of this essay is quite otherwise. First, I would like to determine the conditions under which the author has lived on as a discursive category since his biographical demise in 1968. Second, I would like to carve out a theoretical space from which

From *The Acoustic Mirror: The Female Voice in Psychoanalysis and Cinema* (Bloomington and Indianapolis: Indiana University Press, 1988). Reprinted by permission of the author.

it might be possible to hear the female voice speaking once again from the filmic "interior," but now as the point at which an authorial subject is constructed rather than as the site at which male lack is disavowed.[7] My preliminary step in this double project will be to return to the scene of the Barthesian crime, and to search there for both the murder weapon and the corpse of the deceased author.

———

There is a certain ambiguity about the terms under which the author meets his unmaker in "The Death of the Author." Where—and when— did this major cultural event occur, and through what means? There is a good deal of equivocation in the way Barthes answers these questions. It is "writing," he tells us, that passed the death sentence on the author, but "writing" turns out to mean three very different things. It refers simultaneously to what Derrida has promoted under the rubric of *écriture*,[8] to modernist literature, and to that activity of productive reading which would be elaborated by Barthes one year later in *S/Z*, a book which is forcefully anticipated in "The Death of the Author" through the quotation from "Sarrasine" with which it begins.[9]

"The Death of the Author" initially characterizes writing as a system of graphic traces cut adrift from a phenomenological moorings—as "the black-and-white where all identity is lost, beginning with the identity of the body that writes."[10] According to this account, writing automatically enacts the death of the author by virtue of its iterability—by virtue of its capacity to be reactivated as discourse in the absence of its writer.[11] Since the figure of the author as a person "behind" the text has never been more than a rationalist, empiricist, and positivist illusion, all that is necessary to dissolve that figure is to repeat the vital lesson of Jakobsonian and Benvenistian linguistics[12]—the lesson that "the speech-act in its entirety is an 'empty' process, which functions perfectly without its being necessary to 'fill' it with the person of the interlocutor: linguistically, the author is nothing but the one who writes, just as *I* is nothing but the one who says *I*; language knows a 'subject,' not a person, and this subject, empty outside of the very speech-act which defines it, suffices to 'hold' language."[13] However, it is important to note that although Barthes argues for the loss of the author's "identity," he does not entirely erase the authorial figure. The author's body remains as the support for and agency of écriture.

"Writing" also designates a very specific group of literary texts, conjured up somewhat paradoxically through a catalogue of talismanic names:

Mallarmé, Valery, Proust, Baudelaire.[14] Significantly, this part of Barthes's argument is hedged about with contradictions, contradictions that intimate that the modernist (or premodernist) text may not be as inimical to authorship as he would have us believe. Not only does he rely heavily upon certain proper names, but at one point he suggests that the modernist text does not so much kill the author as move him from the center to the margins of the stage.[15] At another closely adjacent point, Barthes suggests that if the text *does* murder the author, it also presides over his rebirth. Of course, this new author bears scant resemblance to his precursor; he is voiceless, he is an impersonal scriptor rather than a psychological coherence, and his existence is absolutely coterminous with the text. However, like the author-as-individual-person, the author-as-scriptor would seem capable of assuming a corporeal form, since we are given a quick glimpse of his dismembered hand:

> The modern *scriptor* is born *at the same time* as his text; he is not furnished with a being which precedes or exceeds his writing, he is not the subject of which his book would be the predicate; there is no time other than the speech-act, and every text is written eternally *here* and *now* . . . the modern *scriptor*, having buried the Author, can therefore no longer believe, according to the pathos of his predecessors, that his hand is slower than his passion . . . for him, on the contrary, his hand, detached from any voice, borne by a pure gesture of inscription (and not of expression), traces a field without origin—or at least with no origin but language itself, i.e., the very thing which ceaselessly calls any origin into question.[16]

Finally, and most definitively, "writing" designates a way of reading which discloses the cluster or "braid" of quotations that make up a text. The author is here subjected to a double displacement: First, the "voices" of culture replace him as the speaking agency behind the text, and as a consequence unitary meaning gives way to discursive heterogeneity and contestation. Second, because this plurality is activated only through and "in" the reader, he or she supplants the author as the site at which the text comes together. Here again the image of (re)generation is closely linked to that of the authorial dissolution: "the birth of the reader," Barthes writes, "must be requited by the death of the Author."[17] Significantly, this newly emergent reader closely resembles the author-as-scriptor produced earlier in the essay; the former, like the latter, has no history, biography, or psychology, but is merely "that *someone* withholds collected into one and the same field all of the traces from which writing is constituted."[18]

Why must the author be killed three times over, each time with a different murder weapon? And why does he nonetheless persist, in the proper names that herald the modernist text, the fragment of the writing hand, and the image of rebirth? Because, as I would argue, Barthes desires not so much the author's dissolution as his recovery in a new guise. This desire would surface emphatically five years after "The Death of the Author" in *The Pleasure of the Text.* That work relinquishes the author once again as a person and an institution, but reinstates him a moment later as a figure inside the text:

> Lost in the midst of the text (not *behind* it, like a *deus ex machina*) there is always the other, the author. As an institution, the author is dead: his civil status, his biographical person have disappeared; dispossessed, they no longer exercise over his work the formidable paternity whose account literary history, teaching, and public opinion had the responsibility of establishing and renewing; but in the text, in a way, I *desire* the author: I need his figure (which is neither his representation nor his projection), as he needs mine. . . .[19]

The word *figure* marks the return of the authorial body, grasped now not as biographical or corporeal profile but as the materiality of writing. The body of the author has become the (highly eroticized) body of the text.

However, a subsequent passage indicates that the body of the text has undergone in the process of substitution a quite remarkable anthropomorphization, assuming many of the attributes of the human form. This passage effects an even more dramatic reversal of the earlier essay than the passage I quoted a moment ago, since it exhumes the authorial organ— i.e., the voice—which Barthes was at most pains to bury there. Whereas "The Death of the Author" attempts to deoriginate writing by severing its connection to the voice, *The Pleasure of the Text* argues passionately on behalf of what it calls "writing aloud," or "vocal writing." And in the process it conjures up the vision not only of writing-as-voice but of the word made flesh:

> *Writing aloud* is not phonological but phonetic; its aim is not the clarity of messages, the theater of emotions; what it searches for (in a perspective of bliss) are the pulsional incidents, the language lined with flesh, a text where we can hear the grain of the voice, the patina of consonants, the voluptuousness of vowels, a whole carnal stereophony; the articulation of the body, of the tongue, not that of meaning, of language.[20]

Most astonishing of all, Barthes goes on to compare "vocal writing" to the closely miked sounds of speech at the cinema, sounds which permit us to hear "the breath, the gutturals, the fleshiness of the lips, a whole presence of the human muzzle."[21] He characterizes these sounds as an acoustic close-up, but his panegyric also evokes cinema's visual close-up, with its conventional hold on the magnified features of the face. By the conclusion of *The Pleasure of the Text*, the author "lost in the midst of the text" has thus emerged with all the corporeal and vocal palpability of the author "behind" the text, albeit without the latter's biographical and institutional supports.

By fragmenting the authorial body in the way he does—by giving it to us a section at a time (hand, mouth, breath)—Barthes attempts to hold it outside the perspectival frame of classic representation. He also attempts to sustain it outside gender. However, no discourse of the body can foreclose for very long upon sexual difference, which will at the very least function as a structuring absence. Here it is more than that. Sexual difference is the very ground and terrain of Barthes's battle against the traditional author, and of his struggle to install the "modern scriptor" in the other's place.

Although Barthes never definitively says so, the author he seeks to annihilate occupies a definitively male position. As he observes in *The Pleasure of the Text*, the traditional author's "civil status" and "biographical person" exercise a "formidable paternity" over his work, holding it to phallic rectitude and dominant meaning.[22] Barthes dreams of "dispossessing" this author—of stripping him of his paternal legacy. It is in this context that we must read the opening paragraph of "The Death of the Author":

> In his tale *Sarrasine*, Balzac, speaking of a castrato disguised as a woman, writes this sentence: "She was Woman, with her sudden fears, her inexplicable whims, her instinctive fears, her meaningless bravado, her defiance, and her delicious delicacy of feeling." Who speaks in this way? Is it the hero of the tale, who would prefer not to recognize the castrato hidden beneath the "woman"? Is it Balzac the man, whose personal experience has provided him with a philosophy of Woman? Is it Balzac the author, professing certain "literary" ideas about femininity? Is it universal wisdom? Romantic philosophy? We can never know, for the good reason that writing is the destruction of every voice, every origin. Writing is that neuter, that composite, that obliquity into which our subject flees, the black-

and-white where all identity is lost, beginning with the very identity of the body that writes.[23]

The ostensible function of this quotation from "Sarrasine" is to dramatize the way in which language can be said to write itself, even in the most "readerly" of novels, and so to drive a wedge between discourse and its ostensible author. However, this quotation also introduces the metaphor with which Barthes will subsequently characterize the body of the text, and by means of which he will attempt to exorcise the paternal author—the metaphor of a "neuter" or "composite." This metaphor derives its representational force from the figure of Zambinella, a castrato masquerading as a woman.

What does the metaphor of the neuter tell us about the sexual identity of the author whose voice Barthes dreams of hearing through the body of the text? Let us entertain for a moment the most obvious answer to that question, and assume that Barthes's project is to replace the male author with an androgynous author. This is in many respects an exemplary dream, not least because it is self-destructive. One must not lose sight of the fact that Barthes "himself" was culturally gendered as male, and therefore qualified to occupy an authoritative position. Instead, he puts his own sexual and cultural identity under erasure. Rather than speaking "frontally," from the place of the phallus, he constructs *The Pleasure of the Text* on the model of "that uninhibited person who shows his behind to the *Political Father*."[24] "The Death of the Author" negates masculinity even more emphatically, since it presents the scriptor as a man who has not only severed his anatomical link to the phallus, but also assumed a feminine persona.[25]

However, the female subject can participate in this fantasy of sexual and discursive divestiture only in a displaced and mediated way. She can assist the male subject in removing his mantle of privileges, but she herself has nothing to take off. Besides, the striptease has for too long functioned as the privileged metaphor by means of which female lack comes to be textually exposed. Once the author-as-individual-person has given way to the author-as-body-of-the-text, the crucial project with respect to the female voice is to find a place from which it can speak and be heard, not to strip it of discursive rights.

In fact, Barthes's project seems more complex than I have indicated so far, and more aware of what a feminist reader might see as the pitfalls of androgyny.[26] To begin with, there is an implicit acknowledgment in the opening paragraph of "The Death of the Author" that sexual difference can probably be suspended only by modeling both genders on the accepted logic of one of them, and an insistence that if this be the case, "woman" will be the preferred standard. Barthes thus inverts what Luce Irigaray has called the *"hom(m)osexual"* economy of dominant culture.[27]

"The Death of the Author" also facilitates a very different interpretation of Barthes' authorial dream, and one which is closer to my own. When I read the sentence from "Sarrasine" with which Barthes's essay begins, I am always struck less by the accomplished fact of the author's demise than by what would seem to be a crisis within traditional authorship. The passage in question still bears the marks of male enunciation (it is, after all, a fragment of what might be called the discourse of the Woman as Other), but no male voice comes decisively forward to claim it. This crisis is precipitated in part by the fact that "she" here refers not to "natural" but to "artificial"—or what I would prefer to call "constructed"—femininity. However, it is also motivated by the fact that the voice has taken up residence elsewhere, that it has migrated from a masculine to a feminine position. The castration which Zambinella undergoes not only "unmans" him, making it impossible for him to speak any longer from a masculine position, but it also produces a *female* singing voice. Significantly, singing is one of the privileged tropes through which Barthes describes "vocal writing," or the author within the body of the text. The Barthesian fantasy would thus seem to turn not only upon the death of the paternal author, but upon the production of a female authorial voice, as well. It would also seem to insist upon male castration or divestiture as one of the conditions of such a production—to insist that insofar as the female voice speaks authorially, it does so at the expense of the system of projection and disavowal through which masculinity is constructed.

I am in fundamental agreement with Barthes that the author who should be the chief object of current theoretical concern is the one who occupies the interior of the text, and I will henceforth refer to that figure as the author "inside" the text. I am less prepared, however, than was the Barthes of 1969 to bracket the biographical author altogether, and will instead attempt to propose a new model for conceptualizing the relation between the author "inside" the text and what I will henceforth call the author "outside" the text.

The 1972 postscript to Peter Wollen's *Signs and Meaning in the Cinema* provides a useful starting point for conceptualizing the author "outside" the text. "Fuller or Hawks or Hitchcock, the directors, are quite separate from 'Fuller' or 'Hawks' or 'Hitchcock,' the structures named after them, and should not be methodologically confused," he writes there.[28] Wollen does not deny a relation between the director and the cinematic structure that manifests itself in the films that bear his name, but he gives theoretical priority to the latter rather than the former; the author "outside" the text thus becomes a kind of projection of the author "inside" the text, rather than the other way around. Moreover, even as a projected figure, the extratextual author has undergone a diminution; whereas the earlier edition of *Signs and Meaning in the Cinema* describes him as the mental receptacle within which the alchemy of artistic production occurs, here he is only a catalyst within a much larger and more heterogeneous process of production. Wollen leaves no room whatever for intention, insisting several times over upon the unconscious status of the authorial contribution:

> The structure is associated with a single director, an individual, not because he has played the role of artist, expressing himself or his own vision in the film, but because it is through the force of his preoccupations that an unconscious, unintended meaning can be decoded in the film, usually to the surprise of the individual involved. The film is not a communication, but an artifact which is unconsciously structured in a certain way. *Auteur* analysis does not consist of a re-tracing a film to its origins, to its creative source. It consists of tracing a structure (not a message) within the work, which can then *post factum* be assigned to an individual, the director, on empirical grounds.[29]

The 1972 postscript also helps us to reconceive the author "inside" the text. That figure is no longer identified with the primary level of cinematic meaning. Instead, his is only one among the many and disparate voices that "speak" the text, voices that are now associated with discourse rather than "noise."[30] With the authorial structure no longer functioning to unify the film in which it appears, the cinematic text also undergoes a theoretical transformation. It is no longer impossible to conceive of it as a stable or essential entity, since it becomes a different "experience" with different readings. The cinematic text is not only destabilized, but dispersed; the centripetal image of a film centered around authorial meaning gives way to the centrifugal image of codes engaged in an endless dialogue with other codes, a dialogue that transgresses textual boundaries. It is probably not necessary to add that Barthes casts a long shadow over the 1972 postscript.

Psychoanalysis also plays a key role in Wollen's redefinition of authorship. Within the later account of authorship, it is not only the director
who is unconscious of his contribution to a given film, but the film, as
well. Like a dream, the cinematic text proffers a series of more or less plausible and coherent representations, behind which is concealed the author
"inside" the text, now conceived as an organizing cluster of desires:

> What the *auteur* theory argues is that any film, certainly a Hollywood
> film, is a network of different statements, crossing and contradicting
> each other, elaborated into a final "coherent" version. Like a dream,
> the film the spectator sees is, so to speak, the "film façade," the end-
> product of "secondary revision," which hides and masks the process
> which remains latent in the film's "unconscious." Sometimes this
> "façade" is so worked over, so smoothed out, or else so clotted with dis-
> parate elements, that it is impossible to see beyond it, or rather to see
> anything in it except the characters, the dialogue, the plot, and so on.
> But in other cases, by a process of comparison with other films, it is
> possible to decipher, not a coherent message or world-view, but a struc-
> ture which underlies the film and shapes it, gives it a certain pattern
> of energy cathexis.[31]

Although the notion of the film text as the site of contestation between
multiple codes has much in common with *S/Z*, Wollen breaks away from
Barthes in positioning the authorial signature as the latent, and hence
ultimate or final, level of cinematic organization (albeit not, as we are
cautioned, of meaning). The 1972 postscript also differs from the Barthes
of "The Death of the Author" and *The Pleasure of the Text* in the way it
defines that signature; here the author resides not in the body of the text,
but rather "behind" or "beneath" it.

Although the word *structure* recurs in this passage, it is overshadowed
by a more general emphasis upon process, evoked both through the multiple references to the dream-work, and through the identification of
authorship with a "pattern of energy cathexis." A dynamic model of authorship thus takes the place of the earlier structuralist model;[32] desire
replaces binary opposition as the element that is seen to persist from
work to work within any given authorial corpus. The notion of authorship
as a "pattern of energy cathexis" also forces a further reconceptualization of the author "outside" the text, and of his relationship to the author
"inside" the text; although the former is for all intents and purposes a
projection of the former, he is at the same time the point from which
desire issues, and so a kind of absent or empty origin.

Feminist film theory and criticism have manifested only an intermittent and fleeting interest in the status of authorship within the classic text. One of the earliest essays to approach authorship through a critic of sexual difference was, of course, Laura Mulvey's "Visual Pleasure and Narrative Cinema" (1975). Although the first half of that essay focuses on spectatorship, its second half uses the notion of the author as a mechanism for distinguishing between two very different specular regimes, one of which it associates with Sternberg, and the other with Hitchcock. There are moments in Sternberg's films when no fictional gaze mediates the spectator's access to Dietrich's image, and where the construction of that image as a fetish cannot be explained through an ideological spillage from the look of a character onto the look of the camera, implying instead an authorial eye behind the visual apparatus:

> Sternberg plays down the illusion of screen depth; his screen tends to be one-dimensional, as light and shade, lace, steam, foliage, net, streamers, etc., reduce the visual field. There is little or no mediation through the eyes of the main protagonist. On the contrary, shadowy presences like La Bessiere in *Morocco* act as surrogates for the director, detached as they are from audience identification.[33]

Mulvey also positions Hitchcock as the speaking subject of his films, attributing their voyeurism to the intensity of their author's obsessions, noting that "Hitchcock has never concealed his interest in voyeurism, cinematic and non-cinematic."[34]

In an even earlier essay, "Women's Cinema as Counter-Cinema" (1973), Claire Johnston emphasizes the importance of the auteur theory for feminism, suggesting that its polemics have "challenged the entrenched view of Hollywood as monolithic," and have made it possible to see that the "image of woman" does not assume the same status in all films made within that system of production.[35] Johnston also poses the possibility of female authorship within classic cinema by juxtaposing the names of Dorothy Arzner and Ida Lupino with the ubiquitous Howard Hawks and John Ford.

In a monograph published in 1975, Johnston elaborates more fully upon the notion that Arzner's films bear the marks of female authorship. However, although she argues that what she calls "the discourse of the woman" provides Arzner's work with its "structural coherence," she is far from attributing to this discourse the binary logic which Wollen identifies with the films of certain male auteurs. Johnston suggests that the female authorial voice makes itself heard only through disruptions and dislocations within the textual economy of classic cinema—i.e., *through breaks within its systematicity and binary logic.* Significantly, Johnston suggests that these disruptions and dislocations may occur at the level either of a film's story or its enunciation:[36]

> In Arzner's work, the discourse of the woman, or rather her attempt to locate it and make it heard, is what gives the text its structural coherence, while at the same time rendering the dominant discourse of the male fragmented and incoherent. The central female protagonists react against and thus trangress the male discourse which entraps them.[37]

Sandy Flitterman has also suggested that feminist theory would do well to rethink authorship within the Hollywood text, which she conceptualizes in terms of discourse. In "Woman, Desire, and the Look: Feminism and the Enunciative Apparatus in Cinema" (1978), she stresses the importance of Bellour's work on enunciation in *Marnie,* and argues that any foregrounding of authorship within the classic text functions at least momentarily to subvert "the subject-effect that the apparatus is designed to produce and to conceal" by both raising and answering the question: "Who is speaking?"[38]

However, one looks in vain to feminist work published in *Camera Obscura* for a further elaboration of this point. Although that work is heavily indebted to the notion of film-as-discourse, it largely occludes the role of the author within dominant narrative cinema. One of the most striking examples of this occlusion is Jacquelyn Suter's "Feminine Discourse in *Christopher Strong.*"[39] Suter makes absolutely no room in her discussion for the authorial subject. Indeed, the name "Dorothy Arzner" is mentioned only once, along with the date of *Christopher Strong.* This is surprising, since Arzner was one of only two women to direct sound films in Hollywood during the studio period, a fact that would seem of some relevance to a feminist analysis of one of her films—especially when the stated aim of that analysis is to uncover a feminine discourse. However, instead of looking for ways in which Arzner might be said to "speak" *Christopher Strong* differently from the ways in which Hitchcock "speaks" *Marnie,* Suter focuses on two distinct and seemingly anonymous levels of the text—on what she calls the "patriarchal discourse," and on what she calls the "feminine discourse."

Because of the way she conceptualizes each of these discourses, Suter's feminist reading would have to be characterized as dystopian. In effect, she associates the "patriarchal discourse" with the film's formal and narrative articulation, and its "feminine discourse" with the voices and transgressive desires of two of its female characters, Cynthia and Monica. Because Suter assumes enunciation to be absolutely coterminous with that formal and narrative articulation, the "patriarchal discourse" emerges as a metalanguage, capable of neutralizing any disruptions at the level of character or narrative, while the "feminine discourse" is consigned in a completely unproblematical way to the inside of the diegesis.[40] Suter at no point broaches the possibility that the latter discourse might also provide mechanisms through which an author "outside" the text could "speak" her subjectivity—the possibility, that is, that authorship might be inscribed not merely though the camera, or such an obviously reflexive diegetic indicator as the look, but through those forms of identification and textual organization which are generally assumed to be "secondary," and which hinge upon a variety of characterological and narrative devices. Her theoretical model thus closely replicates the Hollywood model, which identifies the male voice with enunciative exteriority, and the female voice with diegetic interiority.

Suter's textual analysis is extremely persuasive, and it is difficult to argue with the conclusions she draws from it. However, the presupposition that *Christopher Strong* is enunciated like any other classic Hollywood film—i.e., from an exclusively male speaking position—guides and coerces her reading. The very different reading of Arzner's work proposed by Claire Johnston is clearly made possible by the assumption that an emphatically female authorial voice at least to some degree speaks Arzner's films, and that there can never be an absolutely smooth fit between such a voice and the dominant Hollywood model. This may very well be a situation where the cinematic apparatus in its complex totality speaks the film one way, in terms of the systematicity and binary logic that Suter notes, dominating and determining what has been widely taken to be the enunciative level, but where authorial desire seeks out another kind of language, finding a way of expressing itself through diegetic elements. The debate around *Christopher Strong* may also provide the occasion to rethink the absolute priority that recent film theory has given to cinematic specificity, particularly camera distance, angle, and movement and shot-to-shot relationships, and to consider whether there may not be enunciative elements elsewhere, as well—enunciative elements which can best be uncovered through returning to the issue of authorship, and by reposing the question: "Who (or what) is speaking?" To assume, as Suter seems to do, that the cinematic apparatus is the only conceivable "speaker" of a Hollywood film is to risk sealing over all kinds of localized resistance, which—as Foucault tells us—may well be the only form resistance can possibly take.[41]

Not surprisingly, this tendency to think of dominant cinema in mono-lithically phallic terms leads Suter to reject the latter altogether:

> Undoubtedly, the fact that we can locate certain formal transgres-sions in a film advances our knowledge of what might constitute a feminine discourse. But we should be aware that isolated interrup-tions do not necessarily deconstruct the narrative discourse in any significant way. It seems that a systematic rethinking of the entire terms of narrative logic, a reformulation of its elements into an order different from what has come to be known as the classic text, may allow the feminine to express itself forcefully.[42]

What Suter proposes in place of *Christopher Strong* is *Jeanne Diel-man, 23 Quai du Commerce, 1080 Bruxelles* (1975), a film whose formal as well as thematic operations deviate markedly from the classic para-digm. Significantly, the turn to experimental cinema marks the reemer-gence of the author. Chantal Akerman figures conspicuously in this part of Suter's analysis, both as the director of *Jeanne Dielman* and as its enun-ciator ("Akerman, in showing a woman's daily routine in all its banality, breaks with convention because these images do not necessarily function to advance the narrative. . . . Akerman says that she found a plot *because* she wanted to show certain gestures in women's lives that are customar-ily left out of films").[43]

I have dwelt at such length upon Suter's extremely interesting essay for several reasons. It helps us to keep in mind that no film is entirely "spoken" by its ostensible author, and, in the case of dominant cinema, there are an enormous number of other productive elements, not the least of which is a whole textual system which often persists intransigently from one directorial corpus to another. Only a director "speaking" from a position as smoothly aligned with the cinematic apparatus as Hitchcock—i.e., from a position of phallic dominance—would be able to identify his own "vision" so fully with the textual system of Hollywood that the latter can seem the extension of the former. Other authorial subjects might well find themselves speaking against the weight of the textual system through which their films are largely articulated. If authorial enunciation within the classic film text is equated with that text's macrologic, the theorist may quite simply be unable to "hear" authorial voices that speak against the operations of dominant meaning, since those voices are much likelier to manifest themselves through isolated formal and diegetic irregularities than through formal systematicity.

A second reason why I have so conspicuously featured the Suter essay is that it dramatizes certain tendencies that are indicative of much recent writing on cinema by women. To the degree that feminist theory and criticism of the late seventies and eighties concerned themselves centrally with authorship, they shifted attention away from the classic text to experimental cinema, and specifically to experimental cinema made by women. The author often emerges within the context of these discussions as a largely untheorized category, placed definitively "outside" the text, and assumed to be the punctual source of its sounds and images. A certain nostalgia for an unproblematic agency permeates much of the writing to which I refer. There is no sense in which the feminist author, like her phallic counterpart, might be constructed in and through discourse—that she might be inseparable from the desire that circulates within her texts, investing itself not only in their formal articulation, but in recurring diegetic elements.

A brief essay by Janet Bergstrom on *Jeanne Dielman* is a case in point.[44] Bergstrom contends that there are two discourses in Akerman's film—one feminist, and the other deriving from a suppressed or "acculturated" femininity. The first of these discourses is that "spoken" by the director herself through the "permissive" look of the camera, and the second is that associated with the character of Jeanne Dielman. Bergstrom argues that in eschewing the logic of the shot/reverse shot, the film works both to foreground the feminist discourse and to keep it separate from the feminine discourse. There would thus seem to be no possibility of "contamination" or slippage from one side to the other. Bergstrom further isolates the author from her central female character by referring to her in quick succession as a "marked controller" and a "controlling eye."[45]

I am not nearly as certain as Bergstrom that *Jeanne Dielman* manages to distinguish so sharply between feminism and femininity, or that the author "outside" the text occupies the position of a transcendental seer, resting in easy detachment from the woman whose gestures are so meticulously recorded. To do Bergstrom justice, her own language ultimately works to erode the absoluteness of the division she draws, and to suggest that the feminist author is at least partially defined through her female protagonist. She characterizes the relationship between Akerman's stationary camera and Jeanne Dielman as "obsessive" and "fascinated,"[46] adjectives which point to a certain psychic spillage between author and character. This spillage indicates that the ostensible object of speech is

in this case also the subject of speech, and as such at least partly consti-
tutive of the author-as-speaking-subject, even though the camera never
adopts Jeanne Dielman's point of view.

As with most critiques, there is a barely concealed polemic here. I
have been arguing over the last few pages for two rather contrary things—
for a greater theoretical attentiveness to the ways in which authorship is
both deployed and limited within the experimental text, and for the development of hermeneutic strategies capable of foregrounding rather than
neutralizing female authorship within the classic film, where it is in danger of being occluded altogether. Of course, the obvious problem with
respect to the second of these goals is that so few Hollywood films carry a
female directorial signature. How is the feminist writer to proceed?

One possible solution to this difficulty is suggested by Tania Modleski
in a chapter of her book *The Women Who Knew Too Much*. The chapter
in question, "Woman and the Labyrinth," focuses on the relationship
between Hitchcock's *Rebecca* (1940) and the Daphne du Maurier novel
on which it was based. Modleski comments upon Hitchcock's reluctance
to claim that film, which was assigned to him by Selznick, as his own, and
some of the subsequently deleted scenes in the script through which he
attempted to "vomit out" a "whole school of feminine literature."[47] What
emerges from this discussion is a sense of the way in which even a classic film might be riven by conflicting authorial systems, in this case one
"male" and the other "female." But Modleski pushes her analysis even
further than this, arguing that through his forced identification with du
Maurier, Hitchcock found one of the great subjects of his later films—the
"potential terror involved in identification itself, especially identification with a woman." This observation has important ramifications for
our understanding of Hitchcock's status as auteur, indicating that his
own authorial system may be far more heterogeneous and divided than
is generally assumed and that it may, in fact, contain a female voice as one
of its consistent although generally submerged elements.

Modleski bases her case not only on Truffaut's interview with Hitchcock, and the exchanges around the making of *Rebecca* that took place
between Selznick and Hitchcock, but on the narrative organization of the
film itself, which she persuasively shows to hinge upon the whole problematic of identification with the mother. The telling detail which brings
this problematic definitively around again to the question of authorship
is the fact that the character who most fully represents the mother—
Rebecca—figures insistently throughout the film as an "absent one,"
whose signature dominates the image track, but who herself escapes vis-

ibility. As such, it seems to me, she functions as a strikingly literal diegetic surrogate for the speaking subject, and hence very precisely as the subject of speech. What I am suggesting, in other words, is that Rebecca stands in for Hitchcock, in much the same way that Mark Rutland does in *Marnie*, and that in so doing she re-engenders his authorial subjectivity.

Another strategy, deployed with very interesting results by Lea Jacobs in an article on *Now, Voyager,* is to shift the emphasis so sharply away from systematicity and textual macro-logic to disruption and contradiction as in effect to *reauthor* the classic film from the site of its (feminist) reception. This project has much in common with that Barthesian undertaking whereby the "readerly" text yields to the *writerly* one, in that it shifts productively away from the ostensible author to the side of the reader, and places itself on the side of heterogeneity and contradiction rather than unity. However, rather than working to disclose the chorus of cultural voices within the text, it strives to install the female voice at the site of a very qualified and provisional origin (and one which, I would argue, is once again defined through the subject of speech)—the voice, that is, of the female critic or theorist.

I speak of this project as though it were an overt and conscious one, but Jacobs's reauthorship of Rapper's film can be glimpsed only indirectly, through the interpretive process whereby Charlotte is shown to supplant Dr. Jacquith as the speaker of her "own" subjectivity. Her discussion focuses attention on that sequence in *Now Voyager* where Charlotte looks at her image in the café window as the camera cuts back and forth between her and the reflected spectacle. This sequence, Jacobs argues, becomes the occasion whereby the female protagonist "takes the enunciating position with respect to herself through an identification with a man," and so becomes "a self-sufficient sexual and discursive configuration"—something which is seen as disturbing both to the shot-to-shot organization of the films, and to the constitution of the couple which is the form of narrative closure.[48] "*Now, Voyager:* Some Problems of Enunciation and Sexual Difference" mimics this disturbance even as it in a sense creates it. Jacobs, in other words, enacts a discursive resistance to dominant cinema precisely through the resistance which she constitutes Charlotte as having. Charlotte thus functions not just as an enunciator within the diegesis, but as the subject of the speech whereby Jacobs rewrites *Now, Voyager,* and hence as a stand-in for the feminist theorist.

Insofar as a filmmaker can be said to function as one of the enunciators of the works that bear his or her name, those works will contain certain sounds, images, characterological motifs, narrative patterns, and/or formal configurations which provide the cinematic equivalent of the linguistic markers through which subjectivity is activated. However, the linguistic model is insufficient to account for the relationship which is thereby set up between the author "inside" the text and the author "outside" the text. Let us look, by way of example, at the most obvious of authorial references.

A director may turn the camera on his or her face, or the tape recorder on his or her voice, and incorporate the results into a film in the guise of a visual representation, a voiceover, a voice-off, or a synchronized sound and image "totality." Such an authorial citation would seem the closest of cinematic equivalents to the first-person pronoun. However, it also differs from that shifter in one crucial way: whereas the relation between "I" and the speaker who deploys that signifier is based upon arbitrary convention, the relation between the cinematic image of a filmmaker and the actual filmmaker is based upon similitude; it is an iconic representation,[49] and therefore more easily confused with what it designates.

Of course, this is not to suggest that the image is an ontological extension of the material reality it mimics. This is so far from being the case that it actually facilitates something which is in no way intrinsic to the "original"—authorial subjectivity. Indeed, so far from being a mere reflection of the author "outside" the text, it could reasonably be said to constitute him or her as such, in much the same way that the mirror reflection (retroactively) installs identity in the same child.[50]

It is by now a truism of film theory that movies construct viewing subjects through identification. It seems to me that authorial subjects can be similarly constructed, albeit through a wider variety of textual supports than have been so far adduced for their spectatorial counterparts. Identity is, after all, impossible not only outside the symbolic, but outside the imaginary. Even an image which seems self-evidently part of the individual it depicts—which seems nothing more than his or her reflection or photographic imprint—can be claimed by that individual only through identification. And identification, as Lacan cautions us, inevitably turns upon misrecognition.

Through its intimate conflation of the author "inside" the text with the author "outside" the text, this kind of directorial "appearance" often works to promote a second, much less inevitable misrecognition. It is the frequent site, that is, of a narcissistic idealization, through which the filmmaker speaks him- or herself as the point of absolute textual origin. Such is the case in *Marnie,* where Hitchcock not only makes his usual appearance on the image track, but turns to look boldly at the camera and the theater audience, as someone clearly in control of both.

Conversely, an authorial citation of this sort may also become the vehicle for an authorial diminution, a device for representing a film's director as a subject speaking from within history, ideology, and a particular social formation,[51] as it is in *Far from Vietnam* (1967), where Godard turns the camera on himself, rather than "going" to Southeast Asia. As important an authorial critique as this film provides, though, it never really qualifies the filmmaker's ostensible responsibility for its sounds and images, calls his masculinity into question, or suggests that his identity as a speaking subject is radically dependent upon the ways in which it is textually constituted. Although it lacks the reflexive complexity of either *Marnie* or *Far from Vietnam*, Chantal Akerman's voiceover in *News from Home* (1975) deprivileges the authorial voice much more profoundly by rendering it feminine, personal, and informal, and by stripping it of all transcendental pretense.

However, I can think of only one film—the Fassbinder section of *Germany in Autumn* (1978)—in which an authorial "appearance" works not to subordinate the camera and voice-recording apparatuses to the filmmaker, but to subordinate *him* to *them*. It does so by placing at absolute center stage the irrecuperable figure of a director who is not just suffering, desiring, politically conflicted, unjust, and domineering, but a culturally, historically, and *textually* bound subject—by showing that his authorial subjectivity is kept in place only through a compulsive and frenetic productivity. *Germany in Autumn* also hystericizes the body of its author through a veritable theater of grotesque corporeality. This last dimension of the film is as exemplary as the other, since its insistence upon Fassbinder's sagging flesh, putrid breath, and drug and alcohol dependency locates him firmly on the side of a graceless but "readable" spectacle, making it impossible ever again to conflate him with a phallic exteriority. It thus openly declares the author "outside" the text to be nothing more than an effect of discourse.

So far I have focused only on representations which so closely approximate the visual or sonorous features of the filmmaker as to be easily conflated with him or her—with representations which promote the kind of mirror recognition that Lacan associates with "primary narcissism." However, authorial subjectivity can also be brought into play through what both Lacan and Metz would call "secondary identification"—that is, through identification with an anthropomorphic representation which is not, strictly speaking, his or her "own," but that of an other who also happens in this case to be a fictional character. This kind of psychic alignment is brilliantly dramatized in *Scénario du Passion* (1982), where Godard once again turns the (video) camera on himself as he sits in an editing suite taking apart and recombining sounds and images from the film to which the title refers. At a key moment in the tape, he reaches out to the image of Jerzy, the character of the Polish expatriate filmmaker who is clearly a stand-in for Godard-as-director, and locks him in a narcissistic embrace. With that extraordinary gesture, the author who is sitting outside the text of *Passion* looking in is shown to derive all his subjective sustenance from a character who is firmly inside.

A director's relationship with the fictional character who "stands in" for him or her textually may be predicated, as it is not only within *Marnie* but within many classic films, upon a kind of replication at the level of the fiction of those functions generally attributed to the cinematic apparatus— authoritative vision, hearing, and speech. Secondary identification can thus provide another vehicle leading to the imaginary mastery and transcendence. Provided, at least, that the character who sustains this ambition is male, such an identification is completely compatible with dominant cinema. However, a filmmaker's secondary identifications may also depart from that paradigm altogether, and put in place a very different kind of authorial subjectivity—one which, for instance, is much more openly endangered and at risk. I think in this respect of Ulrike Ottinger's fascination with freaks of all sorts, or Marguerite Duras's investment in the figure of the exile.

Finally, the author "outside" the text may find the mirror for which he or she is looking in the body of the *text*—in the way in which his or her films choreograph movement; compose objects within the frame; craft, disrupt, or multiply narrative; experiment with sound; create "atmosphere"; articulate light and shadow; encourage or inhibit identification; use actors; or work with color. The kind of identification I am talking about here is the narcissistic correlative of that "recognition" which permits a reasonably literate moviegoer to say after looking at several shots of *The Red and The White* that "it's Jancso," or after viewing three or four minutes of a Peter Greenaway film that "it's Greenaway." Although the authorial citation is in this case a formal or narrative "image," it is not any the less complexly imbricated with gender, ideology, or history.

Although directors such as Welles, Fassbinder, and Duras speak themselves through their films in virtually all of the ways in which it is possible to do so, other filmmakers may leave their signature only at random points within the diegesis. It would be a mistake to assume that there is no author

"inside" a particular corpus of films simply because they have no distinguishing formal trademark. There is little or nothing about the formal
operations of either Arzner's or Liliana Cavani's work to distinguish it
from other contemporaneous and culturally homogeneous work—little
or nothing, indeed, to indicate a particular preoccupation on the part of
either director with what generally passes for the level of enunciation.
However, even at the level of the fiction, there can be all kinds of authorial spoors.

Of course, tracking these spoors is no simple matter. A reasonably
experienced viewer can readily understand a heavy reliance on primary
colors, collage techniques, and intertextuality to be devices with which
Godard identifies, and even a naïve viewer would immediately understand his "appearance" in *Far from Vietnam* or *Scénario du Passion* to be
an authorial trace. However, a filmmaker's imaginary relation to a given
character is often much less evident, particularly so long as it is theoretically isolated from the closely related issue of desire. The moment has
arrived when I must not only turn to the second of my authorial categories, but abandon the pretense that it can be so clearly separated from
the first. Identification and desire are complexly imbricated with each
other—so much so that it is often possible to uncover the former through
the latter.

But what would the theorist be looking for if she wanted to find what
gives a particular group of films their libidinal coherence? She would be
searching not just for the author "inside" the text, but for the text "inside"
the author—for the scenario of passion, or, to be more precise, the "scene"
of authorial desire. The "scene" to which I refer is what Laplanche and
Pontalis, in an inspired passage from *The Language of Psycho-Analysis*,
call the "fantasmatic," and which they define as that unconscious fantasy
or cluster of fantasies which structures not merely dreams and other
related psychic formations, but object-choice, identity, and "the subject's
life as a whole."[52] The fantasmatic generates erotic tableaux or *combi-
natoires* in which the subject is arrestingly positioned—whose function is,
in fact, precisely to display the subject in a given place. Its original cast of
characters would seem to be drawn from the familial reserve, but in the
endless secondary productions to which the fantasmatic gives rise, all
actors but one are frequently recast. And even that one constant player
may assume different roles on different occasions.

Freud has given us some idea of the kinds of fantasies that most frequently come to organize psychic life in this way. Not surprisingly,
although he attempts to ground most of them in phylogenesis, all of his

examples clearly derive from the Oedipus complex. The list is not, at first glance, very extensive; it includes only the fantasy of the primal scene, the fantasy of seduction, the fantasy of castration, and the fantasy of being beaten.[53] However, this list becomes extremely rich and varied once we have grasped the possible permutations of each fantasy— once all the instinctual vicissitudes have been factored in, the negative as well as the positive Oedipus complex has been taken into account, and theoretical allowance has been made for the fantasizing subject to occupy more than one position in the imaginary tableau. Freud explores the multiple forms which the beating fantasy is capable of assuming for both the male and the female subject in "A Child is Being Beaten," but we have barely begun to calibrate the textual range of any of the others.[54] And, of course, there may well be other fantasmatics than those to which Freud draws our attention.

Insofar as authorial desire manages to invade a particular corpus, it will be organized around some such structuring "scene" or group of "scenes." It seems to me, for instance, that Fassbinder's cinema revolves around the beating fantasy, and that much of Bertolucci's work is libidinally motivated by the male fantasy of maternal seduction. However, these generalizations indicate very little about the actual workings of desire in either body of work, since there are so many ways in which these two fantasies can be elaborated, each with its own consequences not only for object-cathexis, but for identity.

It is at this last juncture that my earlier distinction between authorial identification and authorial desire most completely collapses, since an author's identification with a fictional character will be determined by the subject-position the latter occupies not only within the narrative, but within the fantasmatic "scene" which that narrative traces in some oblique and indirect way. This means that authorial identification and authorial desire are indeed mutually referential—that an investigation of one will sooner or later open on to the other.

Since the subject-position which the author occupies within the cinematic mise-en-scène of desire[55] may well transgress the biological gender of the author "outside" the text, the question of whether the latter speaks with a "male" or a "female" voice can be answered only through an interrogation of the sort I have been urging. At the same time, this libidinal masculinity or femininity must be read in relation to the biological gender of the biographical author, since it is clearly not the same thing, socially or politically, for a woman to speak with a female voice as it is for a man to do so, and vice versa. All sorts of cultural imperatives dictate a smooth match between biological gender and subject-position, making any deviation a site of potential resistance to sexual difference. At stage three of the female version of the beating fantay would indicate, where the subject sees herself as a group of boys being treated as if they were girls (occupying an erotically passive position in relation to the father),[56] biological gender can also figure in complex ways within the fantasmatic "scene."

Although this might seem the end point for an investigation of authorial desire, it is in many ways only the beginning. Laplanche and Pontalis make the crucial point that the fantasmatic is "constantly drawing in new material,"[57] thereby indicating that it is far from closed—that, on the contrary, it is always absorbing the world outside. I would go even further, and argue that it is being continually drawn into new social and political alignments, which may even lead to important "scenic" changes. It is thus important to ask of any authorial desire: How has it assimilated history? And how might it be seen to have acted upon history?

One possible point of entry into the libidinal economy that helps to organize an authorial corpus would be through its nodal points. A nodal point might take the form of a sound, image, scene, place, or action to which that work repeatedly returns, such as Parma and its environs within the films of Bertolucci, dancing within the films of Yvonne Rainer or Sally Potter, or undressing within the films of Cavani. It might also assume the guise of a sound, image, scene, or sequence which is marked through some kind of formal "excess," indicating a psychic condition such as rapture (the revolving door shot with which Leandro Katz's *Splits* concludes),[58] fixation (the frequent close-ups of Terence Stamp's crotch in Pasolini's *Theorem*), or intoxication (the vertiginous play of camera, set, and back projection during the final kiss in Hitchcock's *Vertigo*).

The authorial fantasmatic can also be tracked at the level of the story, at least within those films where story can be said to play even a vestigial role. Like Teresa de Lauretis, I believe that there is always desire "in" narrative,[59] and that in certain cinematic instances that desire can reasonably be attributed to the author "outside" the text. (There is also narrative in desire, or, to put it slightly differently, a fundamentally narrative bent to desire, which is so fully sustained by retrospection and anticipation.) Sometimes the fantasmatic "scene" is sketched by the larger narrative trajectory which is repeatedly mapped by films with the same authorial signature. At other times, as in Duras's *India Song*, or in the films of Mark Rappaport, the fantasmatic "scene" may give rise to an insistently scenic narrative structure.

In *The Archaeology of Knowledge,* Foucault suggests that if a group of signs can be called a "statement," it is because "the position of the subject can be assigned":

> To describe a formulation *qua* statement does not consist in analysing the relations between the author and what he says (or wanted to say, or said without wanting to); but in determining what position can and must be occupied by an individual if he is to be the subject of it.[60]

Until now I have stressed precisely what Foucault seems prepared to dismiss here—the relations between the author and what she has to say, or, to put it rather differently, between the author "outside" the text and the author "inside" the text. But there is a more crucial project than determining the relation between the author and what he or she "says," and that is to establish the position which the reader or viewer will come to occupy through identifying with the subject of a given statement. That position is indeed "assignable" (or reassignable). All of this is another way of saying that the reader or viewer may be captated by the authorial system of a given text or group of texts.

My own fascination with Liliana Cavani's marginal male figures in the book from which this essay comes attests to precisely such a captation— suggests, that is, that I in some way participate in the desire for divestiture that circulates through Cavani's films *Francesco d'Assisi* and *Milarepa,* and that my own authorial subjectivity in some way reflects or replicates the one those texts project. It is of course the case that I pursue the image of a lacking or impaired male subjectivity across the entire breadth of my book *The Acoustic Mirror,* and through a diverse group of texts. However, the moment when my obsession with non-phallic forms of masculinity began was while I was watching and writing about another Cavani film— *The Night Porter.* In some curious way, then, my own authorial voice is indeed a reassigned one, from her to me.

NOTES

1. Roland Barthes, "The Death of the Author," in *The Rustle of Language,* trans. Richard Howard (New York: Hill and Wang, 1986), 49–55.

2. Edward Buscombe, "Ideas of Authorship," *Screen* 14:3 (1973): 75–85.

3. See Raymond Bellour, "Hitchcock, the Enunciator," trans. Bertrand Augst and Hilary Radner, *Camera Obscura,* nos. 3/4: 71–103.

4. Sandy Flitterman, "Women, Desire, and the Look: Feminism and the Enunciative Apparatus in Cinema," in *Theories of Authorship,* ed. John Caughie (London: Routledge and Kegan Paul, 1981), 248. *Theories of Authorship* is an excellent anthology, with authoritative commentary by Caughie. [The concept of the "look" or the "gaze" is frequently

employed by film theorists to refer to the exchanges of glances between characters in a film as well as the look of the spectator at the screen. This activity is thought to involve unconscious desires of a scopophilic nature.—Ed.]

5. ["Dominant" or "classical" cinema refers to a mode of filmmaking typified by Hollywood-style productions which seek to further the illusion of realism by means of strategies designed to render their style invisible.—Ed.]

6. See *Screen* 18:2 (1977): 61–77, for the script of *Riddles of the Sphinx.*

7. [Freud theorized that a boy looking at the nude body of a female imagines that she has been castrated for committing some sin, and that he himself could suffer a similar punishment. Such a punishment, he thinks, could be administered by his father in retaliation for the young male's Oedipal desire to take possession of his mother. The anxieties caused by such fantasies are believed to trigger psychic mechanisms that either cover over or disavow the original traumatic vision or project the violent emotions it arouses onto another. The version of this psychodrama promulgated by French psychoanalyst Jacques Lacan stresses the association between this developmental milestone and language acquisition.—Ed.]

8. [This Barthsian term refers to the way in which any act of writing (or filmmaking) involves the confluence of a heterogenious array of psychic and social determinants.—Ed.]

9. Barthes, "The Death of the Author," 49.

10. Ibid.

11. See Jacques Derrida, "Signature, Event, Context," trans. Samuel Weber and Jeffrey Mehlamn, *Glyph* 1 (1977): 172–97. [Derrida has theorized that all systems of representation involve a continuous play of meaning in which actual graphic signs (the words on the page, the images on the screen) inevitably call up the traces of an unstable, infinitely regressing chain of possible significations.—Ed.]

12. [Roman Jakobson and Emile Benveniste were among those linguists who developed the new science of semiotics, in which language is seen as a system of structures that governs the way in which the human mind interacts with the outside world.—Ed.]

13. Barthes, "The Death of the Author, " 51. [In poststructuralist theory the idea of the individual person has been replaced by the concept of the subject, which is conceived as a network of social and psychic forces that is constituted through language and is constantly in flux.—Ed.]

14. [These early Modernist French writers represented the beginnings of a "writerly" literary style that called attention to the process of composition rather than a "readerly" one which, like classical cinema, aims for invisibility.—Ed.]

15. Barthes, "The Death of the Author," 51–52.

16. Ibid., 52.

17. Ibid., 55.

18. Ibid., 54.

19. Roland Barthes, *The Pleasure of the Text,* trans. Richard Miller (New York: Hill and Wang, 1975), 27.

20. Ibid., 66–67.

21. Ibid., 67.

22. Ibid., 27.

23. Barthes, "The Death of the Author," 49.

24. Barthes, *The Pleasure of the Text,* 53.

25. For a rather different account of Barthes, see Naomi Schor, "Dreaming Dissymmetry: Barthes, Foucault, and Sexual Difference," in *Men in Feminism,* ed. Alice Jardine and Paul Smith (New York: Methuen, 1987), 98–110. Schor finds in Barthes's fascination with the figure of the castrator or neurer a refusal to deal with sexual difference.

26. For one presentation of the feminist case against androgyny, see Jean Bethke Elstain, "Against Androgyny," *Telos* 47 (1981): 5–21.

27. In *This Sex Which Is Not One,* trans. Catherine Porter (Ithaca: Cornell, 1985), Luce Irigaray argues at length that the "use and traffic in women subtend and uphold the reign of masculine hom(m)o-sexuality . . . in speculations, mirror games, identifications, and more or less rivalrous appropriations, which defer its real practice. Reigning everywhere, although prohibited in practice, hom(m)o-sexuality is played out through the bodies of women, matter, or sign and heterosexuality has been up to now just an alibi for the smooth workings of man's relations with himself, or relations among men" (172).

28. Peter Wollen, *Signs and Meaning in the Cinema* (Bloomington: Indiana University Press, 1972), 168.

29. Ibid., 167–68.

30. [A discourse is a coherent body of representations that generates its own interior logic.—Ed.]

31. Ibid., 167.

32. See Brian Henderson, *A Critique of Film Theory* (New York: Dutton, 1980), 206–217, for a poststructuralist critique of both the 1969 version of *Signs and Meaning in the Cinema* and the 1972 postscript. While I am in fundamental agreement with Henderson's remarks about the first of these texts, it does seem to me that the second does much to shift the discussion of authorship in the direction Henderson would like it to move.

33. Laura Mulvey, "Visual Pleasure and Narrative Cinema," *Screen* 16:3 (1975): 14.

34. Ibid., 15.

35. Claire Johnston, "Dorothy Arzner: Critical Strategies," in *The World of Dorothy Arzner: Toward a Feminist Cinema* (London: BFI, 1975), 26.

36. [A film's enunciation is the level at which a narrational or authorial presence behind the story makes itself apparent.—Ed.]

37. Johnston, "Dorothy Arzner," 4. For another "antisystematic" reading of Arzner's work, see Pam Cook's essay, "Approaching the Work of Dorothy Arzner" in the same volume (9–18).

38. Flitterman, "Woman, Desire, and the Look: Femininism and the Enunciative Apparatus in Cinema," in *Theories of Authorship,* ed. John Caughie (London: BFI, 1981), 248. [As conceived by film theorist Christian Metz and others, the cinematic apparatus refers to an array of technological and libidinal structures and institutions within and around cinema that operate at an unconscious level to produce a dream-like state in the spectator; that is, to make her or him into a certain kind of subject .—Ed.]

39. Jacquelyn Suter, "Feminist Discourse in *Christopher Strong,*" *Camera Obscura* 3/4 (1979): 114–18.

40. [The diegesis is the plot of a film.—Ed.]

41. See Michel Foucault, *The History of Sexuality,* trans. Robert Hurley (New York: Pantheon, 1978), 92–102.

42. Suter, 147–48.

43. Ibid., 148.

44. Janet Bergstrom, "*Jeanne Dielman, 23 Quai du Commerce, 1080 Bruxelles,*" *Camera Obscura* 2 (1977): 114–18.

45. Ibid., 117.

46. Ibid., 118.

47. Modleski, "Woman and the Labyrinth," in *The Women Who Knew too Much: Hitchcock and Feminist Film Criticism* (New York: Methuen, 1987).

48. Lea Jacobs, "*Now Voyager:* Some Problems of Enunciation and Sexual Difference," *Camera Obscura* 7 (1981): 89–109.

49. [An iconic representation is related to its source by appearing similar to it.—Ed.]

50. [Lacan theorized that when a small child first sees its image in a mirror, he or she initially misrecognizes this image as a more perfect self. It is only during the Oedipal phase, when the child must negotiate his or her relationship between a desired mother and a feared

father that he or she begins to understand this mirror image in more relational terms. This process forms the basis for the child's acquisition of language.—Ed.]

51. [A social formation refers to the way in which a historical phenomenon is constructed from social determinants.—Ed.]

52. J. Laplanche and J.-B. Pontalis, *The Language of Psycho-Analysis*, trans. Donald Nicholson-Smith (New York: Norton, 1973), 317. Laplanche and Pontalis spell the word "fantasmatic" differently than I have—"phantasmatic."

53. Freud calls the first three of these "primal fantasies" in "A Case of Paranoia Running Counter to the Psycho-analytic Theory of the Disease," in *The Standard Edition of the Complete Psychological Work*, vol. 14, trans. James Strachey (London: Hogarth Press, 1953), 269. I have taken the liberty of adding the beating fantasy to the list. In *Introductory Lectures on Psycho-analysis*, Freud suggests that the primal fantasies were once "real occurences in the primaeval times of the human family," but have since become psychic reality (See *The Standard Edition*, vol. 16, 371).

54. Sigmund Freud, "A Child Is Being Beaten," in *The Standard Edition*, vol. 17, 179–204.

55. This phrase comes from Laplance and Pontalis, *The Language of Psycho-Analysis*, 318.

56. See "A Child Is Being Beaten."

57. Laplanche and Pontalis, *The Language of Psycho-Analysis*, 317.

58. For an analysis of this film, see my "Changing the Fantasmatic Scene," *Framework* 20 (1983): 27–36.

59. For an extended discussion of the relationship between desire and narrative, see Teresa de Lauretis, "Desire in Narrative," *Alice Doesn't: Feminism, Semiotics, Cinema* (Bloomington: Indiana University Press, 1984), 103–57.

60. Michel Foucault, *The Archaeology of Knowledge*, trans. A. M. Sheridan Smith (New York: Pantheon, 1972), 95–96.

Judith Mayne

A Parallax View
of Lesbian Authorship

Diane Kurys's 1983 film *Coup de foudre* (*Entre Nous*) has a devoted following among many lesbians, despite—or perhaps also because of—the fact that the allusions to lesbianism occur from within the securely defined boundaries of female bonding and friendship.[1] Two women, Léna (played by Isabelle Huppert) and Madeleine (played by Miou-Miou), living in post–World War II provincial France discover an attraction for each other (an attraction that is definitely erotic though never explicitly sexual) and eventually leave their husbands to live together. As was widely publicized at the time of the film's release, the friendship of the two women has a strong autobiographical significance, for it corresponds to the experience of Kurys's own mother. At the conclusion of the film, when Léna (Kurys's mother) asks Michel (Kurys's father, played by Guy Marchand) to leave, their daughter—that is, the fictional representation of Kurys herself—is seen watching them. Over the final shot of the film, of Madeleine walking with the children on the beach, a title appears, a very literal authorial signature: "My father left at dawn. He never saw my mother again. It's now been two years since Madeleine died. I dedicate this film to the three of them."[2]

The sudden appearance of the author's signature, within the child's point of view, situates the enigma of the women's relationship in the ambiguous world of childish perception. All of Kurys's films are marked by the connection between storytelling and a female bond that wavers between the homosocial and the homoerotic. Somewhat surprisingly, perhaps, that connection is most strongly marked and articulated in what appears to be, on the surface, the film that departs the most sharply from the distinctly female world central to Kurys's first three films (*Diablo Menthe* [*Peppermint Soda*], *Cocktail Molotov*, and *Entre Nous*). In *A Man in Love* (*Un Homme amoureux*) [1987], the plot centers upon a young actress, Jane (played by Greta Scacchi) whose affair with a narcissistic American movie star, Steve Elliot (played by Peter Coyote), is interwoven with her relationship with her mother (played by Claudia Cardinale), who suffers from and eventually dies of cancer.

While the film follows Jane as its central protagonist, it is not until approximately two-thirds of the way through the film that her voice emerges, quite literally, as the voice of the film, through voiceover commentary. The voiceover is the major component of the film's self-mirroring quality: in the concluding scenes, Jane begins writing a text entitled "A Man in Love. " The voiceover first occurs immediately after a scene in which Jane, in bed with her lover Steve, speaks—seemingly at his request—a fantasy of lesbian lovemaking. Hence, the conditions of the emergence of the female narrator's voice are bound up, narratively, with the lesbian fantasy, a fantasy which offers, within the logic of the film, the possibility of combining two spheres otherwise separate—heterosexual passion, on the one hand, and the mother-daughter bond, on the other.

Some aspects of Kurys's films offer significant revisions of the components of narrative cinema—such as the re-writing of the boys' school scenario (central to two classics of French film history, Jean Vigo's *Zéro de conduite* and François Truffaut's *The 400 Blows*) in her first feature film, *Diablo Menthe* (*Peppermint Soda*); or the exchange of looks between the two women in *Entre Nous*. The self-representation of Kurys (in *Peppermint Soda* and *Entre Nous* in particular), and the representation of female authorship, are far more problematic in the present context, for they consistently evoke and dispel lesbianism simultaneously. Put another way, the "lesbianism" affiliated with Kurys's signature is so framed by the duality of heterosexuality on the one hand, and the maternal bond on the other, that female authorship is foregrounded but not significantly reframed or retheorized outside of that duality.

However, if the popular reception of Kurys's *Entre Nous* by lesbian audiences is any indication, then the film lends itself to the same kind of reading as Barbara Smith offered of *Sula*—a reading based, that is, on the permeable boundaries between female bonding and lesbianism.[3] This is not to say that *Entre Nous* has been defined in any simple way as a "lesbian film." Indeed, whether Kurys's film is appropriately described as a "lesbian film"—permeable boundaries notwithstanding—has been a matter of some debate among lesbians. In a letter to the editors of *Gossip*, a British lesbian-feminist journal, Lynette Mitchell criticizes two essays published in the journal which represent *Entre Nous* as "an unequivocally lesbian film."[4] Mitchell notes that in the film, "the two women are shown admiring each other's bodies and at one point in the film they exchange a swift kiss, but this could just as easily be an expression of deep physical affection as erotic desire."[5] In any case, if *A Man in Love* offers the theory (and *Entre Nous* the practice), then the lesbianism evoked in Kurys's work is not only fully compatible with, but also fully dependent upon, heterosexual fantasy and maternal connections. Put another way, lesbianism is simultaneously a limit and a horizon of female narration and authorship.

In some oddly similar ways, lesbianism is also a limit and a horizon for contemporary feminist work on the female subject. Two of the most common and persistent threads of this work have been, first, the theorizing of a double position for women, as both inside and outside of patriarchal culture, and second, a staging of what is by now a classic fixture of feminist theory, the encounter between so-called American empiricism and French theory. While feminist theories of the subject and of subjectivity are often criticized by lesbians and women of color for being inattentive to the difference that marginalities make, it is not altogether accurate, at least not in the case of lesbianism, to describe the apparent indifference as an absence.

Consider, for example, the by-now notorious dismissal in Toril Moi's *Sexual/Textual Politics* of American black or lesbian feminist criticism: "Some feminists might wonder why I have said nothing about black or lesbian (or black-lesbian) feminist criticism in America in this survey. The answer is simple: this book purports to deal with the theoretical aspects of feminist criticism."[6] Moi proceeds to explain that black and lesbian literary critics are as controlled by the limits of empirical criticism as their straight white sisters; while they may have political importance, their work is theoretically—well, theoretically retarded. Moi does note, however, that these "'marginal feminisms' ought to prevent white middle-class First-World feminists from defining their own preoccupations as universal female (or feminist) problems."[7] By conclusion of her own book, even this vapid concession—from which the term "heterosexual" is, in any case, conspicuously absent—is forgotten. That lesbian criticism doesn't have too much importance—political or otherwise—is demonstrated by Moi's elevation of Julia Kristeva as a model of theoretical feminism, with no mention of the extent to which Kristeva's theorizing establishes the lesbian as bad object, and no consideration that this might be a problem for her feminist usefulness.[8]

This isn't to say that Moi is representative of all feminist explorations of the French-American encounter and the contradictory status of the female subject. Nancy K. Miller, for instance, has noted that Moi "manages to collapse each side of the American/French divide with an astonishing lack of concern for the bodies (and positions) under erasure."[9] Indeed, Miller's own work is far less invested in the simple dualities of simple-minded American feminism versus smart French theory. But here, lesbianism also acquires an implicit function, one defined far more in terms of the pole of attraction (in contrast to the pole of repulsion in Moi's account). In the introduction to her book *Subject to Change,* Miller notes that "[it] may also be that the difference of another coming to writing requires an outside to heterosexual economies."[10] While the term "lesbian" is not used to describe the utopian female communities which figure so prominently in Miller's analyses of women's fiction, the language used is quite evocative of much lesbian writing, and Miller's own reading of Adrienne Rich with Roland Barthes can be read as an attempt both to acknowledge lesbian writing and to redefine the intersections between homosexuality and feminism. Thus, while Miller's avoidance of the term "lesbian" has more to do with the desire to avoid a perilous opposition of "lesbian" and "heterosexual" than to dismiss lesbian possibilities, one is left with a conception of female space with distinct, yet distinctly unspecified, lesbian contours.

Moi dismisses while Miller is more inclusive. However, if the specter of lesbianism does not necessarily haunt feminist theories of the subject, lesbianism has had a signifying function by virtue of its very status as "other"—whether untheoretical other, in Moi, or utopian other, in Miller. It is commonly assumed—and frequently euphemized through phrases like "radical feminism"—that a politically informed lesbian subjectivity participates in the naive affirmation of self, the unproblematic articulation of agency, and the most common refrain of all, essentialism, taken to be characteristic of "American feminism."

Many lesbian filmmakers have engaged with the redefinition and reconceptualization of the cinema, and in so doing have challenged the implicit oxymoron of "lesbian theory" that haunts so many feminist explorations of the subject. But why, one might ask, define these projects in terms of *authorship*, particularly given the suspicious reputation it has acquired—much like lesbianism itself, one might add—for harboring idealized, untheorized defenses of the fictions of identity? Furthermore, within the context of cinema studies, the very notion of authorship is far more evocative of traditional, patriarchal film criticism than even is the case in literary studies, for instance. To be sure, throughout the history of contemporary film studies, there have been calls to rethink and retheorize authorship, from Claire Johnston's insistence in 1973 that auteurism and feminism could function compatibly, to Kaja Silverman's recent critique of feminist film theorists whose ostensible dismissal of the film author is accompanied by the return of a desire for unproblematized agency.[11] Nonetheless, the revision of the concept of authorship has not been a high priority in film studies.

The need to bring authorship into a discussion of lesbian representation is evidenced by a significant body of films in which the filmmaker herself is written into the text, although not in ways that match the common, easy equation between authorial presence and the fictions of identity. There are some lesbian films where this does occur as an affirmative and self-revelatory gesture; Barbara Hammer's celebrations of lesbian love come immediately to mind. But a far more provocative feature of contemporary lesbian filmmaking is the articulation of lesbian authorship as a critical exploration of the very components of subjectivity—self/other relations, desire, and—where lesbianism provides the most crucial challenge to theories of the subject—the relationship between the paradigms of gender and agency, such as the presumed identity between activity and masculinity, passivity and femininity. Chantal Akerman's 1974 film *Je tu il elle,* for instance, is saturated with an authorial presence that explores the possible alignments of the pronouns of its title, and Akerman attempts nothing less than the rewriting of the cinematic scenario that prescribes formulaic relations between those terms along the lines of heterosexual symmetry. Or, to take a related but different example, Ulrike Ottinger has written herself into her films as cameo performances. From the flashback appearance as the dead lover, Orlando, of the title character of *Madame X* to a drunken passerby in *Ticket of No Return,* these appearances revise substantially the assumed equation between authorial fictions and heterosexual oedipal narratives.[12]

Midi Onodera's *Ten Cents a Dance (Parallax)* (1985) is a short (30 minutes) film, divided into three sections (in the catalogue of *Women Make Movies,* the film is described as a kind of "*Je tu il elle* in miniature"). Like other explorations of lesbian representation, *Ten Cents a Dance* is less concerned with affirmative representations of lesbian experience than with explorations of the simultaneous ambivalence and pressure of lesbianism with regards to the polarities of agency and gender. This could of course be taken to mean that the film is, because less "explicitly" lesbian in its focus, less lesbian, period. Indeed, the status of *Ten Cents a Dance* as a "lesbian film" has been crucial to its reception.

For *Ten Cents a Dance* has had a controversial reception history. At the Tenth Annual Lesbian/Gay Film Festival in San Francisco in 1986 for instance, Onodera's film was shown last on a program entitled "Lesbian Shorts," with four other films. By all accounts, the film precipitated something close to a riot, with a considerable portion of the audience booing the film and demanding its money back. If the letters devoted to the screening which later appeared in *Coming Up!*—a San Francisco gay/lesbian newspaper—are representative of the controversy, then *Ten Cents a Dance* was indicative of—to borrow a phrase from B. Ruby Rich—a crisis of naming in lesbian filmmaking.[13] For how could this film, two-thirds of which is devoted to the representation of gay men and heterosexuals, possibly be called a "lesbian film," and advertised as such? More specific criticisms were made as well—that unsafe sex was depicted between the two men, for instance, and that the lesbian scene included a heterosexual woman. The Board of Directors of Frameline, the organizers of the festival, responded that *Ten Cents a Dance* ". . . was not only by a lesbian, but was strongly pro-lesbian, despite a scene by two gay men and a straight couple having sex [*sic*]."[14] The exhibition context required the charge of "not a lesbian film" to be countered with "not only a lesbian film, but a pro-lesbian film." But the reception of the film speaks to a larger issue about lesbian representation, concerning precisely the relationship between lesbianism and the contradictory subject theorized within contrary feminist theory.

Each section of *Ten Cents a Dance* is concerned with a different configuration of sexual desire and language. A split screen is used throughout, so that the two players in every scene are divided from each other. In the first section, two women, while waiting for (or just having finished) dinner in a Japanese restaurant, discuss whether or not they will have a sexual relationship. In the second section, shot from a high angle, two men have sex with each other in a public restroom. And in the final section, a man and a woman engage in phone sex. The use of the split screen creates a wide angle effect, since the top and bottom of the frame are masked, and the two screens appear as if "projected" against a black background, with a dividing line between them. Each scene in Onodera's film captures a sense both of pleasurable duration—depending, of course, upon how you define "pleasure"—and of uncomfortable pauses.

The title of Onodera's film cites the Rodgers and Hart song about a hostess at the Palace Ballroom who sells dances to "Fighters and sailors and bow-legged tailors . . . butchers and barbers and rats from the harbor." The song is a cynical lament, full of bitter resignation and desperation.

The most obvious "match" to the song is the third section of the film, and it would be easy to argue that Onodera equates heterosexual sex with the pathos of sex for sale. But in this respect, *Ten Cents a Dance* has an ambiguous quality—it suggests simultaneously the difference and the analogy between different sexualities. For all of the participants in the film enact rituals of erotic connection and distance.

In any case, the title of the film also reminds us that "Ten Cents a Dance" is not to be taken so literally: the addition of "Parallax" in parentheses, over the right screen, can be read in relationship not only to each of the participants in the respective couples, but in relationship to the distinction between straight and gay, gay and lesbian, male and female as well. If the difference between two points of view allows the "apparent displacement of an observed object" (as the dictionary says), then the "parallax" of Onodera's title refers quite obviously to the way in which lesbian and gay readings take citation and replacement as central strategies. More specifically, the "parallax" view of *Ten Cents a Dance* is evocative of Joan Nestle's insistence—speaking of the difference between "replication" and "resistance" in the appropriation of butch and fem styles—that lesbians "should be mistresses of discrepancies, knowing that resistance lies in the change of context."[15]

Undoubtedly the doubled screen is the most striking visual figure of discrepancy in *Ten Cents a Dance*. The split screen suggests a number of cinematic precedents, such as the stereoscope card—a doubled image which, when viewed at the proper distance, creates the illusion of depth. Other uses of the split screen come to mind as well. In *Pillow Talk* (1959), for instance, split screens are used extensively to juxtapose the telephone conversations of Doris Day and Rock Hudson, frequently with contrasting pink and blue color schemes—which Onodera adapts in her red and blue portrayal of heterosexual phone contact. If the third section of the film is the one most obviously informed by classical Hollywood conventions, all three sections play upon the edges of the frame, particularly in their contrasting functions of reiterating the markers separating the two women (the rose) and rendering oblique the restroom wall and glory hole that separate and connect the two men.

In all three instances, the two views are juxtaposed to disrupt the seamless fit between the participants in sexual dramas. The relationship between the two screens in each section acquires the contours of simultaneous connection and separation. The screen surfaces are figures of permeability and division at the same time. Far from serving as the unproblematized ground for the image, the screen in *Ten Cents a*

Dance becomes a site of tension. This occurs by the doubling of the screens, and by the relationship between the two edges that never quite touch. In addition, the interplay of screen and frame makes the film's representation of sexuality more a question of what is screened, in both senses of the term, than what is unproblematically visible. In the first and last sections of the film, of course, sexual talk obscures the sexual act, but even in the second section of the film, it is the threshold between the two men which is foregrounded far more than sexual acts themselves.

In her recent essay on lesbian representation and Sheila McLaughlin's film *She Must Be Seeing Things,* Teresa de Lauretis distinguishes films like McLaughlin's, which produce "modes of representing that effectively alter the standard frame of reference and visibility, the conditions of the visible, what can be seen and represented" (a description which obviously applies to *Ten Cents a Dance*), from those which provide "sympathetic accounts . . . without necessarily producing new ways of seeing or a new inscription of the social subject in representation."[16] In the latter category, de Lauretis includes films like *Desert Hearts* and *Lianna.* Mandy Merck has described *Desert Hearts* as "steeped in the heterosexual tradition of the active pursuit of the reluctant woman," and goes on to cite a series of rigid dichotomies which structure the film—those of class and geography, for instance.[17]

Such dichotomies have more than a passing relationship with *Ten Cents a Dance,* particularly insofar as the first section of the film is concerned. Merck notes that in *Desert Hearts,* the "brunette is to blonde as active is to passive" dichotomy appears as a stock feature of the genre of the lesbian romance. Dark-haired Onodera casts herself in the role of the "experienced lesbian" having relationship talk with a blonde woman whom she had considered "essentially straight" (the experienced lesbian versus the experimenting heterosexual is another typical opposition described by Merck). Yet Onodera cites the dichotomies in order to disrupt them and suspend them simultaneously. For by casting herself, an Asian woman, in the role of the active pursuer, Onodera reverses one of the most common Western representations of Asians, male or female, as passive and obedient. But that such a reversal cannot function in any simple way as an alternative is made clear in the last section of the film, where the woman assumes the active role, but one which reinforces her own position as sexual commodity. More crucially, the oppositions thus cited never attain narrative or sexual resolution—or rather, only attain resolution by displacement and suspension.

But this displacement and suspension engages a risk, for by focusing on two women talking, *Ten Cents a Dance* could be seen as affirming the popular stereotype that lesbians talk about relationships while men have sex—whether with women or with each other. In other words, *Ten Cents a Dance* could be read as affirming lesbianism as, if not asexual, then at least pre-sexual, or, in the language of much contemporary psychoanalytic theory, as pre-oedipal, as a recreation of the mother-child bond. However, what seems to me most crucial in this representation of lesbian sexuality is the way it is framed—not so much in terms of the scene itself, but rather in relationship to the sexual rituals that surround it.

In the essay mentioned above, Teresa de Lauretis is critical of the tendency, in much writing about lesbianism and feminism and the female subject, to conflate identification and desire. The so-called pre-oedipal, mother/daughter bond can only be regarded as the foundation for lesbianism if the desire *for* another woman is subsumed to the desire to be (like) a woman. As de Lauretis puts it, there is a "sweeping of lesbian sexuality and desire under the rug of sisterhood, female friendship, and the now popular theme of 'the mother-daughter bond.'"[18] Implicit in such accounts is a definition of heterosexuality as mature, adult, and symbolic, whether such accounts are "straight" or symptomatic—really the ways things are, or really the way things are under patriarchy. And heterosexual intercourse becomes the norm against which other sexualities are classified as deviant.

Interestingly in Onodera's film, the possessors of the most explicit (though not completely visible) *sex* are not the heterosexuals but the gay men, and the closest thing to a sexual referent in the film is oral sex, not intercourse. Indeed, orality is one of the sexual common denominators of the film, whether through conversation, smoking cigarettes, or sexual acts. Heterosexual intercourse is thus displaced from its status as the standard of sexuality against which all others are compared. The three sections of the film become, rather, sexual configurations in which orality—so long considered a major attribute of the regressive, narcissistic, homosexually inclined individual (male or female)—figures across the dividing lines of different sexualities.

As de Lauretis suggests, the conflation of desire and identification, and the attendant relegation of lesbianism to the pre-sexual stage serves to reinforce what are ultimately homophobic definitions. At the same time, however, the definition of lesbianism as an extension of female bonding or mother love is one to which many lesbians have been drawn. Within contemporary lesbianism, there are competing definitions of what lesbianism is, from the most intense form of female and feminist bonding (as theorized by Adrienne Rich in her controversial lesbian continuum),[19] to a sexuality that is distinctly different from heterosexuality, whether practiced by men or women. The ironic signature which Midi Onodera brings to her performance—understood here both in terms of her role and the entire film—suggests both of these simultaneously.

In the first section of the film, Onodera is both the "experienced" lesbian discussing the possibility of an intimate relationship with a woman, and an Asian-Canadian having dinner in one of the most popularized Western clichés of Asia, a restaurant. In other words, she appears to occupy a position of some authority. But Onodera defines authorship so as to expose its fictions as well as its desires. For the position that she occupies, on the right side of the screen, is taken up by a gay man engaging in anonymous sex in the next section, and a woman offering phone sex in the last part of the film. Given the extent to which anonymity and sex for sale are defined, in much lesbian writing, as symptomatic of either male sexuality or heterosexuality, the affiliation between Onodera's position and those of the man and the woman in the subsequent scene brackets any simple notion of the woman in lesbian desire as isolated from other forms of sexual desire.

At the same time, of course, the lesbian scene *is* different than the other two, with more emphasis on conversation and the erotics of the look—the latter serving a particularly ironic function, given the extent to which the look has been defined in much feminist film theory as the province of the heterosexual male's possession of the woman. Onodera's ambiguous role in the film, as both author and actor, and as both like and unlike gay men and heterosexuals, thus suggests that the lesbian author is defined as both complicit in and resistant to the sexual fictions of patriarchal culture, and that lesbian irony holds competing definitions of lesbianism up to each other, while refusing to collapse one into the other.

NOTES

1. Thanks to Chris Lymbertos, who provided me with information about the reception of *Ten Cents a Dance;* and Laura George, Lucretia Knapp, and Terry Moore, who read this essay at various stages and offered encouragement.

2. "Mon père est parti au petit jour. Il n'a plus jamais revu ma mère. Madeleine est morte il y a maintenant deux ans. A eux trois, je dédie ce film."

3. Barbara Smith, "Towards a Black Feminist Criticism," *Conditions* 2 (1977): 25–44.

4. See Sibyl Grundberg, "Deserted Hearts: Lesbians Making it in the Movies," *Gossip* 4 (n.d.): 27–39; Lis Whitelaw, "Lesbians of the Mainscreen," *Gossip* 5 (n.d.): 37–46.

5. Lynette Mitchell, "Letter," *Gossip* 6 (n.d.): 11–13.

6. Toril Moi, *Sexual/Textual Politics* (London and New York: Methuen, 1985), 86.

7. Moi, *Sexual/Textual Politics*, 86.

8. See Judith Butler, *Gender Trouble* (New York and London: Routledge, 1990); Teresa de Lauretis, "The Female Body and Heterosexual Presumption," *Semiotica* 67:3–4 (1987): 259–79; Elizabeth Grosz, *Sexual Subversions: Three French Feminists* (Winchester, Mass.: Unwin Hyman, 1989); Kaja Silverman, *The Acoustic Mirror: The Female Voice in Psychoanalysis and Cinema* (Bloomington: Indiana University Press, 1988).

9. Nancy K. Miller, *Subject to Change: Reading Feminist Writing* (New York: Columbia University Press, 1988), 21 n. 16.

10. Miller, *Subject to Change*, 10.

11. Silverman, *Acoustic Mirror*, 209.

12. I discuss at length Akerman's *Je tu il elle* and Ottinger's *Ticket of No Return* in chapter four of my book *The Woman at the Keyhole: Feminism and Women's Cinema* (Bloomington: Indiana University Press, 1990).

13. B. Ruby Rich, "The Crisis of Naming in Feminist Film Criticism," *Jump Cut* 19 (1979): 9–12.

14. "Lesbian (?) Short Raises Storm of Controversy at Lesbian Gay Film Festival," *Coming Up!* 11 (August 1986): 5.

15. Joan Nestle, "The Fem Question," in *Pleasure and Danger: Exploring Female Sexuality*, ed. Carole S. Vance (Boston: Routledge and Kegan Paul, 1984), 236.

16. Teresa de Lauretis, "Film and the Visible" (Paper delivered at the How Do I Look? Conference, New York City, October 1989), 2.

17. Mandy Merck, "Dessert Hearts," *The Independent* 10:6 (1987), 16.

18. de Lauretis, "Film and the Visible," 31.

19. Adrienne Rich, "Compulsory Heterosexuality and Lesbian Existence," in *Powers of Desire: The Politics of Sexuality*, eds. Ann Snitow, Christine Stansell, and Sharon Thompson (New York: Monthly Review Press, 1983), 177–205.

Historical and
Institutional Contexts

Thomas Schatz

"The Whole Equation
of Pictures"

*Walking at dawn in the deserted Hollywood streets in
1951 with David [Selznick], I listened to my favorite
movie boss topple the town he had helped to build. The
movies, said David, were over and done with. Hollywood was already a ghost town making foolish efforts
to seem alive. . . .*
  *But now that the tumult was gone, what had Holly-
wood been?*

—Ben Hecht, 1954

David Selznick had a flair for the dramatic, and no one knew that better
than Ben Hecht. The two collaborated on some of Hollywood's biggest
hits—movies like *Gone With the Wind* and *Notorious* and *Duel in the
Sun*—and often enough the making of those films was as rife with conflict
as the films themselves, thanks to Selznick's ego and his unconventional
working methods. In fact, Selznick, a "major independent" producer in the
age of the big studios, saw his entire career in epic-dramatic terms: David
amid a slew of Goliaths. But in the early 1950s that scenario was changing rapidly. In 1953 Selznick wrote Louis B. Mayer, MGM's recently
deposed studio boss, that all of Hollywood's "old companies" were still
geared to a "business that no longer exists." Selznick felt that everything
from the production studios in Los Angeles to the worldwide marketing
and distribution networks were predicated on a notion of moviemaking—
and of movies themselves—for which there was "no longer a market."

This was scarcely a cause for celebration, since Selznick was learning
how little real independence he had from the entrenched movie companies
and their way of doing business. He was barely fifty years old and his
earlier blockbusters were virtual prototypes for the independent productions that now ruled the marketplace, yet he felt himself going under with

From *The Genius of the System: Hollywood Filmmaking in the Studio Era* (New York: Pantheon, 1988). Reprinted by permission of the author.

the old studios. By the decade's end he was ready to write his own as well as Hollywood's epitaph. Selznick told one of his former partners in 1958 that their "old stomping ground" had become "very mixed up and unhappy." He went on to eulogize the pioneers and moguls, a vanishing breed now that the industry was a half-century old, and he closed with the observation that Hollywood's "big companies" were staying alive only through the momentum and the motion pictures created in earlier years.

The big companies like MGM, Paramount, and Warner Bros. continued to survive, of course—indeed they flourished in the age of television and the New Hollywood. But things had changed since that halcyon era when Selznick and Hecht and Mayer were making movies. Gone was the cartel of movie factories that turned out a feature every week for a hundred million moviegoers. Gone were the studio bosses who answered to the New York office and oversaw hundreds, even thousands, of contract personnel working on the lot. Gone was the industrial infrastructure, the "integrated" system whose major studio powers not only produced and distributed movies but also ran their own theater chains. Something was "over and done with" in the early 1950s, all right, but it wasn't the movies. It was the studio system of moviemaking and the near-absolute power that the studio wielded over the American movie industry. The Hollywood studio system emerged during the teens and took its distinctive shape in the 1920s. It reached maturity during the 1930s, peaked in the war years, but then went into a steady decline after the war, done in by various factors, from government antitrust suits and federal tax laws to new entertainment forms and massive changes in American lifestyles. As the public shifted its viewing habits during the 1950s from "going to the movies" to "watching TV," the studios siphoned off their theater holdings, fired their contract talent, and began leasing their facilities to independent filmmakers and television production companies. By the 1960s MGM and Warners and the others were no longer studios, really. They were primarily financing and distribution companies for pictures that were "packged" by agents or independent producers—or worse yet, by the stars and directors who once had been at the studios' beck and call.

––––––––

The collapse of the studio system was bound to provoke questions like Ben Hecht's—"What had Hollywood been?"—and the answers have been plentiful but less than adequate. Hecht himself answered as so many of his industry colleagues did, with an anecdotal, self-serving memoir laced with venom for the "system" and for the "Philistines" who controlled it—and who paid Hecht up to $5,000 a week for his services as a screenwriter. Hecht was an essential part of that system, of course, though he hardly saw things that way, and his reminiscence was less revealing of Hollywood filmmaking than of the attitudes of eastern-bred writers toward the priorities and the power structure in the movie industry. Hecht's answer did provide yet another piece of evidence to be factored in, along with countless other interviews and autobiographies, critical studies, and economic analyses. But the accumulated evidence scarcely adds up, and our sense of what Hollywood had been remained a vague impression, fragmented and contradictory, more mythology than history.

Promising to change all that, a cadre of critics and historians in the 1960s and 1970s cultivated a "theory of film history" based on the notion of directorial authorship. As the New Hollywood emerged from the ashes of the studio era, proponents of the "auteur theory" proclaimed that what the Old Hollywood had been was a director's cinema. They proclaimed, too, that the only film directors worthy of canonization as author-artists were those whose personal style emerged from a certain antagonism toward the studio system at large—the dehumanizing, formulaic, profit-hungry machinery of Hollywood's studio-factories. The auteurists' chief proponent was Andrew Sarris, who in his landmark study, *The American Cinema: Directors and Directions, 1929–1968,* cast the studio boss as the heavy in Hollywood's epic struggle and reduced American film history to the careers of a few dozen heroic directors. Keying on an observation by director George Stevens that as the industry took shape, "the filmmaker became the employee, and the man who had time to attend to the business details became the head of the studio," Sarris developed a simplistic theory of his own, celebrating the director as the sole purveyor of Film Art in an industry overrun with hacks and profitmongers. The closing words of his introduction said it all: "He [the director] would not be worth bothering with if he were not capable now and then of a sublimity of expression almost miraculously extracted from his money-oriented environment."

Auteurism itself would not be worth bothering with if it hadn't been so influential, effectively stalling film history and criticism in a prolonged stage of adolescent romanticism. But the closer we look at Hollywood's relations of power and hierarchy of authority during the studio era, at its division of labor and assembly-line production process, the less sense it makes to assess filmmaking or film style in terms of the individual director—or *any* individual, for that matter. The key issues here are style and authority—creative expression and creative control—and there were indeed a number of Hollywood directors who had an unusual degree of authority and a certain style. John Ford, Howard Hawks, Frank Capra, and Alfred Hitchcock are good examples, but it's worth noting that their privileged status—particularly their control over script development, casting, and editing—was more a function of their role as producers than as directors. Such authority came only with commercial success and was won by filmmakers who proved not just that they had talent but that they could work profitably within the system. These filmmakers were often "difficult" for a studio to handle, perhaps, but no more so than its top stars or writers. And ultimately they got along, doing what Ford called "a job of work" and moving on to the next project. In fact, they did their best and most consistent work on calculated star vehicles for one particular studio, invariably in symbiosis with an authoritative studio boss.

Consider Ford's work with Darryl Zanuck at 20th Century–Fox on a succession of Henry Fonda pictures: *Young Mr. Lincoln, Drums along the Mohawk,* and *The Grapes of Wrath.* Or Alfred Hitchcock doing *Spellbound* and *Notorious,* two psychological dramas scripted by Ben Hecht and prepared by David Selznick for his European discovery, Ingrid Bergman. Or Howard Hawks working for Jack Warner on *To Have and Have Not* and *The Big Sleep,* two hard-boiled thrillers with Bogart and Bacall that were steeped in the Warners style. These were first-rate Hollywood films, but they were no more distinctive than other star-genre formulations turned out by routine contract directors: Universal's horror films with Boris Karloff directed by James Whale, for instance, or the Paul Muni biopics directed by William Dieterle for Warners. Whale and Dieterle are rarely singled out for their style or artistry, and each would have been lost without the studio's resources and regimented production process. But that doesn't diminish the integrity of films like *Frankenstein, The Old Dark House,* and *The Bride of Frankenstein,* or *The Story of Louis Pasteur* and *The Life of Emile Zola.*

The quality and artistry of all these films were the product not simply of individual human expression, but of a melding of institutional forces. In each case the "style" of a writer, director, star—or even a cinematographer, art director, or costume designer—fused with the studio's production operations and management structure, its resources and talent pool, its narrative traditions and market strategy. And ultimately any individual's style was no more than an inflection on an established studio style. Think of Jimmy Cagney in *Public Enemy,* staggering down that dark, rain-drenched street after a climactic shoot-out with rival gangsters, gazing just past the camera and muttering "I ain't so tough," then falling face-down into the gutter. That was a signature Warner Bros. moment, a narrative-cinematic epiphany when star and genre and technique co-alesced into an ideal expression of studio style, vintage 1931. Other studios had equally distinctive styles and signature moments, involving different stars and story types and a different "way of seeing" in both a technical and an ideological sense. On a darkened, rain-drenched street at MGM, for instance, we might expect to find a glossy, upbeat celebration of life, and love—Mickey Rooney in another Andy Hardy installment, struggling to get the top up on his old jalopy while his date gets soaked, or Gene Kelly dancing through puddles and singin' in the rain. Over at Universal a late-night storm was likely to signal something more macabre: Count Dracula on the prowl, perhaps, or Dr. Frankenstein harnessing a bolt of lightning for some horrific experiment.

These are isolated glimpses of a larger design, both on screen and off. Each top studio developed a repertoire of contract stars and story formulas that were refined and continually recirculated through the marketplace. Warners in the 1930s, for example, cranked out urban crime films with Cagney and Edward G. Robinson, crusading biopics with Paul Muni, backstage musicals with Dick Powell and Ruby Keeler, epic swashbucklers with Errol Flynn and Olivia de Havilland, and in a curious counter to the studio's male ethos, a succession of "women's pictures" starring Bette Davis. These stars and genres were the key markers in Warners' Depression-era style, the organizing principles for its entire operation from the New York office to the studio-factory across the continent. They were a means of stabilizing marketing and sales, of bringing efficiency and economy into the production of some fifty feature films per year, and of distinguishing Warners' collective output from that of its competitors.

The chief architects of a studio's style were its executives, which any number of Hollywood chroniclers observed at the time. Among the more astute chroniclers was Leo Rosten, who put it this way in *Hollywood: The Movie Colony,* an in-depth study published in 1940:

> Each studio has a personality; each studio's product shows special emphases and values. And, in the final analysis, the sum total of a studio's personality, the aggregate pattern of its choices and its tastes, may be traced to its producers. For it is the producers who establish the preferences, the prejudices, and the predispositions of the organization and, therefore, of the movies which it turns out.

Rosten was not referring to the "supervisors" and "associate producers" who monitored individual productions, nor to the pioneering "movie moguls" who controlled economic policy from New York. He was referring to studio production executives like Louis B. Mayer and Irving Thalberg at MGM, Jack Warner and Hal Wallis at Warner Bros., Darryl Zanuck at 20th Century–Fox, Harry Cohn at Columbia, and major independent producers like David Selznick and Sam Goldwyn. These men—and they were always men—translated an annual budget handed down by the New York office into a program of specific pictures. They coordinated the operations of the entire plant, conducted contract negotiations, developed stories and scripts, screened "dailies" as pictures were being shot, and supervised editing until a picture was ready for shipment to New York for release. These were the men Frank Capra railed against in an open letter to the *New York Times* in April 1939, complaining that "about six producers today pass on about 90 percent of the scripts and edit 90 percent of the pictures." And these were the men that F. Scott Fitzgerald described on the opening page of *The Last Tycoon*, the Hollywood novel he was writing at the time of his death, in 1940. "You can take Hollywood for granted like I did," wrote Fitzgerald, "or you can dimiss it with the contempt we reserve for what we don't understand. It can be understood too, but only dimly and in flashes. Not a half dozen men have been able to keep the whole equation of pictures in their heads."

———

Fitzgerald was thinking of Irving Thalberg when he wrote that passage, and it would be difficult to find a more apt description of Thalberg's role at MGM. Nor could we find a clearer and more concise statement of our objective here: to calculate the whole equation of pictures, to get down on paper what Thalberg and Zanuck and Selznick and a very few others carried in their heads. After digging through several tons of archival materials from various studios and production companies, I have developed a strong conviction that these producers and studio executives have been the most misunderstood and undervalued figures in American film history. So in a sense this is an effort to reconsider their contributions to Hollywood filmmaking; but I don't want to overstate their case or misstate my own. Hollywood's division of labor extended well into the executive and management ranks, and isolating the producer or anyone else as artist or visionary gets us nowhere. We would do well, in fact, to recall French film critic André Bazin's admonition to the early auteurists, who were transforming film history into a cult of personality. "The American cinema is a classical art," wrote Bazin in 1957, "so why not then admire in it what is most admirable—i.e., not only the talent of this or that filmmaker, but the genius of the system."

It's taken us a quarter century to appreciate that insight, to consider the "classical Hollywood" as precisely that: a period when various social, industrial, technological, economic, and aesthetic forces struck a delicate balance. That balance was conflicted and ever shifting but stable enough through four decades to provide a consistent system of production and consumption, a set of formalized creative practices and constraints, and thus a body of works with a uniform style—a standard way of telling stories, from camera work and cutting to plot structure and thematics. It was the studio system at large that held those various forces in equilibrium; indeed, the "studio era" and the classical Hollywood describe the same industrial and historical phenomenon. The sites of convergence for those forces were the studios themselves, each one a distinct variation on Hollywood's classical style.

The market strategies developed by Warners, MGM, Universal, and Selznick influenced but in no way determined production operations and house style. The movies were a "vertical" industry in that the ultimate authority belonged to the owners and top corporate officers in New York. But the New York office couldn't make movies, nor could it dictate audience interest and public taste. And whatever the efforts to regulate production and marketing, moviemaking remained a competitive and creative enterprise. In the overall scheme of things, the West Coast management team was the key to studio operations, integrating the company's economic and creative resources, translating fiscal policy into filmmaking practice. This demanded close contact with New York and a feel for the company's market skew, but also an acute awareness of the studio's resources and heavy interaction with the top filmmakers on the lot, particularly the directors, writers, and stars.

Because of the different stakes involved for each of these key players, studio filmmaking was less a process of collaboration than of negotiation and struggle—occasionally approaching armed conflict. But somehow it worked, and it worked well. What's most remarkable about the classical Hollywood, finally, is that such varied and contradictory forces were held in equilibrium for so long. The New Hollywood and commercial television indicate all too clearly what happens when that balance is lost, reminding us what a productive, efficient, and creative system was lost back in the 1950s. There was a special genius to the studio system, and perhaps when we understand that we will learn, at long last, what Hollywood had been.

Timothy Corrigan

The Commerce of Auteurism

As soon as you become that big, you get absorbed.
—Francis Coppola

A foundation of postwar film criticism, auteurism has never been a consistent or stable way of talk about films and filmmakers. When auteurs and auteuristic codes for understanding movies spread from France to the United States and elsewhere in the sixties and seventies, these models were hardly the pure reincarnations (as critics sometimes urged us to believe) of literary notions of the author as the sole creator of the film or of Sartrean demands for "authenticity" in personal expression.[1] Rather, from its inception, auteurism has been bound up with changes in industrial desires, technological opportunities, and marketing strategies. In the United States, for instance, the industrial utility of auteurism from the late 1960s to the early 1970s had much to do with the waning of the American studio system and the subsequent need to find new ways to mark a movie other than with a studio's signature. One might also recognize the crucial contribution to auteurism made by the new social formation of movie audiences in the early sixties: the massive "teenaging" of audiences in Europe and America. In the late sixties the global encounter with traditional forms of authority on campuses and on the streets opened doors in academia to nontraditional disciplines like film studies, and this in turn helped to create a crucial forum and platform for a new international art cinema identified with auteurs like Ingmar Bergman, Luis Buñuel, Michelangelo Antonioni, and Jean-Luc Godard, as well as American auteurs like Arthur Penn and Robert Altman.

The historical adaptability of auteurism, back through the works of early filmmakers like von Stroheim and Eisenstein and forward through the present generation of Spielberg and Cimino, identifies mainly the desire and demand of an industry to generate an artistic (and specifically

Romantic) aura during a period when the industry as such needed to distinguish itself from other, less elevated, forms of mass media (most notably, television). Auteurism offered not just new audiences, retrieved from the modernist art communities, but new cultural sanctions to old audiences, alienated and awash in an indistinguishable spate of media images. Since the 1970s especially, the auteurist marketing of movies whose titles often proclaim the filmmaker's name, such as *Bernardo Bertolucci's 1900* (1976), *David Lean's Ryan's Daughter* (1970), or *Michael Cimino's Heaven's Gate* (1980), aim to guarantee a relationship between audience and movie whereby an intentional and authorial agency governs, as a kind of brand-name vision whose contextual meanings are already determined, the way a movie is seen and received.

I
The Multiple Children of Truffaut:
From Author to Agent

One of the chief mystifications or omissions within early theories and practices of auteurism has been a valorization of one or another idea of expression, mostly disconnected from its marketing and commercial implications.[2] Despite their large differences, theories and practices of auteurism from Astruc and Peter Wollen to Foucault and Stephen Heath, from John Ford to Jean-Luc Godard share basic assumptions about the auteur as the structuring principle of enunciation, an organizing expression of one sort or another. Whether one locates that auteurial presence as a source for stylistic or other textual consistencies and variations or as a figurative authority supplanting a lost or "dead" source (as Barthes would say) in the form of a textual enunciation, the place of the auteur within a textual causality describes a way of organizing spectatorial positions in a transcendent or trans-subjective fashion (142–148).[3] To view a film as the product of an auteur means to read or to respond to it as an expressive organization that precedes and forecloses the historical fragmentations and subjective distortions that can take over the reception of even the most classically coded movie. The often strained attempts to make consistent or evolutionary the British and American movies of Hitchcock or the German and Hollywood films of Fritz Lang are governed by some sense of a historically trans-subjective and transcendent category which authorizes certain readings or understandings of those movies. In David Bordwell's analysis of auteurism as an interpretative cue, the film director "becomes the real-world parallel to the narrational presence 'who' communicates (what is the filmmaker saying?) and 'who' expresses (what is the author's personal vision?)" (211).

Formalist and cognitive critiques of auteurism, such as Bordwell's, can vanquish most of the myths of expressivity in the cinema in favor of more formal and heuristic uses for the auteur. Yet, these too do not fully attend to the survival—and, in fact, increasing importance—of the auteur as a *commercial* strategy for organizing audience reception, as a critical concept bound to distribution and marketing aims that identify and address the potential cult status of an auteur. Today, even these modernist corrections, discussions, or deconstructions of the romantic roots of auteurism need to be taken another step towards recontextualizing them within industrial and commercial trajectories. Illustrating this need to investigate how "the author is constructed by and for commerce," John Caughie has noted that this question has been overlooked since Brecht's 1931 account of *The Threepenny Opera* trial in which Brecht "brilliantly exposes the contradiction in cinema between the commercial need to maintain the ideology of the creative artist and the simultaneous need to redefine ownership in terms of capital, rather than creative investment" (2).[4]

This attention to a commerce of auteurism is especially critical in keeping pace with the auteur as a practice and interpetative category during the last fifteen years, the period when the play of commerce has increasingly assimilated the action of enunciation and expression. Certainly such a revaluation of auteurism as more than enunciatory expression or a heuristic category could and should take place across any of its historical variations and to a certain extent has already been implicit in the social and historical emphasis of a "politique des auteurs." Yet the international imperatives of postmodern culture have made it clear that commerce is now much more just a contending discourse: if, in conjunction with the so-called international art cinema of the sixties and seventies, the auteur had been absorbed as a phantom presence within a text, he or she has rematerialized in the eighties and nineties as a commercial performance of *the business of being an auteur.* To follow this move in contemporary culture, the practices of auteurism now must be re-theorized in terms of the wider material strategies of social agency. Here the auteur can be described according to the conditions of a cultural and commercial *intersubjectivity,* a social interaction distinct from an intentional causality or textual transcendence.

Models of agency are useful here precisely because they are models of intersubjectivity which aim to undermine the metaphysics and the authority of expression and intention, the cornerstones of a stable subjectivity. They delineate a model of action in which both expression and reception are conditioned and monitored by reflective postures towards their material conditions. Charles Taylor, for instance, has argued a model of human agency which foregrounds "second order desires" where the "reflective self-evaluation" of "the self-interpreting subject" has as its object "the having of certain first-order desires" (43, 28, 15). Similarly Anthony Giddens suggests a materialist model of expression as self-reflexive action: the motivation of expressive action, the rationalization of that action, and the reflective monitoring of action concomitantly interact to map the structure of expression as a reflective social discourse which necessarily calls attention to the material terms of its communication. In both cases, agency becomes a mode of enunciation which decribes an active and monitored engagement with its own conditions as the subjective expresses itself through the socially symbolic. In the cinema, auteurism as agency thus becomes a place for encountering not so much a transcending meaning (of first-order desires) but the different conditions through which expressive meaning is made by an auteur and reconstructed by an audience, conditions which involve historical and cultural motivations and rationalizations. Here, the strange array of contemporary auteurs from Francis Coppola to Quentin Tarantino may strategically embrace the more promising possibilities of the auteur as a commercial presence, since the commercial status of that presence now necessarily becomes part of an agency that culturally and socially monitors identification and critical reception.

II
The Auteur as Celebrity

The practice of the auteur as a particular brand of social agency appears most clearly and ironically in the contemporary status of the auteur as star.[5] This idea of the auteur-star vaguely harks back to the earlier avatars of auteurism who were placed in certain aesthetic and intellectual pantheons: from Orson Welles to Robert Bresson, the celebrity of the auteur was the product of a certain textual distinction. As generally consistent as that tradition of the textual auteur is, more recent versions of the auteurist positions have swerved away from its textual center. In line with the marketing transformation of the international art cinema into the cult of personality that defined the film artist of the seventies, auteurs have become increasingly situated along an extra-textual path in which their commercial status as auteurs is their chief function as auteurs: the auteur-star is meaningful primarily as a promotion or re-covery of a movie or group of movies, frequently regardless of the filmic text itself. Like *Michael Cimino's Heaven's Gate*, auteurist movies are often made before they get made; and, like Coppola's *Tucker* (1989), a director's promoted biography can preempt most textual receptions of a movie. In a twist on the tradition of certain movies being vehicles for certain stars, the auteur-star can potentially carry and redeem any sort of textual material, often to the extent of making us forget that mater-ial through the marvel of its agency. In this sense, promotional tech-nology and production feats become the new "camera-stylo," serving a new auteurism in which the making of a movie (like *Fitzcarraldo* [1982]) or its unmaking (like *Twilight Zone* [1983]) foreground an agency that forecloses the text itself. As Godard has parodied it so incisively in recent films like *King Lear* (1989), in today's commerce we want to know what our authors and auteurs look like or how they act; it is the text which may now be dead.

Placed before, after, and outside a film text and in effect usurping the work of that text and its reception, today's auteurs are agents who, whether they wish it or not, are always on the verge of being self-consumed by their status as stars. By this I am not suggesting merely some brand of egotism or self-marketing posture but that the binary dis-tinctions that once formulated most models of auteurist expression against textual organization have collapsed into what Dana Polan has called, in a larger context, the postmodern "evacuation of sense" ("Brief Encounters," 167–187). The oppositional calculus of expression to text, psychology to meaning, or authority to interpretation no longer sustains the contemporary auteur film. Instead, institutional and commercial agencies define auteurism almost exclusively as publicity and advertise-ment, that is, as both a provocative and empty display of material that intercepts those more traditional oppositions. Meaghan Morris has noted (in language similar to Richard Dyer's description of stars), that today "the primary modes of film and *auteur* packaging are advertising, review snippeting, trailers, magazine profiles—always already in appropriation as the precondition, and not the postproduction of meaning" (122–123). To respond to a movie as primarily or merely a Spielberg film is, after all, often the pleasure of refusing an evaluative relation to it. An auteur film today seems to aspire more and more to a critical tautology, capable of being understood and consumed without being seen. Like an Andy Warhol movie, it can communicate a great deal for a large number of audiences who know the maker's reputation but have never seen the films themselves. This, not surprisingly, is what so exasperates neo-romantic Marxist critics of postmodernism who cling longingly to the High-Modernist conception of the filmmaker as expressive artist, to a time before "art becomes one more branch of commodity production" and "the artist loses all social status and faces the options of becoming a *poete maudit* or a journalist" (Jameson, "Reification," 136).

Of the several tacks within the commerce of the auteur-star, the two that are most pertinent here are: the commercial auteur and the auteur of commerce. Although the first category could theoretically include a vast range of stars as directors and directors as stars (Sylvester Stallone, Madonna, Clint Eastwood, and so forth) more purportedly respectable names in this group would include Spielberg, George Lucas, Brian De Palma, David Lean and, with different agendas, John Sayles, Woody Allen, Truffaut of the later years, Lina Wertmuller, the Bertolucci of the latest Academy Awards, and the Spike Lee of Air Jordans. My argument so far would assimilate most of these names since what defines this group is recognition, either foisted upon them or chosen by them, that the celebrity of their agency produces and promotes texts that invariably exceed the movie itself, both before and after its release.

The second category is, I believe, the more intriguing variation on the first, for there a filmmaker attempts to monitor or rework the institutional manipulations of the auteurist position within the commerce of the contemporary movie industry. If normally the auteurist text promotes and recuperates a movie, these filmmakers now run the commerce of the auteurist and autonomous self up against its textual expression in a way that shatters the coherency of both authorial expression and stardom. Motivations, desires, and historical developments—which are frequently dramatized in critical readings of films as at least semi-autobiographical—now become destablized and usually with a purpose: did, one asks, the same Fassbinder who made *The Marriage of Maria Braun* (1978) give us *Querelle* (1982)? While a more traditional auteurist position could describe these changes in perspective and expression according to some coherent notion of evolution, an evaluation of many contemporary filmmakers must admit fissures and discrepancies that consciously employ the public image of the auteur in order to then confront and fragment its expressive coherency.[6]

As a specific example of the contemporary auteur's construction and promotion of a self, I will concentrate on one "semi-textual" strategy often taken for granted in the relation between a filmmaker, the films, and an audience: the interview, which is one of the few, documentable extra-textual spaces where the auteur, in addressing cults of fans and critical viewers, engages and disperses his or her own organizing agency as auteur. Here, the standard directorial interview might be described according to the action of promotion and explanation: it is the writing and explaining of a film through the promotion of a certain intentional self; it is frequently the commercial dramatization of self as the motivating agent of textuality. But it is this image of the auteur that the contemporary auteur necessarily troubles, confuses, or subverts through the agency of commerce.

III
The Economics of Self-Sacrifice:
Coppola

Certainly Francis Coppola is one of the more celebrated and bewildering examples of auteurism as it has evolved through the seventies and eighties. In an essay on the evolution of Coppola's career, Richard Macksey has astutely made the connection between Orson Welles and the more recent child prodigy of Hollywood, the first anticipating and the second following the heyday of auteurism as Romantic expression and independent (if not transgressive) vision. Yet, as Macksey observes, distinctions between the two filmmakers are even more compelling. On the one hand, "Welles has been a presiding model of Romantic genius, the myth of the explosive, comprehensive talent challenging corporate power and ultimately becoming the victim of its own genius." On the other hand, there is Coppola's marketing of that myth:

> If he has inherited something of the Romantic artist's impatience with the system, his powers of persuasion and need to take risks have led him toward the boardroom rather than the garret, back toward the old putative center of power in Hollywood (and the financial centers off-camera) rather than toward exile and "independent filmmaking." His perilous if uncanny power to enlist bankers probably depends upon his temperamental inability to fold in a poker game; movie-making and risk-taking are synomous for him. (2, 3)

As a Romantic entrepreneur, Coppola becomes a self-exiled and stridently independent auteur who claims in one sentence "I need to be a solo guy" and then for *Tucker* humbly surrends the film to George Lucas's "marketing sense of what people want" (Lindsey, 23–27). Straddling the margins of European art cinema and the center of commercial Hollywood, he is one of the original directors of the contemporary blockbuster (*The Godfather* [1972]) and the one whose experimental goals seem most threatened by the financial and commercial exigencies of his blockbuster successes. Jon Lewis explains that as "far back as 1968, four years before *The Godfather* made him the best-known director in America, Coppola predicted that this generation of film school-educated *auteurs* would someday trigger significant change in the movie business"; yet, with the needed special emphasis on finances in Coppola's version of this paradox, the dazzling box-office success of expensive auteurist movies like *The Godfather, Jaws,* and *Star Wars*—the very sort of movies Coppola had once believed would foster a new American auteur industry—led to an industrywide focus on blockbuster box offices revenues. The success of auteur films in the 1970s did not, as Coppola hoped it would, give auteur directors increased access to film financing. Instead, directors became increasingly dependent on studio financing to produce and distribute such "big" films (21, 22). Indeed, this ambivalent double-image as the auteur-star of goliathan productions and the auteur-creator victimized by the forces of those productions defines Coppola's central place within the commerce of auteurism, characterizing him, in Andrew Sarris's off-hand portrait, as a "modern dissonnant auteur" ("O Hollywood!" 51).

Coppola's career has followed an almost allegorical path. It begins confidently as a commercial talent (*Finian's Rainbow* [1968] and *The Rain People* [1969]), transforms itself through the commerce of auteurism (*The Godfather* and *The Conversation* [1974]), suffers the contradictions of that position (*Apocalypse Now* [1979] and *One from the Heart* [1982]), and settles uncomfortably into the aims of the commercial auteur (*Tucker*). Jeffrey Chown has described these commercial pressures and contradictions, beginning with Coppola's first appearance as the auteur-creator of *The Godfather:* "it is curious that the film that put Coppola on the celebrity map, that gave him the magic adjective 'bankable,' is also extremely problematic in terms of authorship. . . . Coppola coordinated diverse creative agents in this production, he was clearly the catalyst for the film's success, but, in a career view, his creative control and originality are far less than in other films that bear his directorial signature" (59). Even Coppola's most artsy and individual film,

The Conversation, demonstrates major industrial complications within auteurism, at least as it is applied to the control of the filmmaker. Walter Murch, who engineered the brilliant soundtrack and much of the editing of that movie, can claim, for many critics, the most important part in that film. With *Apocalypse Now*, moreover, this most celebrated of contemporary American auteurs surrenders the choice of three different endings to a battery of advisors and miles of computer printouts which surveyed the expectations and desires of different audiences (including President Carter). In the most industrial and textual sense then, Coppola has become the willing victim of his successful name: as Chown observes of the critical slaughter that greeted *One from the Heart*, *The Outsiders* (1983), and *Rumble Fish* (1983): "The name Francis Ford Coppola connotes spectacles, Hollywood entertainment combined with artistic sensibility, Italian weddings, and napalm in the morning. Coppola the individual seems stifled by those expectations" (175). As with his capitulations to Army censors for *Gardens of Stone* (1987), self-destruction seems part of his "creative compromises" with the contemporary terms of auteurism.

His commercial compromises with the agency of auteurism mean, more exactly, a kind of sacrificing of that self as a spending and expending. In 1975, Coppola summed up his perspective on auteurism this way:

> The *auteur* theory is fine, but to exercise it you have to qualify, and the only way you can qualify is by having *earned* the right to have control, by having turned out a series of really incredibly good films. Some men have it and some men don't. I don't feel that one or two beautiful films entitle anyone to that much control. A lot of very promising directors have been destroyed by it. It's a big dilemma, of course, because, unfortunately, the authority these days is almost always shared with people who have no business being producers and studio executives. With one or two exceptions, there's no one running the studios who's qualified, either, so you have a vacuum, and the director has to fill it. (Murray, 68)

Coppola's emphasis here on the word "earned" is especially significant since for him the expressionistic privileges of auteurism are directly related to financial actualities of investment and risk: an auteur earns his status by spending himself, and both gestures involve the aggrandizement, demeaning, and "expending" of oneself through a primary identification with the agency and exchange of money. Thus the compliment of a self that is constructed as a financial agency is degradation of that self as *merely* a financial product. For Coppola, "the artist's worst fear is that he'll be exposed as a sham" (Murray, 65), namely, that an audience's financial investment in his agency will be revealed as only commerical advertisement.

This image of self curiously mirrors the obsessive geniuses found in Coppola's liturgical and operatic narratives. From the two *Godfathers* through *Apocalypse Now* and *Tucker*, his visionary characters invariably pursue grandiose spectacles which reflect their desires but which either literally or metaphorically then serve to destroy them. While these spectacles frequently echo their nineteenth-century origins (lavish visuals and operatic soundtracks), the more exact terms of their agency as cinematic characters are the contemporary spectacles of industrial technology as a financial investment (for war, for corporate industry, for the business of the family). *The Conversation* is the most appropriate example: driven by the passions of the protagonist Harry, it is a conversation through technology that leads to the absolute collapse of a sacrosanct individuality. Coppola's description of Harry, the devout and tortured Catholic, could indeed describe Coppola himself as auteur: "he's a man who has dedicated his existence to a certain kind of activity, to technology, and who in a part of his life experiences regrets and realizes that the weapon he uses for others in a certain fashion is destroying the man himself. . . . [T]he single reason for which he is destroyed is perhaps that he has started to question all that" (Belloni, 51). If Hollywood's commercial industry is the financial agency which makes and unmakes Coppola the auteur, Coppola remains driven to invest and lose that self in ever grander forms of its technological spectacle. Perhaps the most extraordinary and thus indicative example of this tendency are Coppola's technological dream projects: a giant domed theater in the Rocky Mountains or an imagined film *Megalopolis* where four elaborate video-films would draw on Goethe's *Elective Affinities* to tell the story of Japanese–U.S. relations.[7]

Not coincidentally, I think, an interview with Coppola becomes a media performance focused on the technology and the business that define and threaten him. Worried about the casual nonchalance of his meeting with this auteur, for instance, one interviewer notes Coppola's immediate identification with the technology of the performance, "I needn't have worried. The minute I switched on my tape recorder, Coppola came to life. This was *work*. First, he corrected the position of the machine, then he fiddled with the volume and tone controls till he had them set to his satisfaction. Finally, he allowed me to question him" (Murray, 54). More generally, Coppola frequently constructs himself in an interview as an entrepreneur orchestrating the forces of technology or as a character lost in the improvisations of Hollywood business. In the same interview, he describes his expectations and frustrations about the Academy Awards, his struggles with Paramount executives to have Marlon Brando cast for *The Godfather,* and then acknowledges that this most famous vehicle for his agency as an auteur had less to do with his control of the film than with submission of self and the loss of energy: "A lot of the energy that went into the film went into simply trying to convince the people who held the power to let me do the film my way" (59).

Ultimately, of course, it is this expenditure of energy as the loss of self that is the contradictory measure of Coppola as auteur. Evaluating the ratio of his position as artist against his possible decision to actually assume the full agency of a studio (which he would do with phoenix-like Zoetrope Studios), he casts himself according to the finances of running a large piece of technology:

> If I were running a studio, it might take me 100 B.T.U.s worth of energy to bend something a quarter inch; if I stay independent and use my own resources, those 100 B.T.U.s could bend something a foot. . . . But look: The average executive of a movie studio may make $150,000 a year, and have a corresponding power, over his company. As a film artist I make much, much more than that and, consequently, have that much more power over my company . . . . Perhaps the wisest thing to do is to use all my energies to make a film that grosses some stupendous amount, then go out and buy a major company and change it from the top. (Murray, 68)

Appropriately, for this elaborate characterization of himself at the turning point in his commercial career, Coppola begins this 1975 interview by claiming "this is my last interview" (54). Within this glossy, high-tech conversation with *Playboy,* he must naturally be given up from the start.

Attempting to synthesize his relation to his movies in the manner of the Big Picture, Coppola's interviews often make him into the film itself. He becomes the presiding genius of the film of himself; however, this genius is represented not in expression or productive control but in expenditure and loss: loss of control, loss of money, loss of vision, and loss of self. His renowned posture as a risk-taker thus becomes a bombastic effacement of any distinguishing differences between his intentions and the films. In 1982, Jonathan Cott asks Coppola about the publicity gained from adopting this posture of loss during the production of *One from the Heart.* His response resembles the hysteric in trouble with his language and the trouble with the distinction between self and the agency for that self:

> The real answer, from my point of view, is that I just say what the facts are; in this case, that I'm working on a film, I'm told that the money's gone, and that if I want to go ahead, I'll have to risk something of my own. And by that point, I'm so far into it that I say okay. . . . And then that tends to be the story that the people who write about me want to go for. If they ask me, "If the picture's a flop, will the company go out of business?" and if I say yes, it's because that seems to be the case. But it's not the idea that I want to push out into the public. In fact, I regret that I'm treated more as a charlatan or a con man than as a professional person, and to be honest, my feelings are hurt. I feel that I'm not reckless or crazy. It's just that I'm primarily interested in making films more than amassing money, which is just a tool. If someone suddenly gave me a billion dollars, for instance, I'd only invest it in my work. I will say yes to anything that seems reasonable to me, and sometimes I get in a little deep because I want to participate so much. (24)

A key moment in this interview, as with others with him, is the appeal for sympathy, not the distance of authority. It elicits a kind of social and psychological identification between Coppola and an imagined interlocutor, like that between a spectator and an actor-victim in an epic movie. For Coppola, the auteur communicates from one heart to another, and, for him specifically, the self-portrayal of the auteur as what has been persecuted and dismissed by the operatic conglomerates who have made him a powerless vehicle become the terms for a sympathetic identification: "I've done so much for them, and yet they resent even putting me in a position where I don't have to go to one of them with my hat in my hand and have them tell me what movies I can or cannot make" (76). At other times, with astonishing dexterity, he rhetorically moves between an image of himself as the powerful agent of a financial and technological machine and an image of the completely insignificant individuality that inhabits that agency:

> You know what I think? I think people are afraid of me, basically. They're afraid if I ever got like too much power, I'd change their lives, and they're right! . . . I'm only a minor representative of the times. I may be a schmuck, but you can be sure that some other people somewhere are going to start doing the same kind of stuff, and the world is

going to change. . . . As for myself, I'm not worried. What the hell! If I don't do it with this film, I'll go and invent some little gadget that will make billions! (Cott, 76)

The sympathetic enlistment of an audience now becomes the path for locating multiple subjectivities ("other people somewhere") within an agency that disallows the authority or stability of any single organizing perspective. In this action, Coppola puts into play the central problem of contemporary auteurism as an interpretive category: while it remains a more powerful figure and agency than ever, it is invariably forced to disperse its authority in terms of its commercial agency.

In the end, Coppola remains the most utopian figure within commercial auteurism, for whom the spectacle of self-destruction becomes a way back to self-expression. For him, the destruction of the authority of the auteur can mean the resurrection of a world of private auteurs, an intimate yet goliathan network of electronic communication. Speculating on the future of new technologies which regenerate themselves through money made and money spent on them, he proclaims a home video exchange which somehow retains the aura of auteurist agency, the expressive "I" becoming a third person plural:

> Everybody will use it, everybody will make films, everybody will make dreams. That's what I think is gonna happen. You'll ship 'em over to your friend, and he'll ship one back. . . . I think that, very shortly, there's going to be a whole new approach to things, and the designers and the architects and philosphers and artists are going to be the ones to help lead the society. (Cott, 76)

IV
The Age and Aging of Auteurs

There are many kinds of auteurs in contemporary culture. And there are many strategies through which a moviemaker can employ the agency of auteurism and by which audiences can use it as a way of understanding films. Both European and Asian filmmakers, for instance, have complicated this category for many years, and one only has to look to German or Chilean/French filmmakers such as Alexander Kluge or Raoul Ruiz to get a sense of the range of such revisions of auteurist practices. In the United States, the "displaced Hollywood auteur," more so than ever before, raises questions that need to be addressed. From Peter Weir and Wim Wenders to Stephen Frears, this group of global filmmakers who move in and out of Hollywood suggests contradictions and alternative descriptions to the history and coherence of auteurism.

In "The Unauthorized Auteur Today," Dudley Andrew has added another dimension to auteurism that needs to be taken into account. Following Gilles Deleuze's suggestion about the relation between an auteur's signature and a temporal "duration," Andrew argues that my primarily spatial relation of the commerce of auteurism, as it plays across public and private space, underestimates the temporal dimension of the auteur. The signature, Andrew posits, "embeds within it—as a hyper-text—a genuine fourth dimension, the temporal process that brought the text into being in the first place. . . . The auteur marks the presence of temporality and creativity in the text, including the creativity of emergent thought contributed by the spectator" (83). Coppola's history as a filmmaker thus resonates through any individual film as a complex presence, and his recent release of *Apocalypse Now Redux* (2001) becomes an unusually visible and dramatic example of how the temporality of auteurism anticipates new films and remakes old ones. Appearing simultaneously with Peter Cowie's *Hearts of Darkness: A Filmmaker's Apocalypse* and a decade after Eleanor Coppola's documentary *Hearts of Darkness* (1991), new films and new documents reclaim a signature film as, now, a director's cut, remaking and revising the name of Coppola as a temporal extension.[8]

In whatever shape and in whatever agency, auteurs are far from dead. In fact, they may be more alive than at any other point in film history. This particular interpretive category has of course never addressed audiences in simple or singular ways. Yet, within the commerce of contemporary culture, auteurism has become, as both a production and interpretive position, something quite different from what it once may have been. Since the early 1970s, the commercial conditioning of this figure has evacuated it of much of its expressive power and textual coherency; simultaneously this commercial conditioning has called renewed attention to the layered pressures of auteurism as an agency which establishes different modes of identification with its audiences. However vast some of their differences as filmmakers may be, they each, it seems to me, willingly or not have had to give up their authority as authors and begin to communicate as simply figures within the commerce of that image. For viewers, this should mean the pleasure of engaging and adopting one more text the surrounds a movie without the pretenses of its traditional authorities and mystifications.

Timothy Corrigan

NOTES

1. See Jim Hillier's introduction to *Cahiers du Cinéma*, 1–17.

2. A collection of the major documents and debates about auteurism can be found in *Theories of Authorship: A Reader*, ed. John Caughie. See also Robert Sklar, *Movie-Made America: A Cultural History of American Movies*, 292–94.

3. See Peter Wollen, *Signs and Meaning in the Cinema*; Michel Foucault, "What Is an Author?" in *Language, Counter-Memory, Practice*, 113–38; Stephen Heath, "Comment on 'The Idea of Authorship,'" 86–91.

4. See Brecht's *Le Proces de quat'sous: experience sociologique*, 148–221 and Ben Brewster, "Brecht and the Film Industry," 16–33.

5. Revealing in its directness is Jospeh Gelmis, *The Film Director as Superstar.* "Over half the movie tickets sold today," he notes, "are bought by moviegoers between the ages of sixteen and twenty-five. They know what a director is, what he does and what he's done" (xvii). A much more sophisticated analysis of that tendency is Sheila Johnston's "A Star is Born."

6. In *Narration in the Fiction Film* David Bordwell recognizes this fragmentation of the auteur but sees it as a mere variation on the traditional auteur-narrator: "The popularity of R. W. Fassbinder in recent years may owe something to his ability to change narrational personae from film to film so that there is a 'realist' Fassbinder, a 'literary' Fassbinder, a 'pastiche' Fassbinder, and so on" (210). Obviously I believe that mobilizing these different agencies within an auteurist category has larger implications.

7. Not surprisingly, the ambivalent identification of the artistic self within the commerce of auteurism and its promise of the great spectacle of self becomes fraught with all the liturgical guilt of sin and self-sacrifice: "I am more interested in technology than I am in content. This, in some circles, is the same as admitting that one is a child molester and likes it. The truth is that I am interested in a content I can't get at. I yearn to be able to move into a world where story and content is available to me; where my ideas connect into a pattern that could be identified as a story. But I truly cannot get there" (Coppola, 3D).

8. Indeed, this temporal dimension of auteurism calls attention to other temporal figurings of auteurs within a commercial and historical agency. A common characteristic of new auteurs like Quentin Tarantino, for example, is the "immediacy" of the career (for Tarantino, made and hailed between 1992 and 1994 with *Reservoir Dogs* and *Pulp Fiction*). Other contemporary auteurs choose different temporal signatures: for example, they may be "historically remade" (as one might argue about Samuel Fuller), or become "proleptic" auteurs whose reputations have been established in advance of their films (like Michael Cimino even before his first film, *The Deerhunter* [1978] was released).

WORKS CITED

Andrew, Dudley. "The Unauthorized Auteur Today." In *Film Theory Goes to the Movies*, ed. Collins, Collins, and Radner (New York: Routledge, 1993).

Barthes, Roland. *Image-Music-Text* (New York: Hill and Wang, 1977).

Belloni, Gabria and Lorenzo Codelli."Conversation avec Francis Ford Coppola," *Positif* 161 (1974): 50–55.

Bordwell, David. *Narration in the Fiction Film* (Madison: University of Wisconsin Press, 1985).

Brecht, Bertolt. *Le Proces de quat'sous: experience sociologique*, 148–221.

Brewster, Ben. "Brecht and the Film Industry," *Screen* 16 (Winter 1976–77): 16–33.

Caughie, John, ed. *Theories of Authorship: A Reader* (London: Routledge, 1981).

Chown, Jeffrey. *Hollywood Auteur: Francis Coppola* (New York: UMI Research Press, 1981).

Coppola, Francis. "The Director on Content," *Washington Post,* August 29, 1982: 30.

Cott, Jonathan. "Francis Coppola," *Rolling Stone,* March 18, 1982: 20–24. 76.

Cowie, Peter. *The Apocalypse Now Book* (New York: DeCapo, 2001).

Michel Foucault, "What Is an Author?" in *Language, Counter-Memory, Practice,* ed. Donald F. Bouchard, trans. Donald F. Bouchard and Sherry Simon (Ithaca, N.Y.: Cornell University Press, 1977).

Giddens, Anthony. *Central Problems in Social Theory: Action, Structure, and Contrast in Social Analysis* (Berkeley: University of California Press, 1983).

Gelmis, Joseph. *The Film Director as Superstar* (Garden City, N.Y.: Doubleday, 1970).

Heath, Stephen. "Comment on 'The Idea of Authorship,'" *Screen* 14:3 (Autumn 1973), 86–91.

Hillier, Jim, ed. *Cahiers du Cinéma: The 1950s* (Cambridge, Mass.: Harvard University Press, 1985).

Jameson, Fredric. "Reification and Utopia in Mass Culture," *Social Text* 1 (1979): 130–48.

Johnston, Sheila. "A Star is Born: Fassbinder and the New German Cinema," *New German Critique* 24–25 (Fall/Winter 1981–1982): 57–72.

Lewis, Jon. *Whom God Wishes to Destroy* (Durham, N.C.: Duke University Press, 1993).

Lindsey, Robert. "Francis Ford Coppola: Promises to Keep," *New York Times Magazine,* July 24, 1998, sec. 6: 23–27.

Macksey, Richard. "'The Glitter of the Infernal Stream': The Splendors and Miseries of Francis Coppola," *Bennington Review* (1983).

Morris, Meaghan. "Tooth and Claw: Tales of Survival and *Crocodile Dundee.*" In *Universal Abandon?: The Politics of Postmodernism,* ed. Andrew Ross (Minneapolis: University of Minnesota Press, 1988), 105–127.

Murray, William. "*Playboy* Interview: Francis Ford Coppola," *Playboy* (July 1975).

Polan, Dana. "Brief Encounters: Mass Culture and the Evacuation of Sense," in *Studies in Entertainment: Critical Approaches to Mass Culture,* ed. Tania Modleski (Bloomington: Indiana University Press, 1986), 167–187.

Sarris, Andrew. "O Hollywood!, Oh Mores!," *Village Voice* March 5, 1985, 5.

Sklar, Robert. *Movie-Made America: A Cultural History of American Movies* (New York: Vintage, 1975).

Wollen, Peter. *Signs and Meaning in the Cinema* (Bloomington: Indiana University Press, 1972).

Marvin D'Lugo

Transnational Film Authors and the State of Latin American Cinema

I
A Geopolitical Aesthetic

Fernando Solanas's *Tangos: el exilio de Gardel* (*Tangos: The Exile of Gardel*) (1985) is a paradigm for an increasingly more common strategy for the development of Latin American authorial cinema sponsored through the agency of international co-productions. In this instance, the film was produced through a financial arrangement between Argentine and French producers, with additional support from Argentina's National Film Institute (INC). But more important than its demonstration of the funding strategies for transnational authorial cinema, *Tangos* self-referentially dramatizes through its diegesis the struggle of works of national cinema operating in a global market.

There is one sequence in particular in which Solanas highlights the problematic nature of Latin American co-productions. A group of Argentine exiles in Paris have just staged a rehearsal of their *tanguedia,* a political tango show that recounts aspects of the chain of disappearances, torture, and exile known as the "Dirty War" inflicted by the military junta in power between 1976–1983. The rehearsal has been staged in an effort to persuade French backers to support this production. After seeing the dress rehearsal, however, the audience is somewhat dismayed; one of them laments that the tanguedia is simply "too Argentine," beyond the knowledge and interest of French audiences.

What the staged audience doesn't seem prepared to appreciate is the very idea of a tanguedia, a concoction of dance and narrative designed by Solanas's characters that self-consciously embodies the strategy of cinemas on the margins generally that use certain popular ethnographic tropes as cultural capital. In effect, the fictional director and performers dramatize those efforts of filmmakers who seek to commodify the signs and artifacts of their national culture as merchandise within the global marketplace. Tellingly, Solanas combines in a single genre two of the most essential of these Argentine tropes: the tango, which since the thirties has proven to be a marketable international commodity for Argentine films; and the Dirty War, a more recent construction of cinematic Argentineness. Ironically, in complaining that the tanguedia is "too Argentine," the staged audience of this rehearsal is suggesting the limits of marketability of what are presumably the most accessible tropes of the national designed specifically for foreign consumption. The frustration of the Argentine performers similarly underscores the discomforting recognition that for such foreign audiences Argentine culture is, at best, merely an exotic entertainment.

What is conspicuously troublesome about Argentine culture for Solanas's fictitious audience is the specificity of national history, as though it were a barrier dividing the spiritual solidarity otherwise shared by French and Argentine artists and intellectuals from the resistant history that cannot be easily assimilated into a Eurocentric cultural scheme except by essentializing it as "Third World." The rehearsal scene thus replicates as plot the very problematic of Solanas's own film, as it must struggle in aesthetic, cultural, and financial spheres to construct the audience for a film and for an entire cinema which, over a very short period of time, has seen the loss of its presumed natural "national" spectatorship.

On a larger scale, *Tangos* also works as a response to the process of globalization the symptomatic cultural effects of which Fredric Jameson describes as "the disappearance of the specifically national cultures and their replacement, either by a centralized commercial production for world export or by their own mass-produced neo-traditional images" (Jameson, 3). Jameson perceives a certain category of film work that emerges as a response to this process, imbued with what he calls a "geopolitical aesthetic," that is, the deployment of mythic narratives through which filmmakers "allegorize how our consumption and construction of the object works in terms of Utopian wishes and commercially programmed habits" with the goal in mind of refashioning national allegory, as he says, "into a conceptual instrument for grasping our new being-in-the-world" (3). Solanas's film indeed demonstrates that diagnostic machinery within the filmic texts as it continually poses questions about the place of national culture within the world system. As such, the film might productively be read as an occasion for the rethinking of the cultural dilemma of globalization from the perspective of the Latin American film author.

II
The National and the Migration of the Audience

The decade of the 1980s saw a dramatic loss of the domestic or national audience of cinema throughout Latin America.[1] The causes have been variously attributed to such factors as economic instability, the progressive impact of competing technologies (video, cable, satellite transmissions), and, more generally, what has been described in shorthand as "global processes." One of the underlying assumptions in nearly all descriptions has been that the "natural" market of national cinemas has been lost, or else has migrated to other media. Embedded in such descriptions is the notion that there is somehow a coincidence of geographic space and the static populations defined by local cinematic production as national communities. Yet, the history of Latin American cinema, once freed from that geographic myth, begins to reveal, as Néstor García Canclini and others have noted, a continuing process by degree of deterritorialization and reterritorialization. García Canclini describes these two processes respectively as "the loss of the 'natural' relation of culture to geographic and social territories and, at the same time, certain relative, partial territorial relocations of old and new symbolic productions" (229).

Yet, before we can begin to understand the nature of the ensuing reconfiguration of Latin American cinemas within the global context, this migration of audience in fact forces us to question exactly what we mean by the concept of the national in terms of audiovisual cultures. While the term "national" cinema has become a catch-all term, variously describing all films made in or financed in a given country, or else films that in some way are perceived to address the question of local culture, the concept of national cinema actually masks an important historical tension between local production and its culture and the international system of film distribution. Kristen Thompson and Thomas Elsaesser, among others, have argued that cinema as an institution has always been international both culturally and economically. Thompson sums up this situation by underscoring that national cinemas are in effect alternatives that ". . . gain their significance and force partly because they seek to undermine the common equation of 'the movies' with 'Hollywood'" (Thompson, 170).

Tom O'Regan, describing the development of Australian cinema as a national alternative to Hollywood, refines this argument by observing that ". . . national cinemas work to be local while streamlining themselves to be of interest to audiences outside of [the national space]" (51). It is, in fact, this duality of the local and the global that has intensely marked the development of cinema throughout its history in Latin America.

Ambrosio Fornet, taking an opposite view, focuses his attention on those historical patterns of development that undermine the restrictive definitions of cinematic production and distribution based on national cinemas as essential categories. He thus argues that "Latin American cinema, from its origins, has been multinational and transcultural" (xvii). While Fornet's argument seems completely to negate the historical value of the national in shaping Latin American film history, a less categorical view would clearly acknowledge a prolonged tension and interface between the local and the transnational, long before the 1980s.

At least two important types of cinematic movement beyond the borders of the local or "national" culture have long existed as patterns for the refiguration of cinematic populations: one was regional cinema marked precisely by films such as Mexican *ranchera* comedies, Argentine tango films, or Brazilian *chanchadas*, that were easily distributed to other parts of the region; the second, and perhaps more promising in light of subsequent co-productions, were those rare films that from time to time actually transcended their region of production and were shown successfully at festivals in Europe, or else distributed commercially there or in the U.S. In Mexico, in particular, the films of Emilio "Indio" Fernández in the 1940s represent such a phenomenon, as do Luis Buñuel's *Los olvidados* (*The Young and the Damned*) (1950) or some of the films of Leopoldo Torre Nilsson in Argentina in the 1950s and 1960s (Pick, 38). These instances are significant since they suggested, even before the contemporary period, the potential prestige and marketability of Latin American cinema through works identified with particular auteurs beyond the region's "natural" market. Taken in the light of the subsequent debates about the force of local or international distribution patterns of Latin American films, such historical antecedents seem to confirm the view that globalization is only a recent stage of the historical development of Latin American audiovisual production that has long manifested itself around the ongoing tension between local and international interests.

III
Globalization and the Privilege of Film Authors

Despite the inconclusiveness of such historical debate, evidence abounds of certain Latin American films that have circulated as though expressly designed to occupy their position as "international" productions. The underlying logic of this phenomenon appears to be that the "nation" as a structure, while perhaps still serving the interests of the state in generating and sustaining a collective mythology, now also serves a particular function as the agent for the promotion of commodities of cultural consumption beyond national borders. Richard Maxwell contends that ". . . infranational and supranational economic regions have their own boundaries despite political nationalisms of whatever size . . . capital produces its own media geography on its march for environments of the highest return. . . . The economic region has no provincial, regional, or national borders" (151). National cinema understood in this context is much less a sacrosanct expression of national culture than a particularized discursive formation, the product of a local film culture intended to represent that culture commercially within but also beyond its own borders.

"What we usually call the global," as Stuart Hall clarifies, "far from being something which, in a systematic fashion, rolls over everything, creating similarity, in fact works through particularity, negotiates particular spaces, particular ethnicities, works through mobilizing particular identities and so on. So there is always a dialectic, a continuous dialectic between the local and the global" (62). It is, finally, this special "use" of difference that has emerged prominently in recent years to respond to the appearance of collapse in these Latin American cinemas through the agency of authorial cinema aligned ever more closely to the national in its transnational commerce. That is to say, certain films seem to attract transnational funding and eventually a transnational spectatorship precisely because of the particular cachet of their directors; directors, in turn, attempt to market themselves beyond their national borders through a particular "marriage" with the agents of the national. Solanas's *Tangos* is clearly a paradigmatic version of this marriage.

But author cinema has long been a problematic category in Latin American film culture. García Canclini contends that artists generally" . . . who have contributed to the independence and professionalizing of the cultural field have made the critique of the state and of the market the axes of their argumentation" (67). Yet, that independence has often revealed a greater antipathy toward the excesses of state authority and despotism than the commercialism of the market. When one looks at the checkered history of cinematic auteurism in the region, one is struck by the pendulum swings from state-supported author cinema to a hybrid form of authorship nurtured under the banner of "New Latin American Cinema," in the sixties, finally to the recent authorial promotions developed as international co-productions.

Latin American filmmakers since the sixties have sought to re-articulate authorship often through a necessary collaboration with state agencies which have fostered their work as part of a national cultural project. This was indeed the case with the efforts to "nationalize" Mexico's film industry through the state's financial support of filmmakers like Felipe Cazals, Jaime Humberto Hermosillo, Paul Leduc, and Arturo Ripstein through the sixties and seventies. A similar alignment of state-sponsored authorial cinema emerged in Brazil under the rubric of Cinema Novo.

In sharp contrast to the state's cultivation of these European-style auteurs were the efforts of the theorists and filmmakers of New Latin American Cinema who sought to contest the aestheticism of European-style auterurism by "transferring the individual agency of authorship to mechanisms encouraging cooperative models" that combined artistic creativity with cultural and social militancy (Pick, 39). Thus, as Zuzana Pick contends, the "Third Cinema" movement, as well as New Latin American cinema generally, saw a curious reaffirmation of the film auteur by men such as Fernando Birri and Fernando Solanas in Argentina, Glauber Rocha in Brazil, and Tomás Gutiérrez Alea and Julio García Espinosa in Cuba, all of whom envisioned some form of film authorship in opposition to neocolonial state authority. This was a notion of authorship mitigated by the practices and goals of production collectives rather than merely of the individual filmmaker's desire for self-expression.

By the mid 1980s, however, film authors whose earlier work had been as divergent as that of Ripstein in Mexico, Solanas in Argentina, and Alea in Cuba, were all, to greater or lesser degrees, positioned in the same relation of identifying with national culture and the demands of the global market. This kind of cultural/aesthetic realignment may be understood as the result of a convergence of various factors: the demise of New Latin American Cinema, the economic crisis that afflicted the principal "national" cinemas in Brazil, Argentina, and Mexico, and the advent of new technologies that competed with and in many instances displaced the traditional venues of cinematic exhibition throughout the region. The result, one may only hypothesize, was the necessary alignment of anti-hegemonic filmmakers with the state even as their works seemed to critique the very order that is easily identified with the state. Ultimately, as we shall see, this contradictory situation, rooted in the status of international co-productions, often provides the impetus for the kind of geopolitical aesthetic of interrogation of which Jameson speaks, understood finally as a form of resistance and renegotiation of the national culture on a number of national and international planes.

These are films that are framed discursively both in their production and exhibition by a dual market imperative, and thus embody the dialectical play of the local and the global understood as a negotiation of the national in the context of world markets. They derive from a particular sensibility which spiritually coincided with the concept of exilic transnational authors, as described by Hamid Naficy as "partial subjects and undecidable multiple objects, these filmmakers are capable of producing ambiguity and doubt about the absolutes and taken-for-granted values of their home and host societies" (124–125).

Consequently, the identity of the author in much recent author cinema is understood, not so much in terms of self-fashioned identity in the romanticized mold of fifties and sixties auteurism, but as the result of a marketing strategy in the sense that Thomas Elsaesser has described it (Elsaesser, 300), with the precise intention of reterritorializing the national cinema in the face of the collapse of those local markets. According to Elsaesser's formulation, as it coincides with the filmmakers of "New German Cinema," cinematic authorship framed by the state for foreign consumption afforded "a principle of coherence among the maze of conflicting economic and cultural discourses."

> In this sense, the author was indeed an institution, in so far as he functioned both as a principle of production coherence and, over time, with the increasing international fame of some of them, also became an "auteur" of the international art cinema. On the side of the author, self-expression became redefined as self-image, leading to a "marketing" of the name as itself the seal of quality and a brand name. (116)

In Latin America, this kind of authorship was to have an understandable attraction, both to those agents of the national cinema (local producers, state agencies, cultural critics), as well as to certain audiences. Not only does a recognizable and esteemed filmmaker serve as an emblematic figure of local cultural pride, but also, as Timothy Corrigan describes, "the increasing importance . . . of the auteur [worked] as a commercial strategy for organizing audience reception, as a critical concept bound to distribution and marketing aims that identify and address the potential cult status of an auteur" (103).

V

Film Authors Performing the Local in Global Markets

A. Modes of Address

Given the cultural and political diversity of Latin American films and the equally diverse intellectual and cultural backgrounds of film authors, efforts to construct a single coherent profile for these filmmakers or a single inclusive paradigm to describe their work, would on the surface seem foolhardy. Yet, it is clear that contemporary Latin American film authors are to more or less a similar degree motivated by the desire to establish a common mode of address to a foreign audience. That audience, however, is most often projected as one shaped by an almost abject ignorance of the nuances of Third World cultures, and are thus often given versions of the national that have been refigured in ways to be accessible to a foreign spectatorship. To compensate for ignorance of local culture or history, filmmakers often return to recognizable genres, specifically melodrama as a rhetorical gesture that bridges the gaps in cultural knowledge. Luis Puenzo's Oscar-winning *La historia oficial* (*The Official Story*) (Argentina, 1985) might well serve as a model of the ways in which genre substitutes for a culturally specific knowledge of local culture. The film ostensibly treats one of the more apalling aspects of Argentina's "Dirty War," the disappearances of pregnant mothers and the eventual covert adoption of their children by families well-connected with the military regime. Instead of dealing with this material as political drama, Puenzo's narrative focuses on the plight of one adoptive mother who is drawn by circumstance into investigating the background of her adopted daughter's birth-mother. The highly-charged plot thus replaces the questions of the human rights abuses of the dictatorship with more "universal" themes of frustrated motherhood and the emotional relations between the heroine and her callous, manipulative husband. Puenzo's approach to his material is not an isolated example. The common move of a good number of these filmmakers has been to transpose certain thematics of the local into a register of humanistic universality. The implicit project is to redraw the affective borders of the nation by aligning certain narratives according to ethical values deemed universal. For instance, a series of Argentine films made in the decade of redemocratization after the Dirty War clearly play on the theme of human rights abuses connected with the military dictatorship, thus evoking the common humanity that links these cultures with the first world. María Luisa Bemberg's *Camila* (1984) uses nineteenth-century political repression under the Rosas dictatorship to tell a romantic story of love and resistance. Miguel Pereira's *La deuda interna* (*The Internal Debt*) (sometimes distributed as *Verónico Cruz*) looks at Argentina's marginalized indigenous population whose fate is recounted in the story of a single orphaned Indian boy, whose death during the Falkland Islands War comes to signify the tragedy of a larger community of marginalized Third World peoples victimized by state repression. Lita Stantic's 1992 film, *Un muro de silencio* (*A Wall of Silence*), perhaps best sums up this strategy when Kate Benson, a British filmmaker, explains to her Argentine hosts that European audiences would be interested in a film about the "disappeared" of the Dirty War because of Europe's own history of Nazi concentration camps.

B. Gender and Reterritorialization

In such works we increasingly find a form of cultural heteroglossia, that is, a "decentering" of appropriately national themes and subject matter so that the narrative may be "read" within a more universal thematic register.[2] One of the most successful efforts to remap the national within this type of cultural heteroglossia have been films that underscore questions of gender that appear to link Latin American society with broader international cultural themes. A filmmmaker like Jaime Humberto Hermosillo, for instance, has been one of the few able to sustain and evolve through a corpus of works over decades as a Mexican auteur. As various critics have noted, Hermosillo's works from the 1974 *El cumpleaños del perro* (*The Dog's Birthday*), has moved progressively toward a more openly gay thematics. *Doña Herlinda y su hijo* (*Doña Herlinda and Her Son*) (1983), Hermosillo's first film with openly gay characters, was marketed overseas as gay cinema, which, in turn, transformed Hermosillo into a highly marketable international auteur, promoted in Europe, for instance, as "the Mexican Almodóvar." Though the gay thematics of his work made it a commercial commodity constructing a non-Mexican market where there was none before, only a few critics noted the very tight and complex alignment of the film's gender politics with a critique of Mexican culture,[3] suggesting that it was not merely the presence of gays that distinguished the film, but moreover the ways that gender issues were used to reveal the dynamics of Mexican patriarchal narratives.

An even more commercially successful model of how gendered address serves the complex project of reterritorialization is to be found in Tomás Gutiérrez Alea's *Fresa y chocolate* (*Strawberry and Chocolate*) (Cuba, 1992). As Paul Julian Smith argues, ". . . the international success of *Fresa y chocolate* (with art-house audiences anxious to reconcile their nostalgia for the Cuban political experiment with their sympathy towards queer romance)" is thus easy to explain (81). The assumption of potential international gay spectatorship for the film, hypothesized in textual analyses, was clearly born out by its international marketing as an example of gay cinema. But the film benefited, as well, from the shaping of other audiences. Given its complex finances, with the Cuban Film Institute (ICAIC) joined by no fewer than four foreign producers—two Mexican partners, the official IMCINE, and the private Tabasco Films, and Spain's TeleMadrid and the Sociedad General de Autores—it was not difficult to understand why the film had to be "designed" to meet the expectations held by its presumed hybrid international audience, positioned at the least to see a version of Cuba somewhat different from the one defined by island audiences.

To that end, quite strikingly, certain domestic definitions of Cuban social reality are thus noticeably reshaped for the foreign market. Note for instance, the curious absence of any reference to Fidel in the film except for his name appearing on a wall outside of the apartment of the gay protagonist, Diego. Indeed, the gay poet, Lezama Lima, *"el maestro,"* as Diego calls him, has replaced Fidel as the central icon of the mise-en-scène. In that same vein, Diego is allowed to take the uptight Marxist, David, on a tour through Old Havana that clearly coincides with the particular relation of Spanish tourism to Cuba. The film, in effect, must be seen, in part, as a commodity designed to contribute to an international tourist curiosity which is itself market-determined.

On an even more striking conceptual level, we note the evocation of a rich urban and cosmopolitan sense of Cuban culture as specified in the film by the Lecuona music. Diego's own exile is even foretold here when he plays for David a recording of "Adiós a Cuba," by Ignacio Cervantes, the nineteenth-century composer exiled by the Spaniards. What is important to note is the way the script actually expands the register of Cubanness by aligning Diego with a cosmopolitan tradition that predates Cuban socialism and is therefore seen as more authentically Cuban than David's notion of culture. We are made to sense this revised notion of the cosmopolitan ideal of Cuban culture as more universal than David's provincial notion of islandness. David's strident *campesino* consciousness lacks any sense of history, having been shaped only by rigid institutional behavior.

One of the film's important ironies for both island and foreign audiences is that Diego's character is more fully steeped in a Cuban-specific sense of culture than David's which projects an imported, sovietized, notion of identity. The immediate Cuban audience thus witnesses a sense of national identity that runs counter to the usual treatments of self and other that ICAIC films had portrayed during the previous three decades. Here, of course, it is important to keep in mind that although the action of the film is set in 1979, it was made over three years after the dissolution of the Soviet empire and thus reflects what amounts to an essential Cuban revision of the idea of Cubanness.

Curiously, ICAIC's Alea and the Alea promoted by the film's international distributors coincide insofar as they focus on cultural capital, that is, cultural exports as hard currency for Cuba and conversely, as capital investment for the foreign market. In this light, as Smith argues, the gay thematics of the film reveals an ideologically contradictory but commercially coherent strategy of marketing Cuban cinema that appears to drive *Fresa* wherein gay-themed material is "couched in the form of cultural tourism"(81) in the effort to exploit a certain international market.[4]

C. Biography

Fresa y chocolate also reveals just how the linkage between the filmmaker and the national cinema confers a particular form of reciprocal coherence to films as they circulate beyond the national space in global markets. The nation's history, understood by a few broad strokes, usually distorted stereotypes, appears to "explain" a given film or filmmaker. Alea's film schematizes the twin motifs of sexuality and repression in ways that play down the historical datedness of the film's dramatic situation, which occurred more than a decade earlier. The potential gaps in the story are thus masked by the false analogy between the aesthete, Diego, and Alea himself, appearing to fight political repression in the name of artistic expression. This same humanizing logic of reading the national culture through the figure of the artist was, in fact, the basis of the earlier misreading of Alea's *Memorias de subdesarrollo* (*Memories of Underdevelopment*) (1968) which was often viewed outside of Cuba as the intellectual's denunciation of the Revolution.

An even more powerful example of the ways in which the biographical persona and the gender themes associated with the filmmaker confer a unity and coherence to the national cinema is the filmic and biographic interplay of the Argentine director María Luisa Bemberg. Bemberg, who wrote a number of screenplays for films by Raúl de la Torre and Fernando Ayala before directing her first film at the age of fifty-eight, had a relatively small filmography consisting of six feature-length films made between 1980 and her death in 1993. This abbreviated corpus, however, brought her resounding international success that exceeded that of most of her Argentine contemporaries. The reason, in part, may lie in Bemberg's development of a series of films that clearly link the local social thematics with issues of the status of women within Argentine society.

Her own first two films, *Momentos* (*Moments*) (1980) and *Señora de nadie* (*Nobody's Lady*) (1982), were made under the dictatorship and the tight censorship imposed by the military regime. It was not until Bemberg's third film, *Camila* (1984), once censorship restrictions were eliminated, that she was to achieve astounding and far-reaching success. The film was an Argentine-Spanish co-production, set during the terrible nineteenth-century dictatorship of Juan Manuel Rosas, and told the story of a young woman of the upper class who transgresses societal prohibitions and falls in love with and eventually runs off with a young priest. In time, the two are hunted down and executed. Nominated for an Oscar, the film cleverly blends personal elements of Bemberg's own feminism with the backdrop of violent political repression.

In no small measure, the film succeeded because of the clear link between its melodramatic tale and the recent history of political repression in Argentina (Ciria, 162). In interviews Bemberg did not shy away from the notion that her films were at least spiritually, if not at times literally, autobiographical. Indeed, her screen works are populated by female characters often drawn from protected upper class backgrounds, as is the case of Charlotte, the diminutive heroine of *De eso no se habla* (*Let's Not Talk About That*) (1993), or women who rebel against their social and marital status as in *Señora de nadie* (1981) or *Camila* (1984), or women such as Miss Mary or Sor Juana Inés de la Cruz who find themselves trapped within the prisons built by the social and gender constraints of conservative Latin patriarchal society. In collaboration with her enterprising producer, Lita Stantic, Bemberg effectively moved toward co-producing her own films with foreign companies, including quasi-official state entities. The twin points of celebrity persona as a film author, that is, as an Argentine and a feminist filmmaker, served a clear purpose of countering the earlier image of a regressive, intolerant Argentina, and of refiguring the national community in light of a more liberal international spectatorship. Her use of international actors in leading roles (Spain's Imanol Arias in *Camila*; Britain's Julie Christie in *Miss Mary*; Italy's Dominique Sanda in *Yo, la peor de todas,* and Marcello Mastroianni in *De eso no se habla*) also helped to expand the potential audience of her work.

The conscious effort to move beyond the "natural" national audience of Argentine cinema is nowhere more apparent than in the film often called her masterpiece, *Yo, la peor de todas (I, The Worst of All)* (1989). An Argentine-French-Spanish co-production, with the Spanish actress Assumpta Serna and the Italian actress Dominique Sanda in leading roles, the film was Bemberg's first incursion into non-Argentine material. A reconstruction of aspects of the life of the famed seventeenth-century Mexican poet, playwright, and intellectual, Sor Juana Inés de la Cruz, the film was based on the intellectual biography of the nun by the famed Mexican poet, Octavio Paz. It told the story of the particular difficulties Sor Juan (Assumpta Serna) had with the ecclesiastical authorities who persecuted her for what she and others saw as her status as a woman. While seemingly a break in period and subject matter, *Yo, la peor de todas* reveals Bemberg's strong authorial signature in its focus on the efforts to force the submission of women to patriarchal institutions, here represented by the Spanish Church officials of colonial Mexico.

The process of reterritorialization in the film, however, works in a very specific way. While the story and its biographical subject are rooted in colonial Mexico, its parallels seem to suggest a reworking of the very same national issues as *Camila:* divine love versus passion; the linkage of a tyrannical Church with the state that persecutes the individual, thereby reinscribing the specific configuration of the Dirty War theme into the narrative. The inclusion of an international cast tellingly opens the narrative up to another suggestive transnational reading. The principal actors include one Catalan actress, two Argentine actors, and an Italian. Yet, aligning these seemingly dispersed figures together is a story that works diachronically and dialogically, emphasizing for Latin American audiences parallels with recent Argentine history, while giving centrality to the broader theme of the problematic status of women in patriarchal society. Bemberg's self-identification with the feminist thematic at the core of her cinema reveals the potential force of the authorial as a way of rechanneling the questions of gender and nation within a wider commercial and discursive field.

D. *Geography*

Though we may point to the eccentricity of contemporary Argentina refigured as Bemberg's Mexican convent or Solanas's Paris rehearsal hall as suggestive evidence of a demarginalization of Latin American cinemas, there remains a marked stratum of tourist imagery that, as Hall has argued, dictates the "place of difference" in Latin American co-productions. As we have already noted, Diego's seemingly gratuitous tour of Old Havana in Alea's *Fresa y chocolate* openly acknowledges that otherwise implicit transnational motivation. Other filmmakers, as well, regularly play off a highly legible, cinematically-known, although not necessarily "authentic" geography as the mark of the national in films that seek to move beyond the local in search of audiences. This may be best exemplified in Arturo Ripstein's *Profundo Carmesí* (*Deep Crimson*) (1996), a neo-noir concoction that revisits the aesthetic triumphs of the principal genres of Mexican Golden Age cinema of the forties, the *cabaretera* and *ranchera* films. But far from paying homage to the likes of Dolores del Río, María Félix, and Pedro Infante, the most internationally known of the actors who populated this geography, Ripstein's film suggests the impoverishment, decay, and corruption that lay just beyond the frame of that artificial cinema. The retro ambience, enriched by cinematic self-reference, enables the filmmaker both to align himself with the already-known geography of stereotypical Mexico for transnational audiences, and yet also to comment on the implications of those falsified images.

A similar strategy of cultural heteroglossia informs *La reina de la noche* (*Queen of the Night*) (1995). Ripstein's deconstructive biography of the *caberetera* singer, Lucha Reyes, balances narrow references to the bolero singer's life and travails which carries a particular range of meanings for Mexican audiences familiar with Reyes's life and songs, with the tawdry mise-en-scène of the film which confirms the international audience's expectations of Mexican cantinas and cabarets.

From the beginning of his collaboration with scriptwriter Paz Alicia Garcíadiego in *El imperio de la fortuna* (*Labyrinth of Fortune*) (1985), Ripstein's cinema has consistently functioned through the deployment of this cultural heteroglossia, particularly as it combines certain expected and clichéd visual and narrative tropes of Latin American culture— poverty, promiscuity, social primitivism—with a deconstructive critical view that suggests the distanced position of alterity from which that clichéd world of underdevelopment is viewed. It may well be for that reason that Ripstein's films increasingly have found ingenious combinations of backers that include the Mexican IMCINE and Spanish and French producers.

To a certain degree, this strategy may well appear merely to cater to an elitist form of tourist cinema, reinforcing stereotypes that maintain the imbalance between First and Third world. Yet, in the more imaginative work of a number of transnational authors, there appears to be a very conscious effort to utilize the particularity of a national landscape in a process of reterritorialization, precisely through the agency of their own transnational authorial identity.

Lita Stantic's *Un muro de silenco* (1992, Argentina) might well stand in for a number of Latin American films that implicitly deal with the questions of geographic location of the nation in the context of a global community not defined exclusively by economics, but in combination with certain universal ethical affinities that are, in turn, mediated by the figure of an authorial figure.

In Stantic's film, a British filmmaker, Kate Benson (Vanessa Redgrave), has come to Buenos Aires to make a film about Silvia Massini (the Mexican actress Ofelia Medina, best known for her performance in Paul Leduc's *Frida*). Silvia is the former wife of one of the "disappeared" in the Dirty War. Kate's presence in Buenos Aires is narratively rationalized in dialogue early in the film that equates the *proceso*, the "Dirty War," with the Nazi extermination camps. Through a complex narrational development wherein Redgrave's character is made the spiritual and narrational double of the woman she is building her documentary film about, Stantic clearly seeks to transform the positionalities of Argentine and *other* within the dynamics of recent Argentine history into sites of interrogation and ultimately of national renewal. The "national subject" is continually linked with the non-aggressive, feminized *other* whose presence remaps the affective boundaries of the national community. Thus the co-production becomes the occasion to rechart Argentina's location in the ethical geography of late twentieth century culture. Of particular note here is the presence of Vanessa Redgrave, embodying both the female film author and the universal social conscience that desires to reposition Argentina within a more humane geography of human rights. Stantic's film, like *Fresa y chocolate*, might best be described as using geography to restage the place of the other in relation to national culture. It follows a pattern wherein the national subject is identified explicitly with a transnational element that effectively resituates the nation from its marginal position within a tight economic geography, transposing it figuratively to broader ethical and social spaces.

This kind of remapping of national geography may well be particular to Argentine authors who perceive in geographic marginalization a range of other issues not entirely unrelated to cultural/artistic or political activity. The politics of isolation, in fact, becomes one of the essential leitmotifs of the films of Adolfo Aristarain who has emerged in recent years as the preeminent contemporary Argentine author. Aristarain's work, beginning with *Tiempo de revancha (Time of Revenge)* (1981) a political thriller which, through veiled references, addresses the question of the dirty war, advances through a plot that continually reinforces the protagonist's spatial isolation. In his later *Un lugar en el mundo (A Place in the World)* (1992), a co-production with Uruguay, Aristarain tells the story of individuals whose very movement to the margins of the national culture— Patagonia—are brought to reflect upon their own bonds of affiliation.

Aristarain's films since the Argentine return to democracy have consistently involved international co-production schemes that have established him as the most internationally marketable contemporary Argentine filmmaker. Perhaps the summa of his work, certainly his most lavishly praised film, is *Martín Hache,* an Argentine-Spanish co-production which embodies in a clearly self-referential manner Jameson's geopolitical aesthetic. In the story of Martin Etchenique, a self-exiled screenwriter living in Madrid who is forced to take in his nineteen-year-old son, also named Martin and therefore nicknamed Hache (for Spanish "h," *hijo* or son), Aristarain has his protagonist ruminate about the nature of father and son relations, filmmaking, and affiliation with one's homeland. Ultimately, the three themes coalesce for Martin, gradually leading the spectator to reflect on the ingredients of identity politics in ways that transcend the usual identification/affiliation with a national community.

Through the elder Martín's uprootedness, especially his obviously successful transplantation to Madrid, as exemplified by his comments that "Madrid is a good place to live," the film seems at first to buttress the ideology of the transnational culture that produced it. Yet, when one night in Madrid, Hache asks his father if he ever misses Argentina, the elder Martín becomes unhinged and responds with a tirade against national affiliations in general and Argentine identity in particular. He derides patriotism and, alluding to the Dirty War, calls Argentina's politics a trap that makes you believe you can change it, when in fact you can't.

As powerful as Martin's denunciation is, the criticism of national affiliation proves to be double-edged, for Martín is portrayed through his contacts with his closest friends and family as a rootless and isolated figure whose critique of allegiance to the nation is merely symptomatic of his own personal displacement. He is criticized for his ambivalence by his lover, Alicia, his son, and his best friend, Dante. At the film's end, when Hache returns to Buenos Aires "to become something," he leaves a videotape for his father, explaining his reasons for wanting to forge his own life. Martín acknowledges his loss, not only of his son, but of his roots, thus confessing a nostalgia not for people, but for places. In this regard, the film poses a contestatory theme in its affirmation of cultural roots and its rejection of the global position that self-referentially defines the character and the film itself.

One of the truly distinctive features of *Martín Hache* is that, thematically, the film occupies the slip-zone of indeterminacy between denying validity to national roots and embracing them. What emerges as the narrative process of the film, therefore, is not the clichéd Argentineness expressed as in a tango lyric as nostalgia, but rather a process of rediscovery of one's place in the world that works for Martín as well for the subsequent Argentine generation symbolically represented by his son, Hache.

The ease with which the action shifts from Buenos Aires to Madrid, and back again seems all part of a constructed geographic seamlessness in which Argentina is "relocated" only a frame away from Madrid; the shift between spaces thus appears both effortless and even desirable. The film appears to discard the larger national history framed by Solanas, Bemberg, and others, for personal history; but importantly, a process is developed whereby that national history is resemanticized within the personal. Here, for instance, while the space of the other is held in a positive light, eventually the film seems to fold back on the issue of exile and the loss of affection for homeland when the elder Martín realizes that, despite his successful repositioning in European culture, the specter of loss and uprootedness follows him.

That same kind of indeterminacy defines the film's apparent self-parodic style. Clearly recycling the formula of the ghettoized Argentine films of the Dirty War theme, it even plays with the sound of tangos for a brief moment. As well, Aristarain adds touches of self-conscious parody of his own professional autobiography and allusions to the celebrity status of Federico Luppi, Argentina's internationally renowned actor, who plays the role of Martín. These are touches that underscore the film's discursive strategy of undermining nearly all of the hallmarks of global film culture in its reaffirmation of the cultural roots of national affiliation that must be balanced with broader global interests.

V
A New Politique des Auteurs

The re-articulation of the notion of the film author within transnational cinema derives from the nature of globalized culture itself wherein, as we have seen, cinema responds less to national cultures than to an emerging recognition of transnational media geography. As Richard Maxwell argues in terms of macroregional television, "The state no longer provides traditional political safeguards for that national culture, but acts as manager of the spreading transnational phenomenon 'in the best interests' of the nation" (Maxwell, 152). In such a fluid context, the film author becomes a privileged site for the transformation of markets, a mediation between the narrowly-defined local culture and the dominant "other" culture. At the interstices of local and global culture, Latin American film authors achieve force as cultural agents through their ability to interrogate those shifts and, as well, to question the place of national culture within this broader global sphere.

NOTES

1. Octavio Getino cites, for instance, statistics suggesting a catastrophic decline in the number of spectators in Latin America and the Caribbean during the decade 1979–1989, falling from an estimated 850 million spectators at the end of the 1970s to between 450–500 million in 1989. In a country by country analysis of film attendance statistics, Getino finds the decline to be on the order of 66 percent in Argentina, and roughly 50 percent in Brazil, Mexico, Cuba and Venezuela. See Getino, 168–69.

2. Bakhtin's formulation of "social heteroglossia" in his *Discourse on the Novel* is telling as he describes a "verbal-ideological decentering [that] will occur when a national culture loses its sealed-off and self-sufficient character, when it becomes conscious of itself as only one among *other* cultures and languages" (Bakhtin, 370). The effects he describes bear a curious relation to the intentionality we find in the strategies of reterritorialization of Latin American filmmakers.

3. For insightful treatments of the film see Daniel Balderston's "Excluded Middle: Bisexuality in *Doña Herlinda y su hijo*" and David Willian Foster's "Queering the Patriarchy in Hermosillo's *Doña Herlinda y su hijo.*"

4. As "the international breakthrough movie for Cuban cinema" it revealed that there exists abroad a market for films, such as Ang Lee's or Gutiérrez Alea's, in which gay-themed material is placed in a national context unfamiliar to the foreign audience, whether that context is Taiwanese-American or Cuban. I shall argue that this desire for homosexuality,

couched here in the form of cultural tourism, is also present in different, domestic form in the project of the film itself: the attempt, persistent but impossible, to incorporate or assimilate same-sex eroticism into the nationalist project of the Revolution, from which it had once been so ostentatiously excluded. (Smith, 81)

WORKS CITED

Bakhtin, M. M. *The Dialogic Imagination,* ed. Michael Holquist (Austin: University of Texas Press, 1981).

Balderston, Daniel. "Excluded Middle? Bisexuality in *Doña Herlinda y su hijo.*" In Daniel Balderston and Donna J. Guy (eds.), *Sex and Sexuality in Latin America* (New York and London: New York University Press, 1997), 190–99.

Beceyro, Raúl. *Cine y política: ensayos sobre cine argentino* (Santa Fe, Argentina: Universidad Nacional del Litoral, 1997).

Ciria, Alberto. *Mas alla de la pantalla* (Buenos Aires: Ediciones de la Flor, 1995).

Corrigan, Timothy. *A Cinema without Walls: Movies and Culture After Vietnam* (New Brunswick, N.J.: Rutgers University Press, 1991).

D'Lugo, Marvin. "Buñuel in the Cathedral of Culture: Reterritorializing the Film Auteur." In *Luis Buñuel's TheDiscreet Charm of the Bourgeoisie,* ed. Marsha Kinder. (Cambridge: Cambridge University Press, 1998), 101–10.

Elsaesser, Thomas. *New German Cinema: A History* (New Brunswick, N.J.: Rutgers University Press, 1989).

Fornet, Ambrosio. "Forward." In *Framing Latin American Cinema: Contemporary Critical Perspectives,* ed. Ann Marie Stock (Minneapolis and London: University of Minnesota Press, 1997), xi–xx.

Foster, David William. "Queering the Patriarchy in Hermosillo's *Doña Herlinda y su hijo.*" In *Framing Latin American Cinema: Contemporary Critical Perspectives,* ed. Ann Marie Stock. (Minneapolis and London: University of Minnesota Press, 1997), 235–45.

García Canclini, Néstor. *Hybrid Cultures: Strategies for Entering and Leaving Modernity,* trans. Christopher L. Chiappari and Solvia L. López (Minneapolis: University of Minnesota Press, 1995).

Getino, Octavio. *La tercera mirada: Panorama del audiovisulatiznoamericano,* 1a. edición (Buenos Aires, Barcelona, México: Paidós, 1996).

Hall, Stuart. "Old and New Identities, Old and New Ethnicities." In *Culture,Globalization and the World-System: Contemporary Conditions for the Representation of Identity,* ed. Anthony King (Minneapolis: University of Minnesota Press, 1997), 41–68.

Jameson, Frederic. *The Geopolitical Aesthetic: Cinema and Space in the World System* (Bloomington and London: Indiana University Press and BFI Publishing, 1995).

Maxwell, Richard. *The Spectacle of Democracy: Spanish Television, Nationalism, and Political Transition* (Minneapolis and London: University of Minnesota Press, 1995).

Naficy, Hamid. "Phobic Spaces and Liminal Panics: Independent Transnational Film Genre." In *Global/Local: Cultural Production and the Transnational Imaginary,* ed. Rob Wilson and Wimal Dissanayake (Durham and London: Duke University Press, 1996), 119–44.

O'Regan, Tom. *Australian National Cinema* (London and New York: Routledge, 1996).

Pick, Zuzana M. *The New Latin American Cinema: A Continental Project* (Austin: University of Texas Press, 1993).

Smith, Paul Julian. *Vision Machines: Cinema, Literature and Sexuality in Spain and Cuba, 1983–1993* (London and New York: Verso, 1996).

Thompson, Kristen. *Exporting Entertainment: America in the World Film Market 1907–1934* (London: British Film Institute, 1985).

Chon A. Noriega

"Our Own Institutions": The Geopolitics of Chicano Professionalism

*The question of violence or non-violence in the struggle
is a misleading one, for while many Chicanos theorize
about the question and never have to confront the
answer, they also avoid facing questions of how to best
utilize the possibilities that are open to them.*
—Jesús Salvador Treviño, 1974[1]

*Social change, real and lasting change, has never been
obtained through the "appropriate" channels.*
—David Morales, 1976[2]

It is difficult to talk about Chicano authorship within Hollywood, except
as a structured absence. There have been very few Chicano and no Chicana directors of feature-length films. According to a Directors Guild of
America report released in 1992, employment for Latino directors
increased from 1.0 percent of all television and film work done in 1983 to
1.3 percent in 1991—an increase of one-third of one percent in almost a
decade. As Director Jesús Salvador Treviño pointed out at the time, at
that rate it would take 300 years for Latinos filmmakers to reach parity
with national demographics. In the same eight-year period, Latina directors worked a total of 27 days, or *one-ten thousandth of a percent* of all
available work.[3]

Given that these insignificant increases result from waning federal
regulation, things have not gotten much better since 1991. By 1999,
Latino directors accounted for 2.3 percent of available work within the
industry. Meanwhile, the Latino community itself grew from 4.5 percent
of the national population in 1970 to 11.5 percent in 2000. When this

exponential population growth is correlated against the modest increases in employment, employment *opportunity* for the Latino filmmakers actually decreased in the film and television industry to nearly one-third the level of the 1970s.[4]

Indeed, there is not much to say about Chicano authorship when approached in the usual terms of auteur analysis. When all is said and done, one must have a text that correlates to a body of work by an author. Without that, we are left with a sociological analysis of the institutional systems that *exclude* particular expressions; we are left explaining why there is no there there for some, when it is so clearly there for others. In short, one can neither do auteur analysis nor reject it by calling a homogenous "authorship" into question. In the remainder of this essay, I will engage another approach, one that examines the emergence of "Chicano cinema" and the possibilities for Chicano authorship as the result of institutional struggles initiated by the filmmakers and directed toward U.S. public television and federal agencies, rather than Hollywood and network television. These same filmmakers also situated these struggles within the context of radical film movements within the U.S. and Latin America.

Between 1974 and 1984, Chicano filmmakers, like their activist counterparts, combined radical and reformist demands directed at the film and television industry. But even as filmmakers' sense of their social function became increasingly radical, their actions operated within a broader "discourse of professionalism" that placed an emphasis on funding sources, production schedules, aesthetic conventions, market analysis and ascertainment, broadcast and syndication, the policy arena, and, above all, an ongoing participation in the social networks or "interpretive community" within which these things meant something. For those Chicanos attempting to work within the mass media, being a filmmaker meant an increasing reliance upon noncommercial funding sources and public broadcasting. Indeed, while later series worked at the crossroads of a pan-Latino national audience, they did so mostly within family-oriented educational and children's *public* programming. Thus, one of the ironies of the discourse of professionalism—as with the discourse of violence— was that while it challenged the corporate mass media in terms of access to the public sphere, social change itself required, not the machinations of a civil society, but a dynamic among those things *outside* civil society: the family, the state, and transnational social movements. It is in this sense that the two epigraphs at the start of this essay, while marking a conflict between activist and professional tactics, express a larger strategy that found expression, first in Ray Andrade's grassroots activism, then in Jesús Salvador Treviño's professional advocacy: one must work within the system *and* outside "appropriate" channels. It was a lesson learned first at school and then on the job, and it would be modified over the next three decades in response to changes in the industry and regulatory arena. In the 1970s and 1980s, Chicano producers mobilized a discourse of professionalism that relied upon state support and public television, situating this reformism vis-à-vis U.S. and Latin American alternative cinemas.

If public television has been the major outlet for Chicano cinema, the two have also been coterminous, intimately bound up in each other's history from the very beginning. This relationship had a profound effect on racial minorities, who acquired "voice" or authorship by way of an elite media culture susceptible to political pressures *because* it lacked both public support and commercial viability. In some respects, however, public television was created for just such a purpose, re-routing more substantive demands away from commercial television without becoming an autonomous alternative in and of itself.

In January 1967, the Carnegie Commission on Educational Television proposed a national public television system that would supplement the commercial networks, producing programs about "all that is of human interest and importance which is not at the moment appropriate or available for support by advertising."[5] While the Commission called for a decentralized system outside government control (rather than an elite "fourth network"), it also reinforced the centrality of the marketplace, particularly in maintaining the distinction between programming and reception. In this way, public television also constituted viewers as passive consumers, rather than as active participants in a public sphere, even though its mandate ostensibly placed public television outside market forces.[6] In November 1967, the Public Broadcast Service Act became one of the last Great Society programs, and the only one concerned with communications. But in establishing the Corporation for Public Broadcasting (CPB), the act defined *public* negatively and in market terms—as "noncommercial" (rather than as a way of understanding how a society constitutes itself through communication)—while it also subordinated the CPB to political pressures and corporate underwriting. Indeed, as an administrative structure, CPB had a board that reflected political appointees rather than community participation, while CPB's effectiveness was limited by its ill-defined interconnection with the Public Broadcasting Service (PBS) and local stations.[7]

Though established in 1967, CPB did not deal with race at the national level until the mid-1970s, when a combination of political and public pressures led it to sponsor surveys of the Mexican-American audience (1973–1974),[8] adopt an affirmative action plan (1975),[9] fund a national Latino public affairs series (*Realidades*, 1975–1977),[10] and, in 1979, provide first-time funds to the Latino Consortium (established five years earlier), the first minority public broadcasting consortium.[11] In the interim, efforts to incorporate Chicanos and other racial minorities within public television came either from grassroot efforts aimed at local stations or from national initiatives outside CPB/PBS. In particular, two funding sources provided the impetus behind the development of national programming aimed at Latinos: the U.S. Office of Education and the Ford Foundation. By 1976, the former had granted nearly 15 million dollars for Latino bilingual children's television series as part of its mandate under the Bilingual Education Act of 1968.[12] In the late 1960s, the latter funded various pilot programs in an effort to develop a model for national Latino public affairs programming.[13] In many cases, these Latino-themed series became the start-up productions of local stations within the newly-minted Public Broadcasting Service, allowing one in particular—KCET-TV in Los Angeles—to emerge as one of five national production centers in the system.[14] By the end of the 1970s, that history, like the funding itself, would be erased from the institutional memory of public television.

The Discourse of Professionalism

By the mid-1970s, minority cinemas shifted to a professionalism that correlated not to social protests or state and foundation intervention—both of which were then in decline—but to the idea of a community within the nation and of pan- or transnational cultural formations. Treviño himself would develop and articulate this position through a series of publications over the next decade, wherein he argued that "the films that have resulted are at once an expression of the life, concerns and issues of the Chicano people, and at the same time, the northernmost expression of a political and socially conscious international cinema movement known as New Latin American Cinema."[15] Such claims were more than just rhetorical, insofar as Treviño and others participated en masse in organizational efforts to develop a radical cinema at the national and international levels. These included the U.S. Conference for an Alternative Cinema at Bard College in June 1979, which represented the first such gathering since the 1930s, but which also signalled the end of a class-based leftist politics amid protests from the racial and sexual minorities in attendance.[16] In the mid-1970s, Treviño also participated in the meetings leading up to the first International Festival of New Latin American Cinema in Havana, Cuba, in December 1979, which he and sixteen other Chicano filmmakers attended. Treviño's cultural argument and organizational efforts imbricated minority discourses of cultural identity and civil rights with Third World debates over national identity vis-à-vis neo- and post-colonialism. Film scholars have followed suit with this cultural argument, so that U.S. minorities now factor into most discussions of Third Cinema, but they conveniently ignored the professional discourse that held it all together at a practical level for the filmmakers themselves. Indeed, when looked at from the filmmakers' perspective, one sees that professionalism subordinated the ongoing radical rhetoric challenging the state's legitimizing myths and territorial claims to an overall agenda designed to challenge the government and its policies to intervene on their behalf within the television industry.

Beginning in 1974, Chicano filmmakers formed various organizations as part of a general movement from waning social protests to an emergent professionalism. These included public television syndication (Latino Consortium) and professional groups (National Latino Media Coalition, Chicano Cinema Coalition). But the full range of activities suggests something much more than mere professionalism; or, rather, it suggests the extent to which Chicano filmmakers had to create the discursive and performative contexts within which they could then emerge as professionals and stake a claim to authorship. Thus, in addition to writing for trade and policy-oriented publications, filmmakers introduced the notion of "Chicano cinema" into debates over alternative and independent cinema. Equally important, they also participated in the emerging community-based publications and cultural activities that developed out of the Chicano movement. Treviño and others published in both movement-oriented magazines (*Caracol* and *Chismearte*) and new advertising-based "Latino" general interest magazines (*Nuestro* and *Caminos*).[17] In 1980, the Spanish-language newspaper *La Opinión* published a Sunday cultural supplement on "cine chicano" that brought together and translated many of the formative essays by Chicano filmmakers.[18]

Meanwhile, Chicano and Latino film festivals provided community members with an opportunity to see these films, while they provided the filmmakers with some measure of celebrity and publicity, not to mention moral support, with which to bolster their careers. The main festivals include the Chicano Film Festival in San Antonio, Texas (established in 1975, renamed the International Hispanic Film Festival in the late 1970s, and CineFestival since 1981), the National Latino Film Festival in New York (established in 1981), and the Chicago Latino Film Festival (established in 1985).[19] These and numerous other community- and university-based exhibitions created an important alternative circuit for Chicano independent films. But they also signaled the need for a pan-ethnic, if not hemispheric, framework for public exhibition in order to reach non-Chicano audiences as well as to imbue the public consumption of ethnicity with national and international resonances. In this manner, festivals constructed a viable counter-public in opposition to the mainstream, exchanging the universal appeal of the latter's homogenous subject for the self-selected appeal of a heterogeneous one. In San Francisco, for example, Cine Acción (established in 1980) eschewed a strictly nationalist orientation in favor of an approach that was pan-ethnic, hemispheric, and gender balanced. The group's exhibition efforts have included a regular "cineteca" screening program, the groundbreaking Women of the Americas Film and Video Festival (1988), and the annual ¡Cine Latino! festival (since 1993).[20] By the early 1980s, most public festivals followed the Cine Acción paradigm, even in cities with Chicano-majority populations. In this manner, festival programmers situated the ethnic specificity of individual films within the pan-ethnic and hemispheric viewing context of public exhibition, providing an alternative to the particular-as-universal formula of the mainstream.[21] Here, the particular became *public* against the backdrop of the universal; or, put another way, Chicano films entered America under the aegis of América.

In this same period, Chicano filmmakers began to leave their jobs at television stations in order to form independent production companies. The move was at once a response to the limited opportunities within television stations and an attempt to acquire greater control over the development, production and distribution of Chicano-themed films. The first production companies stemmed from the various settlement agreements and bilingual education funding sources, and were often extensions of advocacy groups such as NMAADC and IMAGE. The McGraw Hill's *La Raza* series helped establish Moctesuma Esparza Productions (1974; now Esparza/Katz Productions). Other production companies included: Ruiz Productions, later InterAmerican Pictures (José Luis Ruiz, 1975–1980); Learning Garden Productions (Severo Perez, 1976–1982); New Vista Productions (Jesús Salvador Treviño, 1977–1978), Chispa Productions

(Daniel, Juan and Susan Salazar, 1978–1981); and, starting with independent works in 1979 and continuing to the present, two Chicana producers who would eventually form their own companies, Sylvan Productions (Sylvia Morales) and Xochitl Films (Lourdes Portillo).

These production companies were located in a "schizo-cultural limbo" where their independent status was measured against an increasing deregulation that would turn them toward the public sector while their rhetoric became simultaneously corporate *and* radical. Chispa Productions in Denver, Colorado, made explicit this dual framework of cultural identity and integrationism.[22] To some extent, this impulse had always been present, but its terms began to change in the late 1970s. In a twist on more nationalist rhetoric, for example, Chispa's Juan Salazar situated *mestizaje* within a reformist vision of American culture:

> We are the last ingredient to make the American Dream real. . . . I believe that the Mestizo . . . is the real existential, modern, paradoxial man [*sic*]. He is bilingual, bicultural, divided. We must find a way to reconcile the divisions, to explore our lives, to understand ourselves and to give the other culture a way of understanding us.[23]

By the end of the 1980s, public television programming changed in several significant ways as deregulation both increased corporate funding and decreased the commitment to local community-oriented production. In essence, the local disappeared, replaced by public affairs programming funded by transnational corporations (mostly in finance or electronics), made outside PBS and its major production centers, and offered direct to local stations at little-to-no cost. Whereas local public affairs programs had served as a vital forum for debate within racially and economically diverse urban populations, these programs reflected elite concerns, consisting of either corporate showcases (*Adam Smith's Money World, Wall $treet Week,* and *Nightly Business Report*) or conservative talk shows (*Firing Line, The McLaughlin Group,* and *One on One*). As William Hoynes concludes, "these programs exist in such abundance because of a convergence of two factors: local public television stations' need to obtain inexpensive programs, and the desire of corporate funders to have such perspectives aired on a regular basis."[24] If the local had been replaced by corporate production of "public affairs" programs, CPB/PBS likewise came under an increasingly corporatist framework, calculating "risk" in production decisions not in terms of some notion of the public interest or even of ratings, but per the concerns of corporate underwriters, local station managers, and conservative legislators.[25]

It is in this period that Latino producers left local stations and became independent producers, often shifting from public affairs to cultural affairs programs, since the latter allowed racial minorities to "cross-over" into a national audience, in large part by dropping the politics and entering into the realm of the aesthetic, wherein, *pace* Horace, one both instructs and delights at some remove from the social formation. The public sphere— as exemplified by the local public affairs programming of the early 1970s— had become privatized around corporate-funded business news and corresponding ideological commentary. What Latino and other minority producers faced, then, was an instance in which the cultural not only challenged the corporate, but did so while standing outside a public sphere within which to participate in political debate and decisionmaking. If pundits and politicians bemoaned the rise of cultural and identity politics, pointing fingers at PBS and the national endowments, they conveniently ignored the fact that such "politics" were the only available strategy for minority groups seeking access to the mass media. They also ignored the fact that PBS and the national endowments already served their own interests to a much greater extent than those of the minority groups that they blamed.

Meanwhile, local stations dropped the minority public affairs series format and began "cherry-picking" from the consortium package, slotting individual programs around the PBS national schedule and corporate-funded syndicated series.[26] The Latino Consortium went from being a syndicator of locally-produced programs packaged into regular series to becoming a "weak access point" for independent producers "where we couldn't even tell the filmmakers when they were going to be broadcast."[27] In the event, regular CPB funding did secure institutional status for the Latino Consortium, ensuring its long term survival, while providing an access point, however weak, for the Latino independent producers who had left local stations since the mid-1970s. When Ruiz returned to the Latino Consortium in 1989, he would remake it into an independent entity within public television, one that attempted to participate in the system's new entrepreneurial zeitgeist. In the interim, Chicano producers would continue efforts to build a coalition with other Latino groups in order to acquire a critical mass with which to address the nation-state. Since Chicanos, like Puerto Ricans and Cuban Americans, were understood in regional and not national terms, they turned to "Hispanic" or "Latino" as a necessary fiction for engaging the national. These terms offered neither identity markers nor de facto political categories; instead, they represented the bumpy road of coalition building among diverse groups unable to achieve a national representation in their own name or in their own image.

Addressing the Nation-State

By the time *Realidades* went off the air in 1977, Executive Producer Humberto Cintrón realized the need for a pan-Latino organization in order to secure ongoing "Latino" funding at the national level. The series itself provided the foundation for such advocacy, since it both established a national network of local producers and provided an arena for working out a pan-ethnic coalition based on identifying differences and shared concerns. In the period between *Realidades* and CPB funding of the Latino Consortium, Cintrón and other Latino producers used the National Latino Media Coalition (NLMC) as a platform for challenging CPB/PBS policy. The NLMC represents a hybrid advocacy group, starting in the early 1970s as an outgrowth of the media reform movement, but becoming more producer-oriented by the time the group incorporated in April 1977.[28] In this respect, NLMC embodies the shift from activism to professionalism, revealing not just the conflicts between the corresponding tactics, locations, and personnel, but also a rather self-conscious attempt to use both outside and inside as part of a larger reform strategy.

By 1973, Chicano-specific efforts to create a national umbrella organization had failed, including the National Mexican American Anti-Defamation Committee and the National Chicano Media Council. In contrast, NLMC emerged through happenstance at a time when Chicanos and Puerto Ricans had come to realize the need to collaborate on areas of mutual concern. In May 1973, during the first meeting between the FCC and minority media reform groups, Latino advocates withdrew as an ad hoc group when they felt that their particular concerns—for example, bilingual programming—were not being addressed. The group demanded and received a separate meeting with the FCC for the next day. The experience convinced the participants of the need to de-couple Latino interests from the catch-all category of "minority," while it also required creating a viable coalition between different Latino groups in order to be effective at the national level.

In creating an organizational infrastructure, the NLMC struck a balance along two axes: Puerto Rican and Chicano; and activist and producer. The chair position alternated between the two major ethnic groups, while the board consisted of representatives from six regions. Furthermore, as the bylaws specified, "No more than three of the six regional representatives are to be employed within the media industry and to earn more than twenty percent of their income from that industry."[29] In many respects, however, the bylaws signaled the increasing presence and influence of media producers within the coalition. In April 1975, the coalition held its first national conference in San Antonio, Texas, followed by ones in Los Angeles (April 1976) and New York (April 1977). The first conference, as Treviño notes,

> would turn out to be this free for all because everybody was polarized. It was Chicanos against Puerto Ricans, and Texas Chicanos against California Chicanos. I mean, it was just a madhouse. . . . But, you know, actually what happened at that time is that a lot of friendships were formed, like with Raquel. Since then we've worked very closely together over the years.[30]

Thus, by the second conference, Cintrón and other producers identified NLMC as a way to lobby public television, government agencies, and Congress. Thus, rather than pursue litigation per the media reform of the early 1970s, the NLMC engaged in a strategy to integrate professionals within the administrative structure and funding protocols for public television. In this way, the NLMC played an instrumental role in several concessions on the part of CPB: the appointment of Louis P. Terrazas to the Board of Directors, the hiring of José Luis Ruiz as a consultant for the development of another national Latino series, and NLMC participation in the CPB's Advisory Council of National Organizations (ACNO). These efforts, and the NLMC's resignation from ACNO in September 1976, coincided with congressional budgetary pressures on CPB over its EEO record, providing the group with some leverage.[31]

In the end, when Ruiz recommended another public affairs series using the magazine format, CPB decided upon a dramatic series, awarding research and development grants to four projects during 1977: *Oye Willie* (Lou De Lemos), *Bless Me Ultima* (José Luis Ruiz), *La Historia* (Jesús Salvador Treviño), and *Centuries of Solitude* (KERA-TV).[32] The CPB delayed decisions on the subsequent production of pilot programs, leading Treviño and Ruiz to present a written statement to the CPB board in October 1979, followed by protests from a national contingent of Latino producers that November.[33] For Latino producers, as Treviño and Ruiz noted, CPB had exchanged its agreement to develop and fund another series for the endless deferral of "research and development as a way of life," while it also turned to the Latino Consortium as a "panacea for national Hispanic programming."[34] These pressures resulted in short-term funding for pending dramatic projects by Puerto Rican and Chicano producers. In 1980, CPB funded *Oye Willie* for one season, while it also provided partial support for two dramatic features that had already received funds from the National Endowment for the Humanities (NEH): *Sequin* (1981), the pilot program from Treviño's *La Historia* series; and *The Ballad of Gregorio Cortez* (1982). But by December 1980, when Ruiz organized a Hispanic Southwest Regional Conference aimed at facilitating additional Chicano projects funded by the NEH,[35] Latino producers had hit a brick wall in terms of public television policy, and the NLMC came to a quiet end. Producers had also identified another funding source in the NEH, one that offered an opportunity to develop and direct feature-length films based on historical events or literary works.[36] In effect, Latino producers looked outside CPB/PBS, making alliances with other governmental agencies, often in order to return with programs for broadcast and syndication within the PBS system. In short, Chicanos joined with Puerto Ricans in order to stake a claim to the nation-state, learning their way around the political and bureaucratic landscape within which public television operated. But these same producers also looked outside the nation-state itself, defining Chicano cinema and their own professional activities within an international context.

Going International

One of the interesting paradoxes of the Chicano movement is that its political discourse continued to look to Mexico, Cuba, and, more generally, the "Bronze Continent" as the necessary backdrop for its efforts to imagine a Chicano community within the political, socioeconomic, and legal structures of the United States. For Chicano filmmakers, this "imagined" location in the Americas became the context for local political action as well as professional reform within the U.S. film and television industries. More than any other media group in this period, the Los Angeles–based Chicano Cinema Coalition (1978–1980) exemplified the mixture of professional, radical, and community-based tactics used to establish the idea of a "Chicano cinema" as well as to create "our own institutions" for production, distribution and exhibition.[37] In its brief existence, the coalition served as a resource for over forty producers, writers, directors and film students and as a platform for protests against exploitation films and industry hiring practices. Members included Jason Johansen, Sylvia Morales, José Luis Ruiz, Luis Torres, Jesús Treviño, and Adolfo Vargas. The coalition held workshops, hosted visiting Latino and Latin American filmmakers, and even screened classic Hollywood films in order to learn about the industry and its cinematic style. Organized protests included detailed press statements upon the release of the gang film *Boulevard Nights* and made-for-television movies *Act of Violence* and *Streets of L.A.* in 1979.[38] The coalition also pressured educational and funding institutions, often successfully incorporating Chicanos into exisiting programs. On December 15, 1978, for example, coalition members met with the American Film Institute (AFI) to discuss the underrepresentation of Chicanos within the organization. In a follow-up letter to the directors on January 10, 1979, the coalition noted that: "(1) there are no Hispanics on the AFI Board of Directors, (2) that only one Chicana has participated in the women's director program, and (3) that only two or three Hispanics have ever participated in the ten-year history of the AFI independent film grant program." Consequently, in late February, three coalition members were awarded AFI grants: Aldolfo Vargas, David Sandoval and Francisco Martinez.[39]

In addition to professional advocacy and membership support, the coalition called for "a Chicano alternative cinema ideology and philosophy which stress the use of film and videotape for the decolonization, independence, advancement, *concientización* and national liberation of the Mexican and Chicano people in the United States."[40] The development of such an aesthetic was seen as "intrinsically linked" to the alternative cinema movements of other ethnic groups in the United States as well as in Latin America and the Third World.[41] The coalition was not alone in making this argument, insofar as Cine Aztlán (Santa Barbara) and Francisco Camplis (San Francisco) had earlier placed the emergent film practice within the context of Third World politics.[42] Interestingly, both were heavily influenced by Jesús Treviño—the former incorporating his research for *¡Ahora!* into its publication, the latter drawing upon an extensive interview with Treviño.

In any case, the connection between ethnic and Third World politics found resonance in the concurrent scholarship by Mario Barrera, Carlos Muñoz Jr., Rodolfo Acuña and others who described the barrio as an "internal colony."[43] The difference between "internal" and "external" colonialism was not so much geographical as legal: Chicanos had the same "formal legal status" as all other United States citizens. But, as

Barrera et al. argued, the conditions of colonialism remained the same: "Internal colonialism means that Chicanos as a cultural/racial group exist in an exploited condition which is maintained by a number of mechanisms . . . [and] . . . a lack of control over those institutions which affect their lives."[44] In "Notes on Chicano Cinema," Johansen articulated the cinematic counterpart to an internal colony model implicit in all the manifestos: "Hollywood cinema is one of intellectual colonization." For this reason, all three manifestos opposed Hollywood while looking to revolution in Latin America as the appropriate international catalyst and context for Chicano cinema: "[O]ur films should strive to connect our struggle internationally. . . . Our films should prepare Raza for that eventuality" (Camplis); "La Raza filmmakers have an international responsibility . . . to unify Raza interpretations with the total human circumstance in a class structured society" (Cine-Aztlán); and "Given the ability of the medium to reach a wide audience, Chicano film must remain linked to and be an integral part of the revolutionary process" (Johansen).

But if the manifestos rejected Hollywood, they nonetheless relied upon the terms of its liberal humanist discourse in order to effect or prepare audiences for international revolution: "Yet, our struggles, hopes and dreams are universal because we are human beings" (Camplis). There was also a simultaneous rejection of the "liberal" filmmakers who sought change or reform from within the established modes of production and distribution, and the call for a "radical" practice that sought revolution based upon an assumption of Hollywood-type distribution. This contradiction manifested itself, also, in the practical efforts of the Chicano Cinema Coalition to seek access to the U.S. film and television industry while also developing relations within Latin America on the basis of an antithetical position toward Hollywood.

The manifestos, then, reveal the way in which Chicano political thought built upon a Third World politics of national liberation, while, at the same time, focusing its efforts on the politics of incorporation vis-à-vis existing U.S. social institutions. In fact, in the case of Camplis and Cine-Aztlán, their understanding of New Latin American Cinema was almost entirely limited to its manifestos, which were translated and reprinted in *Cineaste* in 1970.[45] Thus, if their rhetoric was international and revolutionary, their political orientation was actually grounded in the more immediate experience of the Chicano movement circa 1974. It was not until Jason Johansen published his "notes" in 1979 that Chicano filmmakers, under the direction of the Chicano Cinema Coalition, started to develop a concrete relationship or "active solidarity" with the films and practioners of New Latin American Cinema.[46] But the imagined solidarity served a purpose, too. In the expression of an oppositional political and aesthetic stance, the Chicano film manifestos, like those of the Chicano movement itself, provided an alternative geography or conceptual space within which to approach U.S. institutions.[47]

In this respect, José Limón's application of Harold Bloom's concept of the anxiety of influence to the Chicano movement offers some insight.[48] But whereas Limón identifies the Mexican Revolution of 1910 as the object of the movement's anxiety of influence, it is perhaps more historically accurate to argue that anxiety over the more prevalent "Gringo" influences movitated Chicanos to research and identify models in the Mexican and Cuban revolutions. Likewise, Chicano filmmakers' appeal to New Latin American Cinema masked a considerable anxiety over the all pervasive influence of Hollywood, an anxiety also expressed in the manifestos of New Latin American Cinema. For Chicano filmmakers, especially those who lived and worked in Los Angeles, Hollywood constituted *the* U.S. film and television industry, one from which they remained excluded, except as stereotypes. The Chicano Cinema Coalition and other community-based groups reiterated that point in organized protests against *Walk Proud* (1979), a gang film starring Robby Benson in brownface. Shot on location in Venice, the film production increased tensions between the police and the local Chicano community.[49] It is within this context that Chicano filmmakers theorized, sought out, and developed *other* influences.

Post-revolutionary Cuba provided both rhetoric and experience for the development of the Chicano movement's radical politics as well as its reformist achievements, starting with Luis Valdez's trip to Cuba in 1964 as part of a student delegation. For filmmakers, however, the most lasting impact has been the result of Treviño's involvement with New Latin American Cinema. In 1974, Treviño was recruited into the Cuban-sponsored Comité de Cineastas de América Latina (the Latin American Filmmakers Committee), an international committee of a dozen or more filmmakers committed to the advancement of New Latin American Cinema. The committee met six times between 1974 and 1978, and worked toward the organization of the Annual Festival of New Latin American Cinema, which premiered in December 1979, in Havana, Cuba. At its sixth meeting—held in Havana, July 12–17, 1978—the committee issued a declaration about the festival, and, in the second paragraph, spelled out the relationship of the Chicano filmmakers to New Latin American Cinema:

Igualmente nos declaramos solidarios con la lucha llevada a cabo por el cine del pueblo chicano, manifestación cultural de una comunidad que combate por afirmar su identidad de raíz latinoamericana en medio de la opresión y discriminación a que es sometida en el territorio de los Estados Unidos de Norteamérica. Esta realidad casi o totalmente desconocida por una gran parte de nuestros pueblos, o que ha llegado a ellos a través de las tergiversaciones de la información imperialista, tiene hoy sus cineastas, cuenta ya con un conjunto de obras y demanda de nostros el compromiso de fortalecer los lazos histórico-culturales que nos unen a ella, contribuyendo a la difusión de sus filmes, de sus experiencias y de sus luchas.

[We also declare our solidarity with the struggle of Chicano cinema, the cultural manifestation of a community that combats the oppression and discrimination within the United States in order to affirm its Latin American roots. This reality remains almost or entirely unknown by most of our people, or reaches them through the distortions of the imperialist news media. Yet today (the Chicano community) has its own filmmakers and films, and demands of us the commitment to strengthen the cultural-historical ties that join us together, contributing to the dissemination of their films, their experiences and their struggles.][50]

The Chicano Cinema Coalition led a delegation of seventeen Chicano filmmakers and media advocates to the first festival.[51] Puerto Rican producer Raquel Ortiz also attended. As Treviño explains, "it was a real eye opener experience for a lot of Chicanos that went, because for the first time they were seeing a lot of Latin American—not just Cuban—cinema."[52] One of those who attended was Eduardo Díaz, soon-to-be director of the San Antonio CineFestival, who adds:

The organizers of the event had certainly opened up their perspective—Chicanos were regarded as a nation of Latin American derivation living within the confines of the United States. The Festival even programmed a special series of Chicano films and honored it with a special poster (a wonderful graphic depicting the thorns of a bright green cactus tearing away at an American flag).[53]

The Chicano films screened received an award as a group, and Treviño's *Raíces de sangre* (Mexico, 1977) won the award for best feature script. In subsequent years, Chicano cinema functioned as a national category within this and other Spanish-language festivals. In this manner, Chicanos continued to participate in the festival—for example, as jurors—as well as in a new Cuban film production program established for students from Third World countries in January 1987. Graciela I. Sánchez from San Antonio participated in the first eighteen months of the program, producing the first documentary in Cuba to deal with homosexuality: ". . . *no Porque Lo Diga Fidel Castro*" (1988).[54]

While the experience in Cuba seemed to confirm the predictions of the earlier film manifestos, the social context for racial and radical politics in the United States had changed quite a bit since the heyday of the Chicano movement and of New Latin American Cinema.[55] Contacts with Latin America did foster an increased international political perspective in the 1980s, although it is difficult to separate this perspective from the filmmakers' increased awareness of and attention to the international film market and festival circuit. In this respect, the Festival of New Latin American Cinema served an important symbolic role in doubling the "location" of Chicano cinema, making it into a movement that was at once reformist and revolutionary. But rather than constitute a contradiction, this dual location provided Chicano filmmakers with an effective political strategy within the United States. Chicano cinema both juxtaposed and straddled two locations, America and América, not so much as a matter of an either/or choice (even though it was presented and debated as such), but rather as an attempt to define tightly-coupled oppositional terms—nationalism and assimilation; revolution and reform—so that the one would inevitably produce the other. In this manner, early successful reforms came about as a result of shifting the center leftward during public protests and press statements, providing filmmakers with a vantage point from which to negotiate for more moderate goals within the film and television industry and related social institutions. Without a doubt, such a strategy put Chicano cinema on the map in both a literal and figurative sense, constructing an alternative to Hollywood. But it was an alternative in both senses of the word, something different from Hollywood, yet something that also aspired to take its place.

NOTES

1. Jesús Salvador Treviño, interview by Francisco X. Camplis, n.d. (circa 1974), 3. Transcript in Treviño Collection, M634, Box 13, Folder 10, Department of Special Collections, Stanford University.

2. David Morales, "Media in El Paso," Committee for the Development of Mass Communications, distributed in Media Action News Service, vol. 1176 (November 1976), np.

MALDEF Collection, M673, Box 121, Folder 9, Department of Special Collections, Stanford University.

3. United States Commission on Civil Rights, *Racial and Ethnic Tensions in American Communities: Poverty, Inequality, and Discrimination—Los Angeles Hearing*, Executive Summary and Transcript of Hearing Held in Los Angeles, California, June 15–17, 1993 (Washington, D.C.: U.S. Government Printing Office, November 1998).

4. See Chon A. Noriega, ed., *The Future of Latino Independent Media: A NALIP Sourcebook* (Los Angeles: UCLA Chicano Studies Research Center, 2000); and the Congressional Hispanic Caucus Institute, *2000 Issues Conference Policy Recommendations* (Washington, D.C., 2001).

5. Carnegie Commission on Educational Television, *Public Television: A Program for Action* (New York: Harper & Row, 1967), 1.

6. See Patricia Aufderheide, "Public Television and the Public Sphere," *Critical Studies in Mass Communication* 8 (1991): 168–83.

7. For more on the history of public television in the United States, see Robert K. Avery and Robert Pepper, "The Evolution of the CPB-PBS relationship, 1970–1973," *PTR: Public Telecommunications Review* 4:5 (September–October 1976): 6–17; idem., "An Institutional History of Public Broadcasting," *Journal of Communication* 30:3 (Summer 1980): 126–38; Robert Pepper, "The Interconnection Connection: The Formation of PBS," *PTR: Public Telecommunications Review* 4:1 (January–February 1976): 6–26; Willard D. Rowland, Jr., "Continuing Crisis in Public Broadcasting: A History of Disenfranchisement," *Journal of Broadcasting and Electronic Media* 30:3 (Summer 1986): 251–74; John Witherspoon and Roselle Kovitz, *The History of Public Broadcasting* (Washington, D.C.: Corporation for Public Broadcasting, 1987), a report originally published in *Current*; William Hoynes, *Public Television for Sale: Media, the Market, and the Public Sphere* (Boulder, Colo.: Westview Press, 1994); and B. J. Bullert, *Public Television: Politics and the Battle Over Documentary Film* (New Brunswick, N.J.: Rutgers University Press, 1997).

8. Nicholas A. Valenzuela, *Media Habits and Attitudes of Mexican-Americans: Surveys in Austin and San Antonio* (Austin: Center for Communication Research at the University of Texas, June 1973); Frederick Williams, Nicholas A. Valenzuela, and Pamela Knight, *Prediction of Mexican-Americans Communication Habits and Attitudes* (Austin: Center for Communication Research, University of Texas, June 1973); and Nicholas A. Valenzuela, *Public Television and the Mexican-American Audience in the Southwest*, CPB/OCR Report 214 (Washington, D.C.: Corporation for Public Broadcasting, Office of Communication Research, January 1974).

9. *Affirmative Action Plan* (Washington, D.C.: Corporation for Public Broadcasting, 1975). Two years later, however, Congress took CPB to task for its continued poor record of minority and female employment. See "Authorizations Tied to Improved EEO Efforts," *CPB Report*, the Newsletter of the Corporation for Public Broadcasting, 8:9 (May 2, 1977): 1; "Public Broadcasting Authorization Process," *CPB Report*, 8:9 (May 2, 1977): 2; "Capitol Hill Tells CPB to Shape Up Minority Records or Money May Be Difficult to Get," *Broadcasting*, February 14, 1977, 58.

10. José García Torres, "José García Torres & Realidades," interview by Aurora Flores and Lillian Jiménez, *Centro de Estudios Puertorriqueños Bulletin* 2:8 (Spring 1990): 31–43.

11. "Latinos and CPB: In Quest of National Programming," *Chicano Cinema Newsletter* 1:6 (August 1979): 2–3. CPB policy formally recognized the minority consortia in 1980.

12. "ESAA Funding of Bilingual Programming," *PTR: Public Telecommunications Review*, 4:4 (July–August 1976): 25. See also, Eric Wentworth, "Bilingual TV Funds Resumed Cautiously," *Washington Post*, July 3, 1973, B1, B9.

13. Gerald Astor, *Minorities and the Media*, a Ford Foundation Report, November 1974.

14. KCET acknowledged this fact in the timeline that accompanied a series of articles celebrating its tenth anniversary in 1974; although, to my knowledge, it has not done so since then, while the articles themselves do not acknowledge issues of racial diversity as part of the station's history. See James L. Loper, Art Seidenbaum, and Cecil Smith, "The KCET Story: Reminiscences of the First Ten Years," *Gambit*, program guide for KCET/Channel 28 (October 1974): 20–24. The timeline is published on pages 26–29. In addition to the awards received by the series, the timeline states that on October 1968, "KCET emerges as national production center with national broadcast of *Canción de la Raza*."

15. Treviño, "Chicano Cinema Overview," *Areito* no. 37 (1984), 40.

16. See "400 Media Activists Meet at Alternative Cinema Conference"; "Alternative Cinema Conference," *Chicano Cinema Newsletter* 1:3 (May 1979): 1; Jesús Salvador Treviño, "Alternative Cinema Conference: Optimism, Realistic Expectations," *Chicano Cinema Newsletter* 1:4 (June 1979): 1. The event did result in ongoing connections between *Jump Cut* editors and Chicano filmmakers. Treviño and others later contributed articles to *Jump Cut*, while co-editor John Hess wrote various pieces on Latin American cinema for *Cine Acción News* throughout the 1980s.

17. Carlos Morton, "Why There Are No Chicano Filmmakers: Plática de José Luis Seda y Antonio Ogaz," *Caracol* 2:11 (July 1976): 18–19, 5, 16; Umberto Rivera, "Film Notes," *Chismearte* 1:2 (Winter/Spring 1977): 20–24; Marcelo Epstein, "Film and Industry," *Chismearte* 1:2 (Winter/Spring 1977): 25; Ron Arias, "Getting on the Set," *Nuestro: The Magazine for Latinos* 1:7 (October 1977): 18–21; "Stage and Screen: Struggles Behind the Scenes," *Nuestro: The Magazine for Latinos* 3:3 (April 1979): 19–20; "Feature Section on Chicano Films," guest edited by Jesús Salavador Treviño, *Caminos* 3:10 (November 1982): 6–20.

18. "Cine chicano primer acercamiento," *La Opinión*, November 16, 1980, Cultural Supplement.

19. In addition to programming information, the festival catalogues include essays, often providing early critical work on issues related to the films and filmmakers. Other annual festivals include Cine Estudiantil in San Diego (established in 1994, renamed Cine in 1998), Cine Sol Latino Film Festival in Harlingen, Texas (established in 1993), East Los Angeles Chicano Film Festival (established in 1995), and the Los Angeles International Latino Film Festival (established in 1997). See Ray Santisteban, "Notes on the Hows and Whys of Latino Film Festivals," *AHA! Hispanic Art News* 167 (July/August 1998): 12; and Ethan van Thillo, "A Guide to Understanding Chicano Cinema and Organizing a Chicano Film Festival," Senior Thesis, Latin American Studies, University of California, Santa Cruz, Winter 1992. For an early overview of Chicano film festivals, see Yolanda Broyles, "Chicano Film Festivals: An Examination," in *Chicano Cinema: Research, Reviews, and Resources*, ed. Gary D. Keller (Binghamton, N.Y.: Bilingual Review/Press, 1985), 116–20.

20. In addition to its festival catalogues, Cine Acción publishes *Cine Acción News* and *CineWorks: A Latino Media Resource Guide*, a directory of members' films and videos.

21. The exception seems to be university-based exhibitions, which build upon a Chicano studies and student group constituency.

22. William Gallo, "Chicano Filmmakers Strike Vivid Spark of Life," *Rocky Mountain News*, January 18, 1980, section III, 5, 11. This shift is complete by the late 1980s, as filmmakers reject an "ethnic" label as artists and place their Chicano-themed work within an "American" or "universal" context. Thus, in 1987, Luis Valdez explained, "I want to be part of the mainstream—as myself." See the interview, "An Artist Who Has Blended Art and Politics," *El Tecolote* (San Francisco Mission District), October 1987, 9 ff.

23. Gallo, "Chicano Filmmakers."

24. Hoynes, *Public Television for Sale*, 105.

25. Ibid., 94.

26. Personal interview with José Luis Ruiz.

27. Ibid.

28. See Guernica, "The Development of the National Latino Media Coalition"; and "National Latino Media Coalition (NLMC): A Progress Report," *Reporte,* Newsletter of the Texas Chicano Coalition on Mass Media, 1:1 (February 1977): 5–6.

29. Quoted in Guernica, "The Development of the National Latino Media Coalition," 30.

30. Personal interview with Jesús Salvador Treviño.

31. "Latino Coalition Resigns from CPB Advisory Council," *Access* 44 (October 26, 1976): 3. For information on congressional pressure on CPB, see note 29.

32. Treviño's *La Historia* series was loosely based on the earlier "La Raza History" segments produced for *¡Ahora!* in 1970. For scripts of "La Raza History" and materials related to the *La Historia* proposal, see Treviño Collection, M634, Boxes 1–5, Department of Special Collections, Stanford University.

33. Treviño and Ruiz, "Hispanics and Public Broadcasting." See also Treviño's account and funding information in his article, "Latinos and Public Broadcasting: The 2% Factor," *Jump Cut* 28 (1983): 65.

34. Treviño and Ruiz, "Hispanics and Public Broadcasting," 5–6.

35. José Luis Ruiz, ed., *Media and the Humanities,* proceedings of the Hispanic Southwest Regional Conference, December 4–7, 1980, San Diego, California.

36. Since these films were intended for theatrical release, I consider them at greater length as part of another book on Chicano media and public exhibition. For excellent production histories of *The Ballad of Gregorio Cortez* (1982), *El Norte* (1983), and *Stand and Deliver* (1988), see David Rosen, *Off-Hollywood: The Making and Marketing of Independent Films* (New York: Grove Weidenfeld, 1990). Severo Pérez and Paul Espinosa's . . . *and the Earth Did Not Swallow Him* (1994) is the most recent feature film to have been funded through NEH.

37. In addition to Cine-Aztlán and Cine Acción, the Los Angeles-based Emancipation Arts (established 1978) represented a multiracial and feminist nonprofit corporation that included coalition member David Sandoval. See the newsletter, *Emancipation Arts* (Spring 1980), which includes their manifesto, "Toward a Multinational Film Movement," and an account of their feature-length documentary project, *Valley of Tears.*

38. Chicano Cinema Coalition press statements: March 23, 1979; and November 15, 1979. In addition to a detailed, step-by-step list of reasons the coalition objected to the films, the television movies were cited as "acts of psychological violence against the Latino community," a phrase the press quoted often.

39. "CCC Meets AFI," *Chicano Cinema Newsletter* 1:2 (February 1979), 2.

40. "The Los Angeles Chicano Cinema Coalition: Statement of Purpose," *Chicano Cinema Newsletter* 1:2 (February 1979), 8.

41. Ibid. See also Jason Johansen, "Notes on Chicano Cinema," *Chicano Cinema Newsletter* 1:4 (June 1979): 6–8.

42. Cine-Aztlán, "Ya Basta Con Yankee Imperialist Documentaries," *La Raza Film Bibliography* (Santa Barbara, Calif.: Cine-Aztlán, 1974), 20–25; and Francisco X. Camplis, "Towards the Development of a Raza Cinema," in Tobias and Sandra Gonzales, eds., *Perspectives on Chicano Education,* (Stanford, Calif.: Chicano Fellows/Stanford University, 1975), 155–73. I cite from the excerpted version of Camplis's manifesto, which appears in *Tin Tan Magazine* 2:5 (June 1977): 5–7. These two manifestos, along with the one by Jason Johansen, are reprinted in Chon A. Noriega, ed., *Chicanos and Film: Representation and Resistance* (Minneapolis: University of Minnesota Press, 1992). Subsequent citations of these three manifestos will be in the text itself. For a related statement from an influential Chicano poet and visual artist, see José Montoya's presentation to the First Annual Chicano Film Series at Stanford University in January 1979: "Thoughts on La Cultural: The Media, Con Safos, and Survival," *Caracol* 5:9 (May 1979): 6–8, 19.

43. Mario Barrera, Carlos Muñoz, Jr., and Charles Ornelas, "The Barrio as Internal Colony," *Urban Affairs Annual Reviews* 6 (1972): 465–98, rpt. in F. Chris Garcia, ed., *La Causa Politica: A Chicano Politics Reader* (Notre Dame, Ind.: University of Notre Dame Press, 1974), 281–301; Rodolfo Acuña, *Occupied America: The Chicano's Struggle Toward Liberation* (San Francisco: Canfield Press, 1972).

44. Barrera et al, "Barrio as Internal Colony," in Garcia, *La Causa Politica*, 289. By the mid 1970s, Chicano scholars re-evaluated and critiqued the internal colony model and its role within the university and the community. Some scholars looked to either an increased class analysis or a return to a traditional colonial model. For a recent critique of the legal basis of the internal colony model, see Tomás Almaguer, "Ideological Distortions in Recent Chicano Historiography: The Internal Model and Chicano Historical Interpretation," *Aztlán: A Journal of Chicano Studies* 18:1 (Spring 1987): 7–28.

45. Translations of these manifestos appeared in the Summer 1970 and Winter 1970–1971 issues of *Cineaste*. See also Michael Chanan, ed., *Twenty-five Years of the New Latin American Cinema* (London: British Film Institute and Channel Four Television, 1983).

46. As children, however, these same filmmakers were part of the last Chicano generation to attend movie theaters showing the "classic" cinema of both Mexico and the United States.

47. It is not surprising, then, that these manifestos were written by university students allied with independent producers: Camplis at Stanford University, Johansen at the University of California, Los Angeles, and Cine-Aztlán members at the University of California, Santa Barbara. In fact, Camplis and Johansen were MFA students in film production.

48. José E. Limón, *Mexican Ballads, Chicano Epic: History, Social Dramas and Poetic Persuasions*, SCCR Working Paper Series No. 14, (Stanford, Calif.: Stanford Center for Chicano Research, 1986).

49. For collected press coverage and position statement, see Gang Exploitation Film Committee, *A Reader and Information Packet on the "Gang Exploitation Films"* (Monterey Park, Calif.: East Los Angeles M.E.Ch.A., 1979). See also Daniel G. Solorzano, "Teaching and Social Change: Reflections on a Freirian Approach in a College Classroom," *Teaching Sociology* 17 (April 1989): 218–25.

50. "Declaración del Comité de Cineasta de America Latina," *Cine Cubano*, 8:3 (1977–1978): 45–46. Translation mine. The declaration was translated by Ralph Cook and reprinted in *Cineaste* 9:1 (Fall 1978): 54. In Cook's version, he inserts references to the Chicano movement. The original text, however, refers to the Chicano "community," and not the "movement," whose militant phase had already come to an end.

51. For press accounts of Chicano participation in the festival, see Patricia Aufderheide, "Latins, Exiles, U.S. Chicanos Attend Havana's Film Fest," *Variety*, December 19, 1979; and Clyde Taylor, "Special Report—Cuba: A Festival," *Chamba Notes: A Media Newsletter* (Summer 1980): 1–3. Essays by Treviño and Johansen, along with a filmography by Héctor Garza, were later translated and published in a collection documenting the New Latin American Cinema: *Hojas de Cine: Testimonios y Documentos del Nuevo Cine Latinoamericano* (México: Fundación del Nuevo Cinema Latinoamericano, 1986).

52. Personal interview with Treviño.

53. Eduardo Diaz, "Chicano Film Festivals," unpublished paper, August 1990, 7. Cited with permission of the author.

54. Personal interview with Graciela I. Sánchez, San Antonio, September 29, 1992. Enrique Berumén from Los Angeles entered the program in January 1988, staying for six months.

55. Coco Fusco's brief historical trajectory for New Latin American Cinema speaks to Chicano cinema as well: "Times have changed, and manifestos have given way to deeper reflection and commentary, the signs of a movement in the process of assessing itself. More recent films are generally less sweeping, and often less polemical, but the finest of them

continue to combine aesthetic innovation and social commitment." In Coco Fusco, ed., *Reviewing Histories: Selections from New Latin American Cinema* (Buffalo, N.Y.: Hallwalls Contemporary Arts Center, 1987), 4. For critical accounts of New Latin American Cinema in relation to its earlier manifestos, see Paul Willemen, "The Third Cinema Question: Notes and Reflections," *Framework* 34 (1987): 4–38; Ana M. López, "An 'Other' History: The New Latin American Cinema," in *Resisting Images: Essays on Cinema and History*, ed. Robert Sklar and Charles Musser (Philadephia: Temple University Press, 1990), 308–30; Patricia Aufderheide, "Latin American Cinema and the Rhetoric of Cultural Nationalism: Controversies at Havana in 1987 and 1989," *Quarterly Review of Film and Video* 12:4 (1991): 61–76; B. Ruby Rich, "Another View of New Latin American Cinema," *Iris: A Journal of Theory on Sound and Image* 13 (Summer 1991): 5–28; Catherine Davies, "Modernity, Masculinity and Imperfect Cinema in Cuba," *Screen* 38:4 (Winter 1997): 345–59; and Michael Chanan, "The Changing Geography of Third Cinema," *Screen* 38:4 (Winter 1997): 372–88. Manifestos and key critical works are anthologized in Michael T. Martin, ed., *New Latin American Cinema*, vol. 1: *Theory, Practices, and Transcontinental Articulations* (Detroit: Wayne State University Press, 1997). Volume 2 provides historical accounts of various national cinemas, blurring the boundary between the eponymous film movement and contemporary industrial and independent cinemas. For close textual analysis of major works, see Julianne Burton, ed., *The Social Documentary in Latin America* (Pittsburgh: University of Pittsburgh Press, 1990); and Zuzana M. Pick, *New Latin American Cinema: A Continental Project* (Austin: University of Texas Press, 1993).

Marjut Salokannel

Cinema in Search of Its Authors: On the Notion of Film Authorship in Legal Discourse

Cinema has continually been confronted with the problem of determining who is the actual author of a cinematographic work. This question has been answered differently depending on whether the response was given by the ardent European film-critic supporter of the *politique des auteurs*, by the American corporate lawyer defending the interests of a major Hollywood studio, or by one of the various legal commentators and practitioners who operate in this field. The uncertainty that surrounds the notion of the film author has led not only to debate in film theory and in law, but also to practical problems, with moral and financial consequences for the authors of cinematographic works. This being so, the question of the nature and meaning of film authorship in relation to the day-to-day economic and social practices of film and audiovisual production is not merely of theoretical interest; it also has ramifications for the livelihood and artistic integrity of individuals working in films. The aim of this paper is to examine how the notion of film authorship has been interpreted in the legal discourses of Europe and the United States. As part of this examination, it will be necessary to highlight the mediating processes between the legal definition of film authorship and the notion of the film author in aesthetics and in social discourses relating to film production. As a preliminary, however, it is necessary to pause briefly to consider the notion of the author.

This essay is a revised and updated version of the article "Film Authorship in the Changing Audiovisual Environment," published in *Of Authors and Origins: Essays on Copyright Law*, edited by Brad Sherman and Alain Strowell (New York: Oxford University Press, 1994).

On the Notion of the Author

The notion of the modern artist—the creative genius, the free and autonomous human being who creates unique works of art unhindered by external influences—is a product of the humanist ideas of the Renaissance. It was in the Italian courts of the late fifteenth century that painters and sculptors first began to distinguish themselves from ordinary artisans, a move which enabled them to claim a position approaching that of the *savant*, the free and independent individual possessing unique knowledge which would give their work a place among the liberal arts.[1] Prior to this, artists were seen not as members of a specific professional group, but as mere manufacturers or artisans. When the idea of the autonomous and unified subject emerged with the Enlightenment philosophies of the late eighteenth century, the creative genius found its philosophical basis in this subjectivity. The Romantic notion of the author as autonomous subject and creative genius which this subjectivity helped produce has come to occupy a central position in the discourses dealing with artistic practices such as art history, aesthetics, and author's rights.[2]

In the latter part of the twentieth century, these ideas of a universal and autonomous subjectivity have been the object of much critical scrutiny, and this has led, in effect, to the decentralization of the subject. One of the most important lessons to be drawn from these critiques is that there is no universal subjectivity and that it is therefore not possible to generalize from one social practice to another. As Foucault has observed, the concept of the author should not be seen as something which operates in a uniform manner throughout history; rather authors must always be situated in their relevant historical and social context.[3] The disappearance of the author as the origin of the work in literary criticism does not, of course, imply that writers actually vanish, but rather that they are no longer accorded a privileged position as a category of interpretation.[4]

In examining how the notion of film authorship has been interpreted in the legal discourses surrounding it, we must remember that cinema involves the intersection of three concurrent forms of social practice: the artistic, the economic, and the technological. The structure of each of these is determined by a specific set of historical and social conventions, with their own inherent power-relations. In each of them, ideas such as "cinema" and "author" are defined in accordance with the conventions of the respective discourses. For example, in law, where the author is treated as a holder of rights, the meaning attributed to the notion of the author is different from that applied in film criticism, where it is used more as a focus of interpretation. This distinction does not imply, however, that these different forms of social practice constitute autonomous fields of knowledge (in the Enlightenment sense of the word). On the contrary, mediation takes place between them, and it is important to understand the process by which this occurs.[5]

The Work of Art in the Age of Mechanical Reproduction: The Historical, Social and Legal Constitution of Film Authorship

The history of cinema coincides with that of Western industrial society. Indeed, it could be said that cinema was the first new art form of the industrial age. One of the first problems that confronted the new medium was that it did not come within the orbit of the (then) accepted notion of art.[6] Not only did it stand in contradiction to many of the "sacred" attributes of art, it also fell outside the Romantic vision of artistic creation, a vision in which a work of art is characterized by its authenticity and irreproducibility, and by the fact that it is the unique creation of an individual author, an expression of genius. In contrast, a cinematographic work is a product of collective effort, in which no one individual genius is easily distinguished. Moreover, it has no original, or, to be more precise, the negative is the original and the positive merely a copy of it. The matrix and copies of a film have equal artistic value. To paraphrase Benjamin, we may ask whether the invention of cinema has the potential of altering our conception of artistic creation.

Filmmaking as the Interplay of Technological, Economic, and Artistic Factors

Filmmaking is characterized by a precarious interdependence between technological possibilities, economic constraints, and artistic creation, a relationship marked by inherent contradictions. Historically, technology has influenced filmmaking on several levels. For example, most basic ways of making an audiovisual work require sophisticated technological devices. More generally, the invention of photography and the development of cinematography were both preceded by the invention of new, perhaps revolutionary, ways of making images.[7] Today, different ways of manipulating images offered by digital technology are again radically changing the field of audiovisual expression.

However, technology is not a neutral force. The selection of technology requires both economic and artistic, as well as political, choices. Moreover, technology influences the manner in which films are produced. On one level, commercial logic, which demands the maximization of profit, dictates that only the most economically favorable technologies are used. The decision to move from one mode of technology to another should not therefore be analyzed only from the technical point of view; it does not necessarily depend solely on the mere availability of a new technology; it may also be determined by factors such as the desire fully to exploit the older technology which it is to replace.[8] The tendency to colorize old black-and-white feature films shows the ways in which economic calculations impinge upon the artistic integrity of the author of the work. As we shall see, this has had an adverse effect on the recognition of the creator as the author of the work.

The most interesting aspect of technology, for the purposes of this article, is the influence it has had on the division of labor within filmmaking. This can be seen, for example, in the fact that the introduction of sound to cinema altered the standing of sound engineers within the film crew. Similarly, the use of color film imposed new demands on photographers, set-designers, and others working with the external appearance of the film. One of the consequences of this was that the role of actors diminished in favor of the settings and general *prise de vue* of the film.[9] Digital technology has, for its part, brought forth new professionals to central artistic roles, such as traditional and digital special effects designers. The role of the storyboard artist has expanded in connection with digital filmmaking.

The Role of Authors in Different Modes of Audiovisual Communication

The structural transformations that have occurred in the field of audiovisual communications have also had an impact on the notion of the author. Even though the basis of filmmaking remains the same—namely, the human creative effort through which a cinematographic work comes into being—the role of the author in relation to the production apparatus changes as we move from one mode of audiovisual production to another. When the position of the film author is considered in relation to the different institutionalized forms of audiovisual communication, the political and economic aspects of filmmaking technology are also highlighted.[10]

Because photography introduced a new technical method of producing images, it is generally regarded as the forerunner of cinematography. Initially, these images were seen merely as reproductions of nature, produced by tool-like machines, a process in which the photographer played no creative role. Consequently the photographer was not, in an aesthetic sense, seen to be creating anything new, but only imitating or reproducing nature. The photographer was not an artist, an author, but an artisan who made pictures with tools: this applied both to the artistic and to the legal discourse about authors' rights, where the photographer was initially denied the status of a creative author.[11] The ambiguous status of photography in relation to other forms of art has persisted up to the present day.[12]

When *cinema* was first introduced, it was regarded as merely another way of producing images with a machine; the only factor distinguishing it from photography was that the pictures moved. Early cinema was primarily concerned with the production of animated pictures, with no specific cinematic form of representation. This was true both in the field of fiction, as represented by Méliès (who developed his *trucs* from the theatre), and also in the realm of documentaries, as represented by the Lumière brothers. Unlike traditional arts, which were seen to be the product of human creative effort, the creation of genius, cinema was seen merely as an extension of photographic expression, as a way of reproducing reality with the aid of a machine.

Films of the early cinema, shown in fairs to small audiences, were made primarily as entertainment for working-class people. The idea of the film as a form of live entertainment was reflected in French public-order legislation, in which, for censorship purposes, films were treated as *spectacles de curiosités*.[13] Cinema initially presented itself as a popular art form, and it was not until some ten to fifteen years after the invention of this new medium that its artistic quality began to gain prominence. The emergence of a more elitist cinema in turn contributed, in part, to the legitimization of cinema as art. This shift can be seen in the fact that in the 1920s the artistic avant-garde regarded cinema as a new means by which to challenge the established conventions of high art. When artists such as Picasso and Cocteau turned to filmmaking, it was much more difficult for critics and bourgeois audiences to disregard cinema and to continue to see it only as a form of cheap entertainment and diversion for the masses.[14]

The recognition of cinema as an art form was inextricably bound up with the recognition of the film author. In early cinema, the majority of filmmakers did not regard themselves as artists, but rather as manufacturers of cinema. There was no specific division of labor in the filmmaking process; films were made by small groups of individuals working co-operatively. In its early years, filmmaking was characterized as an artisanal type of manufacture.[15] The development of cinema from an artisanal practice into a fully fledged industry took only twenty years or so from the time that the first moving pictures were shown in the Lumière brothers' backyard.[16] When a division of labor began to occur in filmmaking, it initially did so along similar lines in both America and Europe.[17] First, the role of the cameraman was separated from that of the general filmmaker who took care of the creation of the film as a whole—as author, director, and editor, as well as producer and distributor.[18] The central role of the cameraman, which can perhaps be attributed to the technical skill required to use the new technologies, did not last long. In order for the cinematographic work to attain an artistically coherent form, it was necessary for someone to take control of the creative process as a whole. This was the task of the director. While directors took on an organizing role in the work process, they were, with the exception of a few avant-garde filmmakers, rarely designated "author" of the work. The reason for this lack of recognition was that since early cinema was closely connected to theatrical expression, the role of the director was equated, initially at least, to that of the stage director.[19] That is, a director was still seen more as a metteur-en-scène, who provided the underlying literary work with its filmic representation, than as an actual *réalisateur*,[20] a creator of a new, independent work.[21] With further division of labor, the role of the screenwriter was differentiated from that of the director (although it was common—and still is—for the writing of the script and the directing to be done by the same person, especially in Europe).

A further structural change occurred in the field of audiovisual expression with the introduction of television. It was a change that had profound consequences for the way audiovisual works were both produced and distributed.[22] Television largely replaced cinema as a form of entertainment for the mass public. However, even though cinema lost some of its audience to the easily accessible private television set, television provided a valuable channel for secondary exploitation of feature films and thus considerably expanded the size of the original audiences. Though the relationship between film and television production differs in Europe and America, consideration of broadcasting companies has become an indispensable part of the way in which the contemporary feature film business functions on both sides of the Atlantic.

This transformation has also had implications for the film author. In public service broadcasting companies, film authors have become government functionaries, with all the benefits and disadvantages attached to such positions.[23] However, these positions are occupied by only a small percentage of the people working within film. The vast bulk of those filmmakers who may be regarded as film authors continue to work for broadcasting companies only on a freelance basis, if at all. Television has also introduced a hierarchical structure to the audiovisual field: classical cinema now represents the high realm of artistic creation, the seventh art in its purest form, with television as the "opiate of the masses," cheap popular culture. The overall effect has been to confirm and reinforce ideas of film as an art form and film directors as authors.

Although video technology has led to a major transformation in the field of audiovisual expression, influencing both the means of production and distribution of audiovisual works, it has not, to any notable extent, affected the division of labor within professional filmmaking. Although by enabling more flexible working methods, video has facilitated work in smaller units and introduced new people into the area, it has not altered the tasks of individuals within that process: screenwriters, directors, cameramen, and editors are still required for filmmaking—although one person may perform several of these roles. Digital technology has, however, changed the division of labor within the film production process to a certain extent. As noted above, for example, the role of special effects designers is highlighted in the digital filmmaking process. Generally speaking, digital technology, which makes it possible to postpone the final artistic decisions about the film to the post-production period, has accentuated the later stages of the process.

Emergence of Film Authors

In the United States, the central role of the director lasted only a few years; then the producer took over control of the filmmaking process.[24] From this point on, the U.S. film industry developed on an industrial basis: it treated its personnel, whether artistic or technical, like workers in the automobile industry. Not only were artistic personnel salaried employees, they were also denied any privileges based on the specific nature of their creative work. In this respect, Hollywood has never recognized its authors. In contrast, in most European countries, creative individuals who worked within filmmaking have been accorded a special status. The divergence of film production and associated legal practices in Europe and the United

States may be attributed to various factors: socioeconomic and cultural differences, as well as differing ideological views on cultural production. In this connection, however, it must be noted that independent film-making in the United States operates very much along the same lines as in Europe.

Although the point of rupture between European and American cin-ema can be traced to the establishment of the producer-dominated system in the United States, the recognition in Europe of film as an art form, on an equal footing with other forms of art, did not come easily. Avant-garde artists were indeed recognized as authors of their films, but this occurred only at the margins of filmmaking. The majority of films continued to be seen as forms of popular entertainment, devoid of any particular artistic significance. Cinema was still without its authors. Although a number of directors were recognized for their artistic talent in the first half of the twentieth century, this was insufficient to change the artistic status of the profession as a whole. Indeed, it was not until the 1950s, with the birth of the French New Wave (*Nouvelle Vague*), that the film author assumed an unquestioned position of prominence within the filmmaking process.[25]

The politique des auteurs advocated by the group of young critics associated with the French magazine *Cahiers du Cinéma* argued that the cinematographic film was primarily the creation of its director, who, as a consequence, should be regarded as its author.[26] The French New Wave shifted the line that divided the creative work from the process of adap-tation and execution in filmmaking. Whereas the task of the director had previously been seen as merely to translate or adapt the underlying lit-erary work or script into a filmic representation, it was now viewed as the creative heart of the film; the rest of the film crew were seen as mere executors of the director's orders. Even if the director did not participate in the writing of the script, he or she was said to provide it with its ulti-mate filmic existence. Though the scriptwriter was recognized as the co-author of the film, the director remained its principal creator. By imposing the notion of a single unifying author on the cinematic discourse, the representatives of the French New Wave wanted, among other things, to give cinema the status of art. According to Darré, the French New Wave marked an important point of rupture in the French discourse around cinema. Prior to its development, only a few famous authors such as those of the 1920s avant-garde were recognized as such; after the emer-gence of the French New Wave, however, the director came to be seen, a priori, as the author of the film, even before it had begun to be shot. In other words, all films, irrespective of their artistic quality, came to be considered as film d'auteurs.[27]

Some ten years after the French New Wave, the New German Cinema shifted the notion of the author to a central position in the German film-making process. The author championed by the German *Autorenfilm* differed in a number of ways, however, from the author of the French New Wave.[28] While the politique des auteurs of the French New Wave was based on the Romantic notion of the author as the creator of the work, the German *Autor* was a more political figure who challenged the cinema as an institution while attempting to benefit from the system in which it operated. (German filmmakers had to define themselves as authors in order to obtain government subsidies for their films.) In order to be able to retain their independence vis-à-vis the commercial film industry, direc-tors/writers had to have full creative and executive control over film pro-duction, which meant, in turn, that they also had to assume the tasks of producer. Thus, many German filmmakers who belonged to the gene-ration of the New German Cinema felt closer to the small entrepreneur, the artisan of the early cinema, than to the Romantic author.[29] Despite the multiplicity of functions that converged under the author figure invoked by the New German Cinema, the German Autor, like its French counter-part, was defined as the director of the film.[30] The German Autor can thus be seen to have been used as an ideological weapon in a struggle to secure a viable position in the financing and production apparatus of filmmaking in Germany. The term "Autor" denoted an independent filmmaker holding a critical position vis-à-vis the commercial cinema and the system of government funding without which that cinema could not survive. The notion of the author in New German Cinema thus served to unify the different practices which conditioned filmmaking in Germany.[31]

Juridical Constitution of Film Authorship

Juridically, cinema first attracted the interests of legislators as a poten-tially subversive medium which had to be regulated so as to maintain public order: it had to be controlled for the purposes of government cen-sorship.[32] As long as cinema was not regarded as an independent art form, the question of copyright protection did not arise.[33] As cinema was grad-ually accepted as art, its status within law began to pose problems. Since the traditional legal institution of authorial rights is based on the Romantic notion of the author, on the idea of unified subjectivity represented by the creative genius, it is not surprising that artistic works made by a number of individuals collaborating to varying degrees posed problems for the system. Added to this difficulty is the fact that the film negative is, as it were, a matrix from which positive works can be reproduced almost limitlessly. The fact that the capital needed for the production of a film is considerably greater than that required in most other fields of artistic production also worked against the recognition of the rights of film authors. The intertwining of artistic work and economic investment which generates so many conflicts in the filmmaking process also makes itself felt in the legal protection of cinematographic creation. For all of these reasons, cinema did not easily fall within the accepted meaning of art (defined in terms of its individuality, uniqueness, scarcity, and freedom from economic determinations). Thus, it is not surprising that the legal configuration of cinematographic works within the system of authors' rights long remained a controversial issue.

The Civil Law–Based European System

The early years of cinema in France provide us with a good example of the struggles that occurred in the attempt to get cinema recognized in law as an autonomous field of art as this scenario was played out on the European continent. Film, as an independent art form, did not exist for the French courts at the beginning of the twentieth century. The early decisions dealing with silent films treated movies as mere mechanical works whose production could not be traced to any particular person but only to a machine. Cinematographic works were considered either as a series of photographic images or as a type of dramatic work. In the latter case, it was the author of the underlying dramatic work who was given authors' rights in the work as a whole.[34] French law initially limited itself to protecting the authors of dramatic works against illicit cinematographic reproduction. It was not until sound was introduced into film that the French courts began to recognize cinematographic works as having an autonomous existence.[35]

Before being accorded independent artistic status in the laws of individual European countries, cinema had already entered the international legal framework as a result of the revision of the Berne Convention, agreed to in 1908 in Berlin. This did not mean, however, that cinematographic works were recognized at the international level as independent artistic works, for they were still treated as mere adaptations, which could be given protection as original works only if they could be regarded as genuine representations of the personality of their creator. Cinema had thus not yet fully entered into the category of literary and artistic works within the European community. It was not until the 1948 revision of the Berne Convention in Brussels that films were recognized as independent works in their own right.[36] Even today, there is still no definition with regard to the author of a cinematographic or audiovisual work in the international copyright conventions.[37]

Whether to Protect Human Work or Economic Investments?

Although cinematographic works in Europe eventually made their way into the category covered by authors' rights, this did not mean that the actual authors of the work gained protection. Film producers have continually claimed that legal protection should be instituted for *their* benefit: that is, that they should be treated as the first owners of the copyright in the cinematographic work. Such a claim is, however, in direct contradiction with the basic principles of the European civil law tradition of authors' rights. Historically, much of the discussion concerning authorship of cinematographic works has been obscured by doctrinal debates about the legal status of such works: whether they should be considered as collaborative, in which case the collaborating authors would have the authorship in the work; or whether they should be considered as collective, which would mean that all the rights would lie in the hands of the producer.[38] Underlying these debates was a more fundamental question: Should authors' rights protect the individual creators of the work or the economic investment involved in its production?

Most European countries did not take a firm stand on whether to grant the legal rights in a cinematographic work to its director or to its producer until the latter part of this century. It was not until 1957 in France and 1965 in the Federal Republic of Germany that it was affirmed in legislation that the original rights in a cinematographic work belonged to the actual creators of the work following a civil law tradition known as authors' rights or moral rights.[39] Under the copyright regime prevailing in the common law countries of America and Great Britain, it was the producers who succeeded in their demand that they be recognized as sole owners of the copyright in cinematographic work—a position which has been somewhat weakened in the U.K. by the 1988 Copyright, Designs and Patents Act (CDPA).[40] Even in the civil law countries on the European continent, the legal recognition of film authors did not resolve all the problems connected with rights in audiovisual works. In particular, the question of how the actual "author" was to be defined in this context remained unanswered.

Defining the "Film Author"

In trying to determine who should, from a legal point of view, be considered the author of a cinematographic work, the starting point in continental Europe has been the fundamental principle of authors' rights, namely that those who provide the original creative effort in the generation of the work should, prima facie, be considered authors of the work. This definition is apparently best suited to artistic works in the traditional fields of art (such as the plastic arts or literature), where there is only one or, at most, a small number of persons creating the work. Where several people have made differing contributions to the film, it is of little help to attempt to measure the importance or quality of the effort that each has put into the filmmaking process.[41] Not only would this be difficult from a practical point of view; it also runs counter to one of the fundamental principles of authors' rights, namely that the artistic merit of an individual work must have no bearing on its legal protection.[42] The basic principle of authors' rights implies that creativity as such is insufficient to raise an individual to the status of author. Rather, since authors' rights protect the form and not the content of the work, it is necessary to show that an author is not only creative, but also responsible for the ultimate form that the work takes. In relation to cinema, this principle provides some assistance in determining which of the individuals working on a film may be granted authors' rights in it.[43]

As we have seen, the French New Wave and the German Autorenfilm ushered in an era in Europe in which the film director is routinely treated as the author of the film. In film production it is generally accepted that it is the director who provides the film with its ultimate cinematic form. As Lyon-Caen and Lavigne remark of the role of the director in the creation of the film:

> the film is first and foremost his work, the expression of his own personality. . . . It is he who performs the essential creative act: the transformation of a text into images; the director is the only one whose contribution cannot be individualized—it is the film as a whole which is his. And it is not inconceivable that one day he will be acknowledged as the sole author of the cinematographic work.[44]

In the jurisprudence of the European civil law tradition, the director of a film is granted authorship.[45] The legal position of other creative individuals who assist in the production of the film varies in different national laws. While the screenwriter and the writer of the dialogue are granted rights in their respective contributions to the work (and usually in the cinematographic work as well), practice varies with regard to whether they are also treated as the authors of a pre-existing work (as in Germany) or as co-authors of the film (as in France and Italy). The same uncertainty applies to the composer of the score.[46]

The legal position of those who participate in a more technical manner—cameramen,[47] cutters, light and sound operators—is more uncertain. Although these individuals see themselves as skillful (technical) professionals, they also seek artistic recognition for their work. This leaves them in a paradoxical position: while as technicians they are not entitled to the protection conferred by authors' rights, they enjoy the security and benefits provided by their professional status. In most countries in the European union non-artistic film workers are in principle denied authors' rights in the cinematographic work; if they are accorded any rights, these depend on the amount of creative input that they contribute to each individual film.[48]

One of the main arguments used to oppose the granting of rights to the various creative contributors to cinematographic works is that such a move would hamper the commercial exploitation of films. Without wishing to promote the Romantic concept of the author, we must nevertheless take care not to overlook the dangers inherent in providing authors' rights to the multitude of individuals who contribute to the production of a film. If all those who contribute to the film production process were able to claim authorship in the work, this might lead to a dilution of the concept of authors' rights. Authors' rights should not be seen as a means of supplementing salaries, as a mechanism to recoup financial consideration for the use of artistic works.[49] We must not forget that the basic focus of authorial rights in the European civil law tradition is the protection of the specific relationship between authors and their works. The relevant question to be asked in this context would be: Who should be able to exercise the exclusive rights in the film? If every technical professional could have the right to prohibit the distribution of a given film by claiming that it infringes upon his or her rights, this could raise unnecessary uncertainties with regard to licensing the exploitation. Civil law countries have tried to overcome this problem by providing producers with a safeguard in the form of a presumption with regard to the transfer of rights to them.[50]

In terms of moral rights protection we could ask: Whose personality does an infringement of the cinematographic work undermine? New modes of exploiting and altering films have made this question more pertinent than ever: films are being transferred to digital media, they are being shown in different versions in order to attract larger audiences, they are interrupted by commercials and thereby transformed into vehicles for advertising.[51] It could be that it is in relation to the issue of securing the moral prerogatives of authors—the specific bond between authors and their work—that the major need to define the author of the cinematographic work arises. Who bears the ultimate responsibility for the artistic quality and integrity of the cinematographic work? Whose personal integrity is at stake when a film is mutilated or distorted?

In Europe courts have recognized the vulnerable position that film directors occupy in attempting to defend the artistic integrity of their works and at the same time to secure the best possible distribution for them. One Italian appellate court, for example, held that breaking a feature film up with commercials infringed the moral rights of its director.[52] A similar conclusion was reached in relation to the application of a television station's logo to a film.[53] The most notorious case, however (which also highlights some of the fundamental differences between the civil law tradition of authors' rights and the Anglo-American copyright system), concerns the colorization of the black-and-white American feature-film *The Asphalt Jungle,* directed by John Huston and based on a story co-written by Huston and Ben Maddow. After the death of Huston, the film was colorized by the production company Turner Entertainment. The heirs of Huston and Maddow wanted to prevent the transmission of the colorized version on French television. The legal issue was whether the director and the scriptwriter were able to claim authorship of the film in France, and consequently whether, by virtue of the moral rights they could claim under French law, they could prevent the distribution of the colorized version in France—even though the film had originally been made under U.S. copyright law according to which the director and screenwriter did not have any moral rights in it. The French high court ultimately ruled not only that all authors, irrespective of the country in which their works were first published, might claim authorship in the work in France by "the single fact of its creation," but also that they are invested with moral rights according to French law. The French court also held that both film directors and screenwriters must be recognized as the creators of their work—a right which is confirmed as a human right in international law and as a part of the international legal order (*ordre public international*). Furthermore, the court declared that the application of French statutes relating to the protection of moral prerogatives of authors is mandatory (*impératif*).[54]

The impact of the decision of the French court goes well beyond the boundaries of the case. By giving the author of a work the right to claim authorship in France, irrespective of national legislation, it places the Continental concept of authors' rights on a level with other human rights. As Bernard Edelman eloquently remarks: "the creation as such is now protected just as liberty, communication of ideas or physical integrity: it constitutes a human right integrated as part of the organization of society."[55]

Harmonization of Film Authorship in the European Union

The designation of the principal director as a film's author a priori was consolidated by the European Union in its harmonization policy relating to authors' rights in audiovisual works. The directive on rental and lending rights states: "For the purposes of this Directive *the principal director of a cinematographic work shall be its author.* Member States may provide for others to be its co-authors" (Directive 92/100/EEC).[56] Similar provisions have also been incorporated into the directive on satellite broadcasting and cable retransmission (Directive 93/83/EEC).[57] These two directives mark the first steps towards the harmonization of the legal notion of film authorship in the European Community. The harmonization was concluded in the 1993 directive on the duration of protection for copyright works (Directive 93/98/EEC) which states that "*the principal director of a cinematographic or audiovisual work shall be considered as its author or one of its authors.*"[58] In addition, the directive says that the length of protection for audiovisual works is to be calculated not only in terms of the life of the director but also with reference to the life span of the other creative contributors to the film (the principal director, the author of the script or the dialogue, and the author of a musical score created especially for a cinematographic or audiovisual work). The Commission was very clear in stating that this directive meant the *complete harmonization of authorship in audiovisual works in the [European] Community.*[59]

The final harmonization of film authorship in the European Union represents a compromise solution aiming to leave intact the underlying principles of both authors' rights legislations and copyright legislations.

Even European countries belonging to the copyright traditon (that is, the United Kingdom and Ireland) are now obliged to consider the principal director of an audiovisual work as one of its authors. They may, nevertheless, preserve their existing regulations in which producers are also granted an original copyright in audiovisual works and other audiovisual fixations.[60] In other words, within the European Community the notion of film authorship now always includes the principal director—even though other participants in the filmmaking process may also fall under this rubric. In civil law countries certain other persons involved in the creation of a film, such as the screenwriter and the composer of the original film music, are also considered film authors. In contrast, in the European common law countries, though the producer is considered the primary author of a film, its director must also be now recognized as an author of the cinematographic work.[61]

The U.S. Copyright System

Following the fundamental principles common both to the protection of authors' rights and to the copyright system, the U.S. Copyright Act of 1976 confers authorship, in principle, upon the author or authors of a given artistic work.[62] According to the Copyright Act the law protects original works of authorship,[63] but the term "authorship" is defined in various ways, depending on the category of works in question. In *Community* v. *Reid* the Supreme Court of the United States states that *"[a]s a general rule, the author is the party who actually creates the work, that is the person who translates an idea into a fixed, tangible expression entitled to copyright protection."*[64] In general terms, the authors of the work are thus determined in the same way as in the civil law system.

However, the U.S. law recognizes certain exceptions to this general rule, most notably in cases where works have been created by contractual arrangement or other similar relations. In such cases they are defined as "works made for hire." Audiovisual production represents one of the typical fields where creators are not considered as original rightowners in their works but rather as working "for hire" in consequence of which the employer—the film producer—is considered as the author of the work.[65] Even though the way the fictional authorship in the U.S. Copyright Act is constructed differs somewhat from that of the British CDPA, the end result remains the same: it is the producer of the audiovisual work who is considered as the original right-owner or, in terms of the U.S. Copyright Act, the "author" of an audiovisual work.[66] The definition given in the law with regard to the work made for hire covers a wide spectrum of various forms of employment and other work relationships, and the relevant case law has tended to give the law an even broader interpretation than the original intention of the legislation would suggest.[67] According to the work-made-for-hire doctrine it is the employer who is regarded as the author of the work, and the rights of the actual creator of the work are given no recognition.[68]

This doctrine means that according to the U.S. law the author of a work made for hire is the employer, which for audiovisual works means the producer. The authorship of the employer or other person for whom the work was prepared is statutory and may not be contractually transferred to anyone else after the fact. It means that given the certain objective factors spelled out in the law, a work must be considered as made for hire.[69] However, even if authorship may not be contractually transferred at a later date, the initial ownership of rights may be subject to such transfer. This arrangement presupposes that the agreement under which the employee is to own rights in the work must be in writing and signed by both parties.[70] *Goldstein* has interpreted this stipulation to mean that such an agreement can only confer the initial ownership of rights, not a transfer of authorship per se.[71] This stipulation means that in terms of the U.S. Copyright Act authorship and initial ownership of rights in an audiovisual work are two distinct notions and must be treated separately. In addition, the authors of audiovisual works could acquire the ownership of other specific rights contractually from the producers through similar means. The principle is thus exactly the reverse of that governing authors' rights-based laws, according to which it is the producer who has to acquire the rights to the film, not the creators.[72]

A contribution to an audiovisual production by a screenwriter, director or cameraman may be considered work for hire if it fulfills the specific criteria set by the law. There has to be a written instrument signed by both parties in which the parties agree that the work shall be considered a work made for hire.[73] An agreement reached before the work has begun with a contract signed after the work is underway or even after its completion may be sufficient.[74] Even if the prerequisites set out in the law with regard to works commissioned for use as a part of a motion picture or other audiovisual work are not satisfied the work may still be regarded as made for hire under the general rules set by the law in § 101 according to which a work prepared by an employee within the scope of his or her employment is regarded as a work made for hire. In this case it must be established that the general requirements for such works are satisfied.[75] Thus, by virtue of his or her status as the original right-owner, the audiovisual producer enjoys a stronger position than his or her counterparts in the literary field (the publishers) in relation to the continuous right to control the exploitation of the work.[76]

In the United States the relationship between filmmakers on the one hand and producers on the other is regulated under labor legislation. The transfer of exploitation rights and the residuals accruing from the exploitation are, together with salaries and general employment terms, negotiated between the respective guilds representing different categories of rightholders and producers' organizations.[77] In these negotiations the parties may use the usual means and tactics of collective labor negotiations, including strikes.[78] At the collective level the guilds have been able to negotiate residuals for re-uses of the material as well as merchandising rights and other derivative rights to an extent which exceed, in practice, the level of remunerations received for these uses by, for example, average Nordic writers and directors.[79] As a result of this system, American filmmakers have achieved very satisfactory financial benefits from almost all forms of exploitation of their works in spite of the lack of protection under copyright law, benefits which many of their European colleagues look upon with envy. Having said this, it must, however, be noted that these substantial financial returns for the right-holders are due not so much to the legal system as to the size of the North American audiovisual industry, which far exceeds that of any other country in the world.

———

Even this superficial overview of the regulation of authorship in motion pictures and audiovisual works in the United States reveals the fundamental structural difference resulting from a legal approach which differs from that of the European civil law tradition of authors' rights. Under U.S. law the persons creating the film are not granted any authorial rights at the legislative level and all rights are concentrated in the hands of the producer, whereas in the civil law countries the persons creating an audiovisual work are considered its authors. This distinction is often presented as an insurmountable barrier between the two systems of protection. In reality, the two regimes are much closer than is often supposed and have reached more or less the same outcome by different means.[80]

By Way of Conclusion

To summarize we can say that the notion of the film author has performed a similar function in various social, economic, and legal discourses in different historical situations: it has served as a unifying element between different social practices. According to Deleuze, "author" is a notion which refers to the work of art. The function of the author, in turn, is to distinguish between art as a multiplicity of creative and liberative emotions and art as commercially produced works geared for mass consumption. The task of *cinéma d'auteur* is to foster the distribution of films that cannot stand up to competition from commercial cinema because they are less accessible to the public and to make possible the creation of such films.[81] It seems that in order to confer efficient protection upon film authors, legal discourse tends to assume that it is necessary to raise the status of one of the collaborators above that of the others. The role of the director as the principal film author is reflected in the legal doctrine of continental Europe. By contrast, in the common law tradition of Great Britain and the United States, the notion of a singular film authorship is vested in the film producer.

Thus, in legal parlance, the definition given to the term "author" does not necessarily follow the logic of creative artistic work, and the term itself tends, in some cases, to assume a purely fictional form. The civil law system of authors' rights defines the author as a physical person performing a certain kind of creative work, but "author" in the copyright doctrine refers to a fictional subject operating only within the framework of copyright law. This distinction does not, however, mean that the concept of "author" in copyright law has no point of reference to everyday practices, but rather that these points of reference are determined according to a different logic than in civil law doctrine. In the civil law doctrine the subject of protection is the person creating the work, the author, and what is protected is the authors' specific relation to the work in its personal as well as its economic manifestations, whereas in the copyright system the work is protected as marketable merchandise having only economic relevance to its creators.[82]

Authors serve as a point of reference when speaking of cinema either as art or as an economic practice. In order to ensure that those working in film are able to secure their livelihoods, we need to be able to situate film production in a socioeconomic context. In addition, we have to be able to distinguish those who provide a cinematographic work with its special form as a product of creative effort from those who have otherwise—technically or financially—contributed to its making. It is for these reasons that we need the notion of the film author—not as the Author, the origin of all things, the ultimate Creator, but as a socially determined person, as *l'homme de métier*, without whom we would not have any of the films which enable us to see worlds that would otherwise remain hidden.

NOTES

I would like to thank Susanna Virtanen-Pascal for her insight with regard to the changes brought upon the film production process by digital technology.

1. On the emergence and constitution of a specific artistic field, as defined by its relative autonomy vis-à-vis other sectors of society, see Pierre Bourdieu, "Le Marché des biens symboliques," *L'Année sociologique* 22 (1971): 50–4; and R. Moulin, *L'Artiste, l'institution et le marché* (Paris, 1992), 251–55.

2. Historians have already provided us with valuable analysis of the origins of authorship. See, for example, Roger Chartier, "The Figure of the Author," in *The Order of Books*, trans. Lydia G. Cochrane (Stanford, Calif.: Stanford University Press, 1994), 25–60. Chartier discusses the way knowledge (and power) was circulated and institutionalized around books from the fourteenth to the eighteenth centuries. See also, on literature, Carla Hesse, "Enlightenment Epistemology and the Laws of Authorship in Revolutionary France, 1777–1793," *Representations* 30 (1990): 109; Martha Woodmansee, "The Genius and the Copyright: Economic and Legal Conditions of the Emergence of the 'Author,'" *Eighteenth Century Studies* 17 (1984): 426 ff.; on art, G. Fyfe, "Art and Reproduction: Some Aspects of the Relations between Painters and Engravers in London 1760–1850," *Media, Culture and Society* 7 (1985): 399 ff.; on film, Bernard Edelman, *Le Droit saisi par la photographie* (Paris, 1979), and Molly Nesbit, "What Was an Author?" *Yale French Studies* 73 (1987): 229–57.

3. In studying the function of the notion of the author in different social practices, the methodological approach outlined by Foucault provides an example of how that notion may be used as an epistemological category. Foucault presents the notion as a function of certain discourses in society. The name of the author serves not only as a means of classifying certain kinds of discourses, but also as a unifying element linking different social practices: 'It is situated in the breach, among the discontinuities, which gives rise to new groups of discourses and their singular mode of existence . . . the function of an author is to characterize the existence, circulation, and operation of certain discourses within the society." Michel Foucault, "What Is an Author?" in Josué V. Harari, ed., *Textual Strategies: Perspectives in Post-structural Criticism* (Ithaca, N.Y.: Cornell University Press, 1979), 144.

4. See, for example, Roland Barthes, "The Death of the Author," in *Image-Music-Text*, trans. Stephen Heath (New York: Hill & Wang, 1977), 142–48.

5. Bourdieu provides valuable methodological insights for studying the mediation processes between different fields of cultural production and other fields of social practice. For the legitimation of the artistic field, see Bourdieu, "Le Marché des biens symboliques"; idem., *Les Règles de l'art Genèse et structure du champ littéraire* (Paris, 1992).

6. This being the case, it is not surprising that the acceptance of cinema as one of the major arts was no easy process.

7. The dispersal of television into various modes of audiovisual communication, such as cable television and satellite, was due to the discovery of new means of transmitting moving images through hertzian waves. Video and its further applications represent, for their part, alterations in recording techniques. Digital reproduction means, however, have brought a completely new way of both producing and distributing audiovisual works.

8. See, for example, the time taken to move from silent movies to sound cinema, and, more recently, the commercialization of video discs. P.-J. Benghozi, *Le Cinéma: Entre l'art et l'argent* (Paris, 1989), 64–73.

9. Ibid., 70 ff.

10. Thomas Elsaesser argues that the institution of cinema consists of the following: the social spaces needed to gather the audiences, and the practices regulating the latter's admission; the production companies' competition for access to, and control of, technology; the changes in distribution, away from selling and towards exchange and renting; and the standardization of an agreed commodity equally easily recognized by producers and audiences. What is striking about this observation is that it overlooks the creative aspect of filmmaking, without which films would never come into existence. See "Early Cinema: From Linear History to Mass Media Archaology," in *Early Cinema: Space, Frame, Narrative,* ed. Thomas Elsaesser (London: British Film Institute, 1990), 1–10.

11. See, for example, Edelman, *Le Droit saisi par la photographie,* 50 ff.

12. For example, photographer was recognized at an equal level with other creative authors in the Finnish Copyright Act only in connection with the amendment of the law in March 1995.

13. See G. Lyon-Caen and P. Lavigne, *Traité théorique et pratique de droit du cinéma français et comparé,* vol. 1 (Paris, 1957), 33 ff.

14. For the legitimation of cinema as art, see Y. Darré, "Auteurs et techniciens: Division du travail dans le cinéma français" (thesis, Ecole des hautes études en sciences sociales; Paris, 1982). For the role of avant-garde artists, see 7 ff.

15. For instance, Méliès did not regard himself as an author of films but rather as a manufacturer, an artisan of cinema. He made films in the full sense of the word: he was author and screenwriter, director and choreographer, set- and costume-designer, make-up person, and even actor. He also took care of the technical side of production, from the creation of special effects to the operation of cameras and other machines. He was also responsible for marketing, being both the producer and distributor of all his films. Other filmmakers of the period played a similar role in cinematic production. In some cases, like that of Pathé, the production and distribution of the film was managed by the same person on both sides of the Atlantic.

16. This rapid industrialization can be explained by the fact that American film magnates built the American movie industry around a number of powerful cartels.

17. While recognizing that there is no unified "European" way of producing films, and that film production in individual European countries is impregnated with, and structured by, the specific historical and socio-economic background in each country, I will refer in the text to "European" films. Since a large proportion of the feature films made in Europe today are co-produced by various countries, the concept of national film production has, in any case, become somewhat blurred. According to Michèle Lagny, the appropriate way to classify films today is according to the director of the film (on the assumption that the film is made in the director's own country). See Michèle Lagny, *De l'histoire du cinéma: Méthode historique et histoire du cinéma* (Paris, 1992), 102.

18. At that time, the cameraman also performed functions which today fall either to the director or to various technicians. Staiger dates the cameraman system of production in Hollywood to the period 1896–1907. See Janet Staiger, "The Hollywood Mode of Production to 1930," in David Bordwell, Janet Staiger, and Kristin Thompson, *The Classical Hollywood Cinema: Film Style and Mode of Production to 1960* (New York and London: Columbia University Press, 1985), 116 ff.

19. Staiger claims that the modern stage-director emerged in the 1870s (ibid., 117).

20. It is interesting to note the different connotations of the English and French terms here: "director" evokes the notion of the technical leader or manager of a work process, whereas *"réalisateur"* points to the realization of the cinematographic work as an artistic

totality. As we shall see, this distinction has implications for the extent to which these individuals are recognized as film authors.

21. Given the different roles which stage directors and film directors play, Desbois argues that the latter should not be given the same legal status in the matter of author's rights. He considers that the film director should be regarded as the author of the cinematographic work, whereas the stage director should, in general, be treated as a performing artist, as a holder of rights related to copyright (i.e., neighbouring rights). See Henri Desbois, *Le Droit d'auteur en France,* 3d. ed. (Paris, 1978), 181 ff.

22. Although the concept of an audiovisual work was, in effect, born with televisual expression, a distinction should be drawn between audiovisual and cinematographic works. The category of cinematographic works forms a subgroup of audiovisual works and is usually considered to include, in addition to feature films and short films, films made for television. The definition of the term "audiovisual work" varies according to national traditions of audiovisual production (with slightly different connotations in English and in French). While this distinction is of little practical relevance from the point of view of authors' rights (for example, in the practices adopted by authors' societies in regard to remuneration), the amount an author receives varies according to the type of program. In the following, when the terms "cinema" and "cinematographic" are used, they refer to both feature films and short films.

23. For an account of how the different approaches to production in different sectors of audiovisual production have influenced the way in which those engaged in making the film are remunerated, see B. Miège, *L'Industrialisation de l'audiovisuel* (Paris, 1986), 65 ff.

24. Staiger characterizes the period 1905–1907 as one in which the director system of production prevailed, being followed by the director-unit system, with further hierarchization and division of labor. The latter system dominated filmmaking until 1914. Staiger, "The Hollywood Mode of Production," 117–27.

25. For the social background to the *Nouvelle Vague,* and its influence in the legitimation of cinema as art in France, see Darré, "Auteurs et techniciens," 14.

26. For the impact of the politique des auteurs on film theory, its further developments, and the different approaches to it in Europe and the United States, see John Caughie, ed., *Theories of Authorship* (London: British Film Institute, 1981).

27. Ibid., 51 ff. The influence of the French New Wave is also interesting in terms of the legal recognition of film authors. As we shall see, the creative authors of cinematographic works were granted authors' rights in French law in 1957. Before that, jurisprudence had been wavering as to whether to confer the rights in a film to the author or to the producer of the work. It would be interesting to ascertain what impact the New Wave had on the drafting of the law, and, on a more theoretical level, to examine the mediation processes between the cultural and legal spheres at the time.

28. For the differences between the Nouvelle Vague and the New German Cinema, see Thomas Elsaesser, *New German Cinema* (New Brunswick, N.J.: Rutgers University Press, 1989), 24 ff., 41.

29. For a detailed discussion of the German *Autorenfilm* and its sociohistorical role, see ibid., 74–116.

30. Ibid., 44.

31. Ibid. The political role of "author cinema" has also been very marked in oppositional filmmaking in Spain and in many Latin American countries. See Marvin D'Lugo, "Authorship and the Concept of National Cinema in Spain," *Cardozo Arts and Entertainment Law Journal* 10 (1992): 591 ff.

32. We have already seen how the first laws relating to cinema in France came within the orbit of public-order legislation. See Lyon-Caen and Lavigne, *Traité de droit du cinéma français,* 32 ff. Contemporary cinema has retained its potentially subversive character vis-à-vis government; special censorship legislation relating to audiovisual media still forms

an integral part of the legal institutions regulating the broadcasting and distribution of cinematographic works.

33. One of the foremost functions of the legal institution that was in force before the conferment of privileges by government to creative artists was the control of the production and distribution of texts; in other words, such privileges were also used as a means of government censorship. Government censorship on the one hand, and authors'/publishers' rights over literary and artistic works on the other, were thus two sides of the same coin—namely regulation of the circulation of knowledge in society. For the political function of privileges, see, for example, Marie-Claude Dock, *Étude sur le droit d'auteur,* bk. vii (Paris, 1963), 66–70.

34. For a description of French jurisprudence, see P. Leglise, *Histoire de la politique du cinéma français,* pt. 1 (Paris, 1970), 13 ff.

35. According to the Tribunal de commerce de la Seine in 1933, "The cinematographer has his demands . . . and his own genius is of such a type that one could create of the same dramatic work several cinematographic adaptations, each one having its own style and personality." Cited in Lyon-Caen and Lavigne, *Traité de droit du cinéma français,* 237. See also Leglise, *Historice de la politique du cinéma français,* 207.

36. For the report of the Berlin Congress, see Bureau international de la propriété intellectuelle, *1886–1986: Centenaire de la Convention de Berne* (Geneva, 1986), 180, 213.

37. According to art. 14 bis (para. 2 (a)) of the Berne Convention, the ownership of copyright in a cinematographic work comes under the laws of the country where protection is claimed. This is limited by the fact that para. 2 (b) states that authors may not, in the absence of any contrary stipulation, object to the exploitation of the film by means specified in the Convention. Exceptions are made to this, however, in para. 3, which states that (unless national legislation provides otherwise) para. 2 (b) shall not apply to authors of scenarios, dialogues, or musical works, nor to the principal director. The privileged position accorded to these authors by the convention could be interpreted as implying that they are regarded as the primary authors of the film. On the definition of authorship in the Berne Convention, see Sam Ricketson, "People or Machines: The Berne Convention and the Changing Concept of Authorship," *Columbia-VLA Journal of Law and the Arts* 16 (1991): 1.

38. See, for example, Lyon-Caen and Lavigne, *Traite' de droit du cinéma français,* 261 ff.; Leglise, *Histoire de la politique du cinéma français,* 207 ff.; and Eugen Ulmer, *Urheber- and Verlagsrecht,* 3d ed. (Berlin, 1980), 198 ff.

39. For an overview of the situation in Europe, see Adolf Dietz, *Copyright Law in the European Community* (Luxemburg, 1978), 50 ff. [Continential Europe is governed by a civil law tradition which has fundamental differences from the Anglo-American common law regime.—Ed.]

40. U.K. law here distinguishes between the author of the film, who is deemed to be the first owner of copyright (sect. 9 (2)), and the director of the film, who is granted the moral rights of paternity and integrity (sects. 77, 80). The author of the film is defined as the person who undertakes the arrangements for the making of the film. This could be the director, but most commentators assume that it will be the producer, an interpretation suggested by sect. 172 (2) of the Act. See J. Phillips, "The Concept of 'Author' in Copyright Law: Some Reflections on the Basis of Copyright Law in the United Kingdom," *Copyright* 8 (1990): 26; W. R. Cornish, *World Intellectual Property Guidebooks: United Kingdom* (New York, 1991), 26–30.

41. The institution of authors' rights aims to protect independent creative work. The boundaries of creative work are constantly being reviewed, the latest example being the inclusion of computer programs within the ambit of authors' rights. As far as the tasks of the different individuals working within film production are concerned, we need to be able to distinguish independent artistic work from work which, even if containing artistic elements, is of a subordinate or predominantly technical nature. If authors can be seen as

artistically independent workers in the production of a film, they may also be granted authorship in the audiovisual work.

42. See Lyon-Caen and Lavigne, *Traite de droit du cinéma français,* 272.

43. For a longer discussion of this issue, see Marjut Salokannel, *Ownership of Rights in Audiovisual Productions: A Comparative Study* (London: Kluwer Law International, 1997), III. 6.2.3.

44. Lyon-Caen and Lavigne, 273.

45. See Desbois, *Le Droit d'auteur,* 182.

46. Legislation which provides exemplary (as in France) or exhaustive (as in Italy) definitions of the film author usually encompasses the director, the writers of the script and dialogue, and the composer of the film music. In French law, the person responsible for the cinematographic adaptation of the work on which the film is based is also regarded as the co-author of the film.

47. For the role of the cameraman in the filmmaking process, see, for example, K. Prümm, "Die schöpferische Rolle des Kameramannes," *UFITA* 118 (1992): 23; and from the point of view of authors' rights, P. Hertin, "Die urheberrechtliche Stellung des Kameramannes," *UFITA* 118 (1992): 57.

48. For an overview of the situation in Europe, see Dietz, *Copyright Law,* 50; for France, Desbois, *Le Droit d'auteur,* 177, and Lyon-Caen and Lavigne, *Traité de droit du cinéma français,* 271 ff.; for Germany, K. Bohr, *Die Urheberrechtsbeziehungen der an der Filmherstellung Beteiligten* (Berlin, 1978), Ulmer, *Urheber-und Verlags recht,* 200 ff., G. Fromm and W. Nordemann, *Urheberrecht* (Stuttgart, 1988), 365, and S. Lütje, *Die Rechte der Mitwirkenden am Filmwerk,* (Baden-Baden, 1987), 66; and for the Nordic countries, M. Salokannel, *Häviävät elokuvan tekijät* (with English abstract: "The Loss of Film Authors") (Helsinki, 1990), 23 ff., G. Karnell, "Upphovsrätt, närstående rätt ellerallsingen rätt för 'tekniskt medverkande' in audiovisuell produktion," *Nordiskt Immateriellt Rättsskydd* 4 (1991): 457, and Å. Lögdberg, *Auktorrätt och film* (Uppsala, 1957), 97 ff.

49. For a further discussion, see Salokannel, *Ownership of Rights,* III.6.2.

50. See Salokannel, *Ownership of Rights,* in particular Chapter III.

51. This situation has necessitated defensive measures on the part of those whose reputation has suffered the greatest damage as a result of the distortion of a film—namely, the film directors and writers.

52. Judgment of the Rome appellate court, November 16, 1989, in *Germi* v. *Reteitalia, RIDA* 144 (1990): 91. For an extensive commentary on Italian jurisdiction in this area, see T. Collova, "Les Interruptions publicitaires lors de la diffusion de films à la télévision," *RIDA* 146 (1990): 124.

53. "*Marchand et autres c la cinq',*" Tribunal de grande instance de Paris, June 29, 1998, *Revue trimestrielle de droit commercial* 42:1 (1989): 72.

54. The lower French courts recognized the rights of the actual authors of the film to claim authorship in it and consequently to prohibit the showing of the offending version to the public in France. The Cour d'appel reversed the decisions of the lower courts, holding that since American law was applicable to the case, the production company had authorship in the work. This ruling was itself overturned by the Cour de cassation, which ultimately upheld the supremacy of French law in this case. See Tribunal de grande instance de Paris, June 24, 1988 (with note by Bernard Edelman), *Journal de droit international* 4 (1998): 1010; Tribunal de grande instance de Paris, November 23, 1988 (with note by Edelman), *Journal de droit international* 1 (1989): 67; Cour d'appel de Paris, 4e chambre, sect. B., July 6, 1989 (with note by Edelman), *Journal de droit international* (1989): 979; and Cour de cassation, 1ère chambre civ., arrêt n 861, May 28, 1991 (with note by Edelman), *Journal de droit international* (1992): 133.

55. Bernard Edelman, "Applicable Legislation Regarding Exploitation of Colourised U.S. Films in France: The 'John Huston' Case," *IIC* 23 (1992): 629.

56. Art. 2, para. 2, *Council Directive on rental right and lending right and on certain rights related to copyright in the field of intellectual property*, 92/100/CE (emphasis added).

57. *Council Directive on the co-ordination of certain rules concerning copyright and rights related to copyright applicable to satellite broadcasting and cable retransmission,* 93/83/EEC, OJ No. L248/15.

58. *Council Directive harmonizing the term of protection of copyright and certain related rights* 93/98/EEC of October 29, 1993.

59. COM(92) 602 final SYN 395.

60. See more closely Salokannel, *Ownership of Rights*, III.5.1. [A fixation is a legal term referring to the final form taken by a work of art.—Ed.]

61. For the discussion on conferring copyright upon the director of the film in the United Kingdom, see *Merkin and Black*, Copyright and Designs Law, vol. I, Longman Law, Tax and Finance 1996 at 5.9. See also Cornish, *World Intellectual Property Guide Book*, 2d. ed. at UK-30, according to whom a separate copyright exists for the script, for the scenery, and for the costume design of a play or film. On general discussion about regulating ownership of rights in audiovisual works in the United Kingdom, see Salokannel, *Ownership of Rights*, III.10.1.

62. *Community for Creative Non-Violence* v. *Reid*, 109 S.Ct. 2166 (1989) at 737.

63. 17 USC § 102 (a).

64. *Community for Creative Non-Violence* v. *Reid*, 109 S.Ct. 2166 (1989) at 737.

65. According to the law "a work made for hire" is considered to be

> *(1) a work prepared by an employee within the scope of his or her employment; or*
>
> *(2) a work specially ordered or commissioned for use . . . as a part of a motion picture or other audiovisual work . . . if the parties expressly agree in a written instrument signed by them that the work shall be considered a work made for hire. (17 USC § 101.)*

66. In U.S. federal copyright law, cinematographic works treated as works made for hire have all rights invested in the hands of the employer, i.e. the film producer (17 USC, sect. 201(b)). For the legal situation relating to audiovisual works, see, for example, D. Horowitz, "Film Creators and Producers vis-à-vis the New Media: Reflections on the State of Authors' Rights in Audiovisual Works," *Columbia-VLA Journal of Law and the Arts* 13 (1989): 157ff. For the concept of authorship, see 175 ff.

The fact that the persons creating the audiovisual work are not granted authorship in the work, however, does not mean that their creative role as such is overlooked. On the contrary, in the preparatory documents of the law it is explicitly stated that, for example, in connection with *"a broadcasting of a football game with four cameras, and with a director guiding the activities of the four cameramen and choosing which of their electronic images are sent out to the public and in what order, there is little doubt that what the cameramen and the director are doing consitutes 'authorship.'"* (House Report, 52.) Nonetheless, except in the recent Visual Artists Act, which itself accords moral rights of little practical significance, such rights do not exist in U.S. copyright legislation. See, for example, R. Gorman, "Visual Artists Rights Act of 1990," *Journal of the Copyright Society of the USA* 38 (1990): 233 ff; E. Bauck, "Der U.S. Visual Artist Rights Act of 1990: Durchbruch zum droit moral?" *Zeitschrift für Urheber- und Medienrecht* 2 (1992): 72 ff.

67. For the application of the work made for hire provisions of U.S.C. 1976, see *Hamilton, Marci A.*, Commissioned works as works made for hire under the 1976 copyright act: misinterpretation and injustice, Copyright Law Symposium, 1992 no. 38, pp. 181 ff. See also *Goldstein* (1996) at § 4.3., and *Nimmer* (1992) at § 5.03.

68. The status of the employer is confirmed in the law by stating that in *the case of a work made for hire, **the employer or the person for whom the work was prepared is considered the author** for the purposes of this title, **and**, unless the parties have explicitly agreed*

otherwise in a written instrument signed by them, **owns all of the rights comprised in the copyright** (emphasis added). (17 USC § 201 (b).)

69. Cf. *Goldstein* (1996) at 4.3, and *Nimmer* (1992) at § 4 (b).

70. 17 USC § 201(b), see also House Report, p. 121. In *Baltimore Orioles, Inc.,* v. *Major League Baseball Players,* 805 F.2d 663 (7th Cir. 1986) the court held that a mere disagreement with regard to copyright ownership, even if implied in players' contract, benefit plan, and basic agreement, does not meet the requirement of express agreement regarding ownership of rights but *"an agreement which altered statutory presumption that employer own copyright in work made for hire must be express and appear on face of signed written instrument; thus, use of parol evidence to imply provision not found within four corners of agreement is barred."*

71. *Goldstein* (1996) at § 4.3.

72. Before the enactment of the 1976 Copyright Act the screenwriters and composers tried to change the work made for hire rule with regard to audiovisual works to something similar to "shop-right" doctrine in patent law. This change would have meant that the employer could acquire the right to use the employee's work only to the extent needed for purposes of his or her regular business activities, and the employee would retain all other rights on condition that the employee did not authorize any competing uses of the work. Even though it was recognized that such legislation would have improved the screenwriters' and composers' bargaining power considerably, this proposition was rejected as going too far outside of the well established principle in American copyright law according to which initial ownership of rights vests in the employer. (For this discussion, see House Report, 121.)

73. 17 USC § 101.

74. Whether the contract must be both concluded and signed before the work has commenced has been subject to somewhat differing interpretations by the courts. See, for example, *Playboy Enters. Inc.,* v. *Dumas,* 53 F.3d 549 (2d Cir. 1995), and *Schiller & Schmidt, Inc.* v. *Nordisco Corp.,* 969 F2d 410, 412 (7th Cir. 1992). See also *Nimmer* (1992) at § 5.03[B]2[b].

75. For the general requirements under § 201(a) see, for example, *Community for Creative Non-Violence* v. *Reid,* 490 U.S. 730, 109 S.Ct. (1989), for audiovisual productions see also *Hi-Tech Video Productions* v. *Capital Cities/ABC, Inc.,* 58 F3d 1093 (6th Cir. 1995), in which the court reversed the trial court's decision in determining that a commissioned, professionally produced videotape was a work made for hire and held that "[i]n deciding whether individual is an employee or independent contractor, for purposes of determining whether copyrighted work is work made for hire, no single factor is determinate."

76. This is reflected, for example, in the regulation relating to the author's right to terminate the transfer of rights after a certain period (35 years) has lapsed, at which time the rights will revert back to the author, 17 USC § 203 (a).

77. For an excellent overview of the determination of audiovisual authorship in the United States, see John M. Kernochan, "The Response of the United States to the questionnaire on Ownership and Control of Intellectual Property Rights in Motion Pictures and Audiovisual Works: Contractual and Practical Aspects," *Columbia-VLA Journal of Law and the Arts* 20 (1996): 379 ff.

78. For the strike of the Writers Guild, see A. Larner, "The Writers Guild of America Strike of 1988: A Question of Respect," *Columbia-VLA Journal of Law and the Arts* 14 (1989): 75–89.

79. In many cases, at least in the Nordic countries, the audiovisual authors have assigned all these rights in exchange for a lump-sum remuneration or a (illusory) royalty based on net profits of the film. For further information on the way in which the American system operates, see the agreements concluded between the various producers' organizations, on the one hand, and the various guilds, on the other hand (e.g., 1995 Writers' Guild of America Theatrical & Television Basic Agreement; the Screen Actors Guild codified Basic

Agreement of 1989 for independent producers and Screen Actors Guild 1989 television Agreement for Independent Producers, Screen Actors' Guild 1995 Contract on theatrical pictures and television and Screen Actors Guild 1995 Theatrical Films and Television Programs Contract Digest for Extra Performers; and the Directors Guild of America 1996 Basic Agreement).

80. See Salokannel, *Ownership of Rights*, III.10.2.

81. Gilles Deleuze (interview), "Le Cerveau, c'est l'écran," *Cahiers du Cinéma* 38 (1986): 29.

82. For the differences between the two systems on the general level see, for example, *Kéréver* (1990), 133 f.

Case Studies

Tom Gunning

D. W. Griffith: Historical Figure, Film Director, and Ideological Shadow

In 1913 D. W. Griffith took out an advertisement in the *New York Dramatic Mirror*. Having just left the Biograph Company and apparently advertising for a job, Griffith claimed credit for "revolutionizing Motion Picture drama and founding the modern technique of the art." The text of the advertisement listed Griffith's innovations as "The large or closeup figures, distant views as represented first in Ramona, the 'switchback,' sustained suspense, the 'fade out,' and restraint of expression, raising motion picture acting to the higher plane which has won for it recognition as a genuine art."[1] To dismiss this claim to a revolutionary role in film art as mere press agentry is too simple. Resume padding or statement of fact, it provides one of the first accounts that presents Griffith as a prime mover in a transformation of filmmaking.

Griffith's *Dramatic Mirror* advertisement includes, along with the claimed innovations, a list of nearly 150 films that he directed at Biograph (from some 450 he directed for the company). That he provided such a list reveals Griffith's need not only to identify himself as director for the Biograph Company, but also to assert his authorship of specific films. Biograph films carried no credits referring to Griffith in contrast to his later features, which not only bore director credits, but also emblazoned Griffith's name or initials on intertitles. Griffith has been identified as director of these films retroactively, with the 1913 advertisement serving as primary evidence. The degree of Griffith's involvement in all Biograph films during his employment is unclear. After 1909, Biograph hired secondary directors who made films under

From *D. W. Griffith and the Origins of American Narrative Film: The Early Years at Biograph.* © 1991 by the Board of Trustees of the University of Illinois. Used with permission of the University of Illinois Press.

Griffith's announcement of his departure from Biograph in an advertisement in the New York Dramatic Mirror, *December 3, 1913.*

his supervision, and it is not known which of the films made after 1909 they directed.[2]

However, for the years I am investigating, attributing films to Griffith is easier. The date of the introduction of secondary directors is relatively certain. The memoirs of Billy Bitzer,[3] Linda Arvidson,[4] and statements by Frank Powell, the first of these secondary directors, all indicate Powell's first film, *All on Account of the Milk,* was shot on December 9, 10, and 11, 1909. Therefore, we can assume Griffith directed nearly all Biograph films from June 1908 until nearly the end of 1909. The only uncertainty comes at the very beginning of his career. What films (or parts of films) may Griffith have directed before *The Adventures of Dollie* (shot on June 18 and 19, 1908), and did he have a hand in the Mutoscopes after *Dollie?* None of these peep-show films seem to have survived, but Arvidson indicates that Griffith directed a few.[5]

But what does it mean to declare Griffith the director of these films? What was the role of the film director in 1908 and 1909, and did it differ from that in earlier filmmaking? In uncovering the archaeology of the director, one must recall that in theater (from which the term comes) the director is a comparatively recent phenomenon. As Helen Kritch Chinoy demonstrates, the concept of the theatrical director emerged gradually at the end of the nineteenth century.[6] Although precursors of the theatrical director can be found, the director as the unifying force of a production appeared in the late 1800s. Previously, a traditional way of presenting plays, embedded in actors' training and the design of performing space, determined elements that later became the director's responsibility.

With the breakdown of this tradition, directors began to supply the cohesiveness that formerly resided in conventions shared by audiences and theater artists. The director served "to impose a point of view that would integrate play, production and spectators."[7] At end of the nineteenth century, directors emerged who unified productions around conceptions of realism—Antoine, Otto Brahm, the early Stanislavsky, and Griffith's personal model, David Belasco. These realists introduced attention to naturalistic environment, verisimilar acting, and, particularly with Belasco, the use of recent innovations and technology in stagecraft and lighting.

Film appeared soon after the emergence of the director in theater. Popular theater in the United States during the period, exemplified by the "Uncle Tom" shows still touring at the beginning of the century and captured on film by Edwin Porter in 1903, still relied on the traditional staging and acting styles, and certain early films adopted this style. Griffith, as well as other directors who entered film around the same time, came to film from theater, bringing an awareness of the revolution that had occurred in theatrical presentation.

In film, the director was an even more recent concept. In *The Classical Hollywood Cinema*, Janet Staiger describes the first mode of production in the American film industry as "the cameraman system of production," which she dates from 1896 to 1907.[8] Although this describes the actual mode of production which gave much essential control to the man who actually operated the camera, in our context it ignores the important role the production company played in making production decisions and particularly in asserting ownership and authorship of the film. This separation can be elusive, as in Staiger's citing of W.K.L. Dickson, because the first cameramen were often associated with the ownership of the production company and were more than mere employees. The first "Lumière films" such as *The Arrival of the Train at the Station* were actually filmed by Louis Lumière for the production company that bore his family name. Soon however, "Lumière films" were being shot by a group of peripatetic cameramen-showmen—such as Promio and Doublier—and a basic split in film authorship emerged. The extraordinary "Brighton School" of British filmmakers, such as G. A. Smith and James Williamson, were also cameramen-producers.

When we refer to "Méliès films" we are invoking a production company model because, except for some early films, Méliès did not operate the camera. The artisanal conditions of Méliès's productions, in which he exercised close control over all aspects of production—writing the scenario, overseeing the costumes, originating the key "trick" effects, designing the sets, and often performing principal acting roles—make Méliès seem like a film director. But it was as head of a production company that he placed his imprint on his films.

The figure in American film most often cited as a filmmaker before Griffith, Edwin S. Porter, seems to be part of the cameraman mode. It was primarily as camera operator that Porter was employed by the Edison Company, although at points he was also in charge of Edison film production generally. Placing a cameraman in charge of production marks film as primarily a technological product that needed the experience of a machinist, rather than as a dramatic work in need of supervision from someone with theatrical training. In 1904, in a deposition given to the United States circuit court, Porter gave a description of his wide-ranging duties at the Edison Company: the technical tasks of camera work and processing the negative, as well as managing pro-filmic events (specified later in Griffith's contract as director at Biograph) such as selecting locations, "engaging the pantomimic performers," and "instructing them as to the scenes which I wished to have enacted."[9]

However, research by Charles Musser calls into question a sharp division in the United States between the cameraman mode of production and what Staiger terms the "director system of production," which she claims replaced it around 1907. Investigation of Edison payrolls reveals that Porter was paired with other employees from as early as 1901. These men—George S. Fleming, William Martinetti, J. Searle Dawley, who directed *Rescued from an Eagle's Nest* as well as other Edison films, and Wallace McCutcheon Sr., who directed *Daniel Boone*[10]—were primarily men of the theater, who worked with actors and staging. Grace Dawley told Barnet Braverman that her husband's work with Porter followed a strict division of labor. Porter "busied himself with the camera while Searle rehearsed the scene and when he said 'All ready to shoot, Ed,' Ed shot and that was all there was to it."[11] Musser feels that similar collaborative pairings of workers with complementary talents were probably the most typical production in early American cinema, finding evidence for similar pairs at Vitagraph, Essany, and even Biograph. But the early directors did not assert artistic control over the film. As Musser states, the pairs were noted for their basic equality, with each member sticking to his area of expertise.[12] The concept of the director as a unifying force was not a factor.

In later years after leaving Edison, Porter became a director in the sense that Griffith was, overseeing the whole production and using a cameraman to operate the camera. The cameraman, Arthur Miller, recalled that Porter continued to be obsessed with technical details and constantly became involved with the cameraman's tasks, often ignoring the actors.[13] Porter's late films at Edison, which directly precede the work of Griffith at Biograph, show a technical ingenuity, as in the animated titles in *College Chums* (1907) or the split screen in *Cupid's Pranks* (1908), but lack articulation of the dramatic content through filmic means. Though narrative films, they seem more related to the cinema of attractions' display of technological novelties. Porter's technical bent was typical of the earlier era of production and contrasts sharply with the later director's role based on narrativization.

The exact date on which a director, separate from the cameraman, was introduced at Biograph is unknown (if a record of Biograph directors was ever kept, it no longer exists), but it is likely to have come with

Biograph's increased production of fiction films around 1903. Although Bitzer indicates that for his first "staged" (i.e., non-actuality) film he was "director, cameraman, props and writer . . . all rolled up in one," this does not seem to have lasted long if it was ever strictly true. Bitzer refers to Wallace McCutcheon Sr. as "the director of our pictures."[14] The exact chronology of Bitzer's memoirs tends to be hazy, but he seems to indicate that McCutcheon was directing films at Biograph about 1903, which, given evidence that he directed *The Moonshiner* in 1904, seems a likely date.[15] Musser stresses the collaborative team of McCutcheon and Francis Marion during Biograph's early days, with both of them working on the directing, rather than photographing, aspects of filmmaking.[16] By the time Griffith was hired as director at Biograph, directors had long been established; he replaced a series of disastrous tryouts in the position. Bitzer indicates that Wallace McCutcheon Sr., his son Wally McCutcheon Jr., and Stanner Taylor all briefly directed films at Biograph immediately before Griffith's debut.[17]

If Edison and Biograph employed directors well before Griffith, how important is Griffith in the evolution of the director? It seems that specialists were early hired to collaborate with cameramen on the production of American fiction films. However, as the relation between Porter and Dawley shows, these collaborations were based on an esthetic division of labor rather than the dominance of the director. The relation between Bitzer and Griffith became markedly different from that between Dawley and Porter. Bitzer, with a trace of pique, describes Griffith's growing dominance: "Before his arrival I, as cameraman, was responsible for everything except the immediate hiring and handling of the actor. Soon it was his say whether the lights were bright enough, or if the make-up was right."[18] Bitzer's memoirs are filled with the numerous "suggestions" that Griffith made to Bitzer about the visual presentation of scenes.

With the director's new involvement in the visualization of the film, which Dawley's and Griffith's predecessors at Biograph left entirely to the cameraman, the equivalent of the theatrical director appeared in film: a role that integrates elements of production around a unifying center. With Griffith, and most likely other film directors around the same time, the director was no longer an independent expert working with the actors and then relying on the cameraman's expertise for visualization. Rather, the dramatic purpose within a scene determined its visual presentation as well, creating a filmic discourse which expressed dramatic situations. This constitutes the essence of the cinema of narrative integration and the narrator system. Although this new conception of the film director was inspired by the theater director, it dealt with filmic discourse. Whereas Dawley and McCutcheon seem to have restricted their attention to the pro-filmic level of filmic discourse, Griffith directed his attention to the other levels as well—the enframed image and, particularly, editing. Integrating these three levels through narrativization constitutes the role of the director that Griffith pioneered and which shaped the narrator system.

Although theoretically narrativization of film style need not depend on the actual production role of the director, it is historically significant that they appear at the same time. The integrative and dominant role of the director at Biograph was not the simple result of the force of Griffith's personality, but the product of an industrywide redefinition of the film commodity through a new emphasis on film as a fictional dramatic medium.[19] Nonetheless, Griffith responded to these forces with a new production role for the director, undoubtedly inspired by contemporary theater. Nothing in his contract with the Biograph company hints at this change.

Griffith's original director's contract with the Biograph Company specified his involvement with pro-filmic elements and selecting and arrangement of script material.[20] Besides his responsibility for screen stories, his duties as film director included arranging sets or choosing actual locations, selecting performers and overseeing their costuming and makeup, rehearsing performances, and enforcing company discipline. The contract envisions a man with theatrical experience who could arrange and manage what went on in front of the camera. It by no means redefines the relation between director and cameraman. The only section of the contract that could relate to Griffith's new interpretation of his role is the first paragraph, which refers to the "composing, selecting and modifying subjects, stories and plays." Although this seems to refer to the preparation of shooting scripts, Bitzer indicates that Griffith's "composing and modifying" soon extended to the way things were shot and their breakdown into shots that would guide their final edited form.

This contract is possibly identical to those of Griffith's predecessors, and Janet Staiger has indicated that it was typical of other production companies of the period. Although Griffith's understanding of his role as director in determining filmic discourse seems to have been in the vanguard of film practice in 1908–1909, and may have been more intense than that of his peers, it was not an anomaly. The move to the director system was a widespread industrial change, as Staiger has shown, based on economic changes in the industry.

Griffith began his film career at a point of transition which opened new opportunities for the director, and he contributed to this transition through his production practices. But if we have established the importance of Griffith's production role, the implicit claim to authorship contained in the *Dramatic Mirror* advertisement encounters more recent theoretical opposition. In 1913, Griffith retroactively claimed the output of a studio as his corpus, citing it as evidence that he "revolutionized Motion Picture drama." This claim goes beyond production modes and raises theoretical issues.

Film criticism treatment of the director as author (and, for some, treatment of directors at all) has fallen into disrepute. This has been in part a response to the "death of the author" in contemporary literary criticism, as well as a reaction against the often-naive assumptions of certain auteur film critics.[21] Beginning in the seventies, a number of film critics bracketed a director's name with quotation marks, identifying this rubric with the structure found by the critic in a body of texts rather than an actual biological and historical person.[22] This practice not only short-circuited reference to a real person and the consequent understanding of auteur criticism as biographical and psychological, but it also sidestepped objections that the auteur theory provided an unrealistic account of how films were made, inaccurately privileging the director's contribution in a collaborative art form.

My textual analysis basically operates within these revisions of the notion of director/author. The "D. W. Griffith" referred to herein is rarely a biographical, biological person. Griffith stands as the theoretically posited source of the films I am discussing, even though it is known that the original film stories were usually written by someone else, the film was shot by Bitzer or Marvin, and the splices were not made by Griffith's hand. "D. W. Griffith" basically corresponds to Wayne Booth's "implied author." Defined by Booth as the decisive power behind a text, but different from the actual author as a person, the implied author "chooses, consciously or unconsciously what we read; we infer him as an ideal, literary created version of the real man: he is the sum of his own choices."[23] The implied author exists, not outside the text, but as a function of its discourse.

However, as useful as this concept may be in untangling the problems of auteur analysis, it does not address the issues raised by the "death of the author."[24] From this perspective it is not simply the association with a biological person that makes the concept of an author problematic. Critics such as Roland Barthes find that traditional criticism posits the author as a semi-theological figure, the ultimate point of origin of the work and guarantor of its unity and coherence of meaning.[25]

Separating the author as biographical person from the text may be a methodological necessity, but it can also become a historical blind spot. The revisionist redefinition of the author as a critical construct and function of the text insulates films from contact with historical forces. By interjecting the author into the text, or using the concept of text to displace the author entirely (as Barthes may seem to do), we run the risk of endowing it with the theological attributes formerly reserved for the author.[26] The idea of an author can be valuable insofar as it opens texts to historical forces, and pernicious insofar as it insulates films in an ahistorical cult of personality.

As Robert C. Allen and Douglas Gomery have pointed out, the auteur approach deflected attention away from investigation of actual production practices and other historical issues in pursuit of an author's signature.[27] An analysis of art works seeking to reveal subjective experiences, individual world views, or biographical traumas as the true source and ultimate significance of the work has limited historical or esthetic value. Likewise, an all-powerful author who creates works ex nihilo forbids historical understanding. The author as producer is also a product, constrained by the means of production available to him or her and the host of social relations which it is the historian's task to describe. Confining our understanding to Griffith's intentions is not only a critical fallacy but also impoverishes the films' address to us as both spectators and historians. As Hans Georg Gadamer states, the historian's task "is not to understand the subjective intentions, plans and experiences of the men who are involved in history. Rather, it is the great matrix of the meaning of history that must be understood and that requires the interpretive effort of the historian."[28]

It is precisely in this context that David Wark Griffith, the historical and biological person, reemerges. As John Caughie has pointed out, "in placing the author as a fictional figure inside the text, we remove the most accessible point at which the text is tied to its own social and historical outside."[29] Griffith, the actual person outside the text, is important to this work not as a personality who expresses himself through these films, but as a force in their production, through whom other forces enter. Vital to a historical understanding of his films is the Griffith who expressed his admiration for Zola's naturalism in 1907, who styled himself on the muckraking journalists of his time, who worked within the romantic performance idiom of Nance O'Neil, and who tried to imitate David Belasco in the orchestration of details in his playwriting. Griffith as director stands as an important relay for these and other forms of discourse as they enter the Biograph films during 1908 and 1909.

But just as the concept of the director has a historical context, the idea of an author of a film, and particularly understanding a director as an author, exceeds theoretical concerns and plays a historical role. Michel Foucault's essay "What Is an Author?" provides a basis for a historical investigation by focusing on what he terms the "author-function." Foucault points out that the author-function exceeds text-immanent concerns and is determined by the social understanding of discourse. Texts do not obtain authors spontaneously. Authors are attributed through a series of complex operations with links to other institutions, legal and cultural. Further, not all discourses are considered as "authored," and the types of discourse that can possess authors change with the social context.[30]

Griffith's *Dramatic Mirror* advertisement claiming authorship of the films he directed exemplifies Foucault's description of how authorship must be asserted outside the works themselves. Although Griffith did not claim legal ownership, he called for recognition of his authorship. In doing so he also announced that films are an authored discourse rather than anonymous studio products. While Biograph could still assert legal ownership of the films listed—and continued, in fact, to release and rerelease Griffith's films for several years after he had left the company, often invoking his name in publicity—Griffith countered ownership by asserting authorship.

Griffith's advertisement combated the effect of the Biograph Company's policy of anonymity. The lack of credits on a Biograph film, a practice the company maintained long after the rest of the film industry had abandoned it, meant that the host of contributors to its production—actors, scriptwriters, cameramen, technicians, as well as directors—went unacknowledged. However, the films were not issued anonymously. The name of the production company was emblazoned not only on opening credits, but also on all intertitles; it even appeared on interior sets as a trademark. The Biograph Company consciously suppressed all other names associated with their films while it publicized the company itself. In pursuing this policy, the company proclaimed the films as products, complete with trademark, rather than as authored discourse. Although shortly before Griffith's departure in 1913 Biograph eventually followed the practice of other American production companies and announced the names of cast and directors of their films, Griffith's self-promotion responds to the previous occulting of his name and redefines film as an authored discourse.

NOTES

1. *New York Dramatic Mirror,* December 13, 1913, 36.

2. The traditional means for establishing which films Griffith directed during these later years has been Bitzer's claim that all the films he shot were directed by Griffith. Two other sources exist, and others might appear with a detailed search of trade journals from this later period. First, an announcement in *Moving Picture World* of April 5, 1913, states that "David Griffith, the original Biograph producer, is personally directing all Saturday releases," while midweek comedies were directed by Dell Henderson and other releases by Tony O'Sullivan (34). The other source is the Biograph Author's Book preserved in the D. W. Griffith Papers at the Museum of Modern Art Film Library, which records stories purchased by Biograph from 1901 to April 1913. The entries in the book from 1912–1913 often include initials or names next to titles of completed films. These are consistent with the announcement quoted above, so that the initial *H* can be assigned to Henderson, *S* to O'Sullivan, and *G* to Griffith. Some of the films photographed by Bitzer (as indicated in the Biograph Cameraman's Book, also preserved at the Museum of Modern Art) are shown by these other sources to be directed by the secondary directors, although the majority of films Bitzer photographed do seem to have been directed by Griffith. The amount of control Griffith might have asserted over the work of these secondary directors is unknown; the *Dramatic Mirror* advertisement stressed that Griffith "supervised all Biograph productions and directed the more important features" (36).

3. In the *Dramatic Mirror* advertisement, Griffith indicated that he directed all Biograph releases for two years after he began directing. However fairly good evidence exists that secondary directors were working during the first Biograph trip to California in the spring of 1910. Bitzer's comments about these secondary directors is somewhat sketchy and, written decades later, may include some errors. Bitzer lists *All on Account of the Milk* (December 9, 10, 11, 1909) as the first film directed by Frank Powell, the first of the secondary directors. An earlier film, *His Duty* (May 10, 12, 1909) also carries Bitzer's notation "Frank Powell," but this may be intended to indicate that Powell acted in the film (which he did). Powell himself later cited *All on Account of the Milk* as the first film he directed. Bitzer indicates that Powell directed at Biograph until 1911 (when Dell Henderson and Mack Sennett took over), turning out "1 long 1 short" film a week (presumably a full-reel film and a split-reel film). He also notes that Powell's films were shot by Arthur Marvin or Perry Higginson, adding, "Powell's comedies of 1000 ft. length are distinguishable by the actors when any doubt arises, i.e. Walthall, Sweet, Mary Pickford, Lucas would not have been directed by Powell, Henderson or Sennett." But several films Bitzer assigns to Powell do not match this profile. For example, *The Dancing Girl of Butte* is not a comedy and was shot, in fact, by Bitzer himself; and *A Gold Necklace,* a split-reel comedy shot by Marvin in a hasty, improvised style little resembling Griffith and starring Mary Pickford. Bitzer Papers, in the D. W. Griffith Papers, Museum of Modern Art Film Library, New York City.

4. Mrs. D. W. Griffith [Linda Arvidson], *When the Movies Were Young* (1925, repr. New York: Dover Publications, 1969), 109, 139.

5. Arvidson, *When the Movies Were Young,* 69.

6. Helen Kritch Chinoy, "The Emergence of the Director," in *Directors and Directing: A Source Book of the Modern Theater,* ed. Toby Cole and Helen Kritch Chinoy (Indianapolis, Ind.: Bobbs-Merrill, 1976), 1–77.

7. Chinoy, *Directors and Directing,* 3–4.

8. David Bordwell, Janet Staiger, and Kristin Thompson, *The Classical Hollywood Cinema: Film Style and Mode of Production to 1960* (New York: Columbia University Press, 1985), 116.

9. David Levy, "Edison Sales Policy and the Continuous Action Film, 1904–1906," in *Film Before Griffith,* ed. John L. Fell (Berkeley: University of California Press, 1983), 216.

10. Charles Musser, "Pre-Classical Hollywood Cinema and Its Modes of Film Production," paper delivered at the 1989 Society for Cinema Studies, Iowa City; see also J. Searle Dawley file in Braverman material, D. W. Griffith Papers, Museum of Modern Art Film Library, New York City, and Florence Lawrence, "Growing up with the Movies," *PhotoPlay* (November 1914): 40.

11. Grace Dawley to Barnet Braverman, March 12, 1947, Braverman material, D. W. Griffith Papers, Museum of Modern Art Film Library, New York City.

12. Musser, "Pre-Classical Hollywood Cinema," 7.

13. Fred Balshofer and Arthur Miller, *One Reel a Week* (Berkeley: University of California Press, 1967), 48–51.

14. Billy Bitzer, *His Story: The Autobiography of D. W. Griffith's Master Cameraman* (New York: Farrar, Straus and Giroux, 1973), 28, 30, 50.

15. Bitzer, *His Story,* 50–51. McCutcheon is an enigmatic figure and it would be valuable to clarify his role in film history. We know that as a cameraman he shot a number of films for Biograph, both actualities and dramas, in 1903. His last film as cameraman for Biograph was *Wanted a Dog* (1905). He also directed dramatic films during this period. At some point he left Biograph for the Edison Company, where he again directed. A *Variety* notice from January 25, 1908, announced that "Wallace McCutcheon, after several years in the employ of the Edison people has returned to the American Mutoscope and Biograph as producer of their supply of new films. In the same capacity Mr. McCutcheon served the Biograph company when that firm was the first of American film manufacturers" (11). This item contradicts Bitzer's memoirs which do not mention that McCutcheon had left for the Edison Company, nor that he had returned not long before Griffith's debut (perhaps as a ploy in the struggle between Edison and Biograph). More information about McCutcheon's role at both companies is needed for an understanding of the archaeology of the film direcor.

16. Musser, "Pre-Classical Hollywood Cinema," 13–14.

17. Bitzer, *His Story,* 50–51.

18. Ibid., 69.

19. Trade journals are equivocal in their terms for the integrating force responsible for films. Frequently, early reviewers of Griffith's films refer to the anonymous force responsible for them as the "stage manager." But more frequently the term used is the one appearing in *Variety*'s announcement of McCutcheon's return to Biograph—*producer.* Eventually the term *director* does appear. Griffith's own *Dramatic Mirror* advertisement refers to him as both director and producer, although this may be in reference to his double role as actual director of his own films and as supervisor of others.

20. Contract, Lawrence Griffith with the American Mutoscope and Biograph Company, August 7, 1908, D. W. Griffith Papers, Museum of Modern Art Film Library, New York City. The 1909 contract is identical in the passages cited. This contract has also been commented on by John H. Whitney, "The Pragmatic Artist," *Classic Film Collector* (New York, n.d.).

21. Many relevant texts on this issue are assembled in *Theories of Authorship: A Reader,* ed. John Caughie (London: Routledge and Kegan Paul, 1981).

22. Peter Wollen, *Signs and Meanings in the Cinema,* rev. ed., anthologized in *Theories of Authorship,* ed. Caughie, 146–47, as well as Stephen Jenkins, "Introduction," in *Fritz Lang: The Image and the Look,* ed. Stephen Jenkins (London: British Film Institute, 1981), 1.

23. Wayne C. Booth, *The Rhetoric of Fiction* (Chicago: University of Chicago Press, 1961), 74–75. It is curious that although Booth's concept is close to some revisions of the auteur theory, there is not one reference to him in the Caughie anthology. Booth is discussed in relation to the auteur theory in John Belton, "Implied Author and Implied Reader in the Cinematographic Image," in *Cinema Stylists* (Metuchen, N.J.: Scarecrow Press, 1983), 1–8, as well as George M. Wilson *Narration in Light: Studies in Cinematic Point of View* (Baltimore: Johns Hopkins University Press, 1986).

24. Relevant texts would be Roland Barthes, "The Death of the Author," in *Image Music Text*, ed. and trans. Stephen Heath (New York: Hill and Wang, 1977); Michel Foucault, "What Is an Author?" in *Language, Counter-Memory, Practice: Selected Essays and Interviews*, ed. Donald F. Bouchard, trans. Donald F. Bouchard and Sherry Simon (Ithaca, N.Y.: Cornell University Press, 1977), 113–38; Stephen Heath, "Comment on the Idea of Authorship," in *Theories of Authorship*, ed. Caughie, 214–20.

25. Barthes, "The Death of the Author," 147.

26. See Foucault, "What Is an Author?" 119–20: "In current usage, however, the notion of writing seems to transpose the empirical characteristics of an author to a transcendental anonymity."

27. Robert C. Allen and Douglas Gomery, *Film History: Theory and Practice* (New York: Alfred A. Knopf, 1985), 88.

28. Hans Georg Gadamer, "Semantics and Hermeneutics," in *Philosophical Hermeneutics*, ed. and trans. David E. Linge (Berkeley: University of California Press, 1977), 103.

29. Caughie, *Theories of Authorship*, 3.

30. Foucault, "What Is an Author?" 130.

Sumiko Higashi

Cecil B. DeMille and Highbrow Culture: Authorship versus Intertextuality

The Consumption of Culture: Highbrow versus Lowbrow

When Cecil B. DeMille decided to abandon an unspectacular stage career for filmmaking in 1913, he was undeterred by the low repute of one-reelers associated with workers and immigrants in storefront nickelodeons. Such a rash move, however, prompted his older brother, William, a celebrated playwright, to react: "You do come of a cultivated family. . . . I cannot understand how you are willing to identify yourself with a cheap form of amusement . . . which no one will ever allude to as art. Surely you know the contempt with which the movie is regarded by every writer, actor and producer on Broadway." William's condescending attitude toward motion pictures was not unrehearsed. Previously, he had corresponded in a similar vein with Broadway producer David Belasco when Mary Pickford, who had appeared in one of his father's well-known plays, abandoned the stage. The playwright was so contemptuous of films that not even curiosity could induce him to enter a nickelodeon to see one-reel adaptations of his own works.[1] Cecil had the last word, however. A year after the formation of the Jesse L. Lasky Feature Play Company, William himself succumbed to the lure of motion pictures as a new democratic mode of expression. What led to this dramatic reversal of convictions regarding the nature of cinema? What role did Cecil play in persuading not only his playwright brother but respectable middle-class consumers that film was indeed an art form? Put another way, what intertextual relationship existed during the Progressive Era between the legitimate stage and early feature film as a photoplay?

Adolph Zukor, president of the Famous Players Film Company, commented on successful stage productions as a standard for filmmakers when he affirmed in a trade journal: "The moving picture man must try to do as artistic, as high-class, and as notable things in his line of entertainment as such men as . . . Charles and Daniel Frohman were doing in high-class Broadway theatres."[2] A chapter in film history that has yet to be thoroughly investigated, the legitimate theater rather than vaudeville served as a model for the production of feature film exhibited in movie palaces. As a mode of representation legitimating cinema for "better" audiences, multi-reel film adaptations of stage plays constituted a significant industry development that requires a study of the intertextuality of cultural forms in the genteel tradition. Although motion pictures were most likely patronized by the lower as opposed to the upper half of an expanding middle class before World War I, filmmakers like DeMille developed representational strategies for sophisticated audiences conversant with highbrow culture.[3] Pivotal to the success of the Lasky Company was exploitation of the well-known DeMille family name, for it had been associated with the celebrated stage productions of impresario David Belasco. Indeed, DeMille's contract stipulated that he would obtain the motion picture rights to the "plays and scenarios . . . controlled by the . . . DeMille Agency [his mother's company] and the . . . DeMille Estate."[4] Consequently, the director's arrival on the West Coast was part of a wholesale importation of Broadway producers, actors, playwrights, art directors, and music composers to legitimate cinema as art. The production of feature film adaptations was thus based on the name recognition of established writers and stage artists as signifiers of cultural legitimacy. Such an emphasis upon intertextual modes of address, however, rendered the question of early film authorship problematic, a dilemma that was resolved once cinema achieved recognition as an art form in its own right.

Understanding DeMille's contribution to the legitimation of cinema and film authorship first requires a consideration of American cultural practice in relation to class dynamics during the late nineteenth and early twentieth centuries. Concepts of cultural hierarchy that pervade our thinking today, as Lawrence W. Levine argues, did not always exist. For the first half of the nineteenth century, a fairly homogeneous American audience enjoyed such art forms as Shakespearean theater and Italian opera as "*simultaneously* popular and elite." Shakespeare was thus not infrequently "presented as part of the same milieu inhabited by magicians, dancers, singers, acrobats, minstrels, and comics."[5] Similarly, museums displayed "Indian arrows, mammal bones, [and] two-headed pigs alongside casts of Greek sculpture and paintings by Gilbert Stuart and Thomas Sully."[6] Such cultural juxtapositions, seemingly incongruous today but for postmodernism, were emblematic of a social formation that had receded into the past before the Victorian era drew to a close. As a result, American culture was subject during the latter part of the nineteenth century to a process of sacralization accelerated by an increasingly professionalized culture industry and by the impulse of the genteel classes to distance themselves from workers and immigrants. Although the differentiation of cultural consumption according to class was an urban phenomenon that also occurred in Europe, the legacy of evangelical Protestantism and a more secularized Unitarianism predisposed the American patrician elite to recast culture in moral and didactic terms. Furthermore, the influence of Matthew Arnold, who emphasized a perpetual striving for self-improvement in pursuit of human perfection, was not only considerable but had strong religious overtones. Arnold's concept of culture as a force that could transcend individual and group differences was severely tested, however, as the urban scene became increasingly pluralistic. American intellectuals, already concerned about the debasement of cultural forms by the middle class, were undoubtedly alarmed by the practices of the lower orders. As the consumption of culture became an expression of class and ethnic hierarchies, the genteel classes not only attempted to reform the recreation of the lower classes but also mapped out a *cordon sanitaire* for their own forms of conspicuous leisure. Consequently, performances of Shakespeare, opera, and symphonic music for the edification of the elite were elevated above popular entertainment. A sign of the increasing fragmentation of cultural production, the term "legitimate" denoted stage plays enshrined in the pantheon of art as opposed to cheaper amusement such as vaudeville, burlesque, and the circus. Pursuit of recreation and leisure thus became part of social practices that reinforced class and ethnic lines as the mid–nineteenth-century model of a harmonious civic culture receded into the past.[7]

The differentiation of American culture into highbrow and lowbrow—originally phrenological terms based on cranial shapes to equate racial types with intelligence—occurred at a time of demographic change associated with rapid industrial and urban growth. Unprecedented immigration from southern and eastern Europe, which crested in 1907, resulted in a more heterogeneous population in bustling American cities. The arrival of large numbers of seemingly unassimilable immigrants, especially Italians and Jews, and labor unrest culminating in the Haymarket riot and the Homestead and Pullman strikes sparked a revival of nativism. Characteristically, the response of the Anglo-Saxon elite to the centrifugal forces of a market society resulting in fragmentation was to impose cultural and moral order. As arbiters of good taste, they established the canon of legitimate theater, music, and art; validated modes of representation; and dictated audience reception that was respectful. Cultural refinement thus became part of a distinctive style of living in which ritualistic attendance at theaters, concert halls, and museums represented a sign of gentility vis-à-vis urban workers and immigrants.[8]

Since the genteel middle class defined its social identity in terms of its cultural practice, film entrepreneurs intent on escaping the lower-class stigma of storefront nickelodeons were determined to upgrade both production and exhibition. Significantly, their effort to uplift motion pictures coincided with that of the custodians of culture who were motivated by a sense of Progressive reform and moral rectitude. Although historians disagree about the nature of the relationship between these two factions, the attraction of cinema as entertainment for workers and immigrants influenced reformers to establish mechanisms of censorship and to regulate exhibition practices restricting the industry.[9] Ultimately, film magnates, pursuing respectability as well as profit, and Progressive reformers, intent on mediating film spectatorship to educate the urban masses, were at cross-purposes. Whereas the self-appointed elite struggled against the erosion of their authority through a process of sacralization to reinforce the status quo, profit-driven film entrepreneurs developed economic practices, such as vertical integration that resulted in an increasing homogenization of cultural production if not reception. As filmmakers like DeMille exploited the genteel tradition to legitimate cinema, cultural forms became more interdependent and less amenable to concepts validating hierarchies of aesthetic modes. Within this context, the accelerating growth of the leisure industry meant that class and ethnic divisions reinforced by cultural consumption became less distinctive with each succeeding decade. What emerged, therefore, was a significantly different basis for a homogeneous population than had existed in mid–nineteenth-century civic culture. As opposed to a sense of community based upon shared commitment and moral values, twentieth-century popular culture represented the homogeneity of democratized access to commercialized amusement—especially as a form of visual appropriation—if not to actual consumer goods like furniture signifying upward social mobility.[10]

Texts and Intertexts:
A Question of Authorship

The Jesse L. Lasky Feature Play Company, cofounded by former vaude-ville producer Lasky, his brother-in-law and glove salesman Samuel Gold-fish (later Goldwyn), attorney Arthur S. Friend, and DeMille, was quick to announce its strategy to upgrade cinema for respectable middle-class audiences. As *Motion Picture News* reported in December 1913, the pro-duction company would film adaptations of "familiar novels and plays for presentation on the screen."[11] Although the company was named after Lasky because he was the best-known of the four cofounders, DeMille's theatrical legacy represented cultural capital that could immediately be exploited. Adolph Zukor, who merged his Famous Players Film Company with the Lasky Company in 1916, recalled that the DeMilles were "so closely associated with the stage that he was surprised Cecil . . . was becoming associated with the screen."[12] A *Photoplay* writer anticipated Zukor's reaction in 1915: "For more than a generation the name of DeMille has been closely linked with that of Belasco, both synonymous with high altitudes of dramatic art. Consequently when the first DeMille turned to the screen there was marked the beginning of a new epoch in film annals."[13] Profiting from the cultural legacy of his father and brother as well-known playwrights, DeMille quickly attempted to validate his authorship in a related new medium. Problems that he encountered resulted from the questionable status of motion pictures compared to more traditional forms of genteel culture. Although the director was able to establish the validity of his signature within a relatively short period of time, narrative and marketing strategies that exploited stage and literary works proved at first to be a mixed blessing.[14]

Consider, for example, DeMille's first three releases, *The Squaw Man* (1914), *The Virginian* (1914), and *The Call of the North* (1914). All were adaptations of stage Westerns that, in the last two instances, were in turn adapted from novels written by Owen Wister and Stewart Edward White, respectively. A fourth feature, *What's His Name* (1914), was a domestic melodrama based on a minor work by George Barr McCutcheon, a best-selling author whose earlier fiction had been successfully adapted as stage plays and feature films. Significantly, the credits of all four fea-tures attribute authorship to well-known writers, whereas DeMille is only acknowledged as having "picturized" the screen version. Not until his fifth feature, *The Man from Home* (1914), an adaptation of a Booth Tarkington and Harry L. Wilson play about American innocents abroad, did DeMille begin to identify himself in the credits as a producer equivalent to the Belascos of the stage. But his claim to authorship remained tenuous until the industry ceased to foreground writers, signifyng cultural legitimacy, and represented cinema as the artistic expression of the director.

Credit sequences of early Lasky Company features illustrate the extent to which novelists and stage actors rather than directors were privileged as film authors. An intertitle in *The Call of the North,* for example, reads "Mr. DeMille Presents the Cast to Stewart Edward White," author of *The Conjuror's House,* a novel previously adapted for the stage by George Broadhurst. DeMille is seated on the extreme left, at times practically out of the frame, whereas White, seated prominently in the center, meets the costumed actors who represent the characters he portrayed in his novel. Robert Edeson, the Broadway actor starring in the dual role of Canadian frontiersmen, *père et fils,* is introduced last, turns to his left, and shakes the hand of his creator. In *What's His Name,* trumpeted as an adaptation of "The Celebrated Novel by George Barr McCutcheon," Lolita Robertson

Although he directed Kindling, *DeMille's name appears only at the bottom of the ad as director-general of the Lasky Company.*

and Max Figman emerge on screen as poster board characters who come to life. Figman, interestingly, bows to the audience as if he were acknowledging applause on stage. Dustin Farnum, hero of the stage version of *The Virginian*, claimed that he was criticized for prostituting himself in the film adaptation of *The Squaw Man*, but a succession of theatrical stars, including Ina Claire, Marie Doro, Fannie Ward, Charlotte Walker, Theodore Roberts, Thomas Meighan, and Elliott Dexter, appeared in DeMille's early features and became part of the Lasky studio's equivalent of a stock company. Since the appearance of Broadway actors on screen was considered a noteworthy event, trade journals regularly publicized the recruitment of theatrical stars who signed contracts with film studios. In March 1914, *Photoplay* claimed that more actors were abandoning the stage to appear in motion pictures on a permanent basis, a sign of the growing financial profitability as well as increasing cultural legitimacy of the cinema.[15]

Authorship of early film adaptations constructed as intertextual modes of address is an issue complicated by the role of talent behind the camera as well as publicity accorded writers and stage stars. When DeMille boarded a train to film *The Squaw Man* on the West Coast, he had never before directed a motion picture and was thus accompanied by filmmaker Oscar Apfel. Calling attention to this event, the *New York Dramatic Mirror* headlined, "Oscar Apfel to Direct Company Leaving for Pacific Coast Soon," and described the director in a follow-up article as "well-known in film circles." Previously, Apfel had enjoyed a successful theatrical career as stage manager and director of several stock companies and worked with Belasco's assistant director, Will Dean. After leaving the theater, Apfel had also written and directed scores of motion pictures for the Edison Manufacturing Company, the Mutual Film Company, and Pathé Frères Film Company. According to Robert Grau's characterization of the struggle of independent film producers against the Motion Picture Patents Company, which was declared in restraint of trade in 1917, Apfel's Reliance productions for Mutual "contributed more to the 'Independent' cause than any single factor one may name."[16] The Lasky Company had thus recruited a considerable talent for its first filmmaking venture, but DeMille fortunately proved to be a quick study.

A consideration of *The Squaw Man* illustrates some of the basic filmmaking techniques that DeMille learned from Apfel, credited as codirector. Adapted from Edwin Milton Royle's stage play (1905) and starring Dustin Farnum, the film was a melodrama in the tradition of dime novels about the Wild West and foregrounded issues regarding class, ethnicity, and gender. Apfel and DeMille adroitly used parallel editing[17] to narrate the adventures of Captain James Wynnegate (Farnum), British aristocrat turned cowpuncher, who settles on the frontier after assuming blame for a crime committed by the husband of the woman he secretly loves. As evident in *The Squaw Man*, Apfel's filmmaking style was technically advanced and distinguished by composition for depth, a high ratio of medium shots, camera movement for reframing, parallel editing, eye-level shots with occasional use of high angle and even reverse angle shots, superimpositions and split-screen effects to show a protagonist recalling past events, and intertitles as exposition and dialogue, all characteristic of DeMille's early features. Significantly, the use of low-key lighting effects in night scenes with a fireplace or a match as naturalistic light sources are not as dramatic as in later films that would benefit from the expertise of Belasco's former set designer, Wilfred Buckland. Yet such lighting is used in two scenes to convey intimacy in Jim's tabooed relationship with an Indian chief's daughter, Nat-u-ritch (Red Wing), and thus prefigures the way in which DeMille constructed mise-en-scène to express moral dilemmas. Indeed, the director's striking use of "contrasty"

DeMille's chiaroscuro lighting in The Cheat *won him critical acclaim both at home and abroad. Courtesy of George Eastman House.*

lighting in a succession of feature films not only achieved product differentiation for the Lasky Company but also contributed to recognition of his claim to authorship.

The reaction of enthusiastic film critics, who recognized Apfel's work when *The Squaw Man* was premiered in New York, must have been instructive for DeMille as he sought to establish himself as an author in his own right. Aside from this first acclaimed Lasky Company film, the director's collaborations with Apfel were never listed as titles in his filmography. Apfel continued to direct features as one of the studio's stable of filmmakers but was soon eclipsed in reputation by his apprentice. Probably, DeMille, who was extremely competitive with his brother, William, was not predisposed to advance the career of yet another rival. At the beginning of its history, however, the Lasky Company profited from Apfel's mastery to establish a reputation for quality film with its very first release. A *Moving Picture World* critic who admired *The Squaw Man* claimed, "I have not seen Oscar Apfel's name made prominent in connection with this winner, but I recognize his handiwork without difficulty." The *New York Dramatic Mirror* tactfully stated, "As director-general, we presume the first credit for a skillfully directed drama belongs to Cecil B. DeMille, but this need not detract from the honor due Oscar C. Apfel, who, we understand, bore the brunt of the actual work." Indeed, a photograph taken on December 29, 1913, the day shooting commenced on the film, shows Apfel in command as director while DeMille is standing unobtrusively with cast and crew. One account of the production attributes camera angles and editing to Apfel and acting direction to DeMille.[18] Such a division of labor is feasible given noticeable contrasts between *The Squaw Man*, a collaborative work, and *The Virginian*, DeMille's third release, second feature, and first solo effort. An adaptation of Owen Wister's acclaimed bestseller about a Westerner (Dustin Farnum) who delays his marriage to an Eastern schoolteacher (Winifred Kingston) for a shootout, *The Virginian* is the most technically flawed of the director's early features. DeMille violates screen direction in editing several scenes, represents contiguous space in separate shots that are awkward with respect to scale and direction, makes erratic use of fades, and has a lower ratio of medium shots for intimate scenes such as one in which the Virginian bids farewell to a friend about to be hanged for cattle rustling. DeMille's later features, especially *Carmen* (1915), were reedited as reissues, but such was apparently not the case for this Western. Yet *The Virginian* does feature dramatic low-key lighting effects, as in nighttime campfire scenes repeated in *The Warrens of Virginia* (1915)—

a Civil War saga based on William deMille's play—which are absent in *The Squaw Man* and most likely attributable to the genius of Belasco's set designer, Wilfred Buckland.

Although DeMille boasted, "I brought the whole Belasco crew out here . . . the men who had made the Belasco productions great," he attributed Buckland's recruitment as art director to the persuasive powers of his mother, Beatrice DeMille.[19] She was able to capitalize on professional ties dating back several decades because Buckland had acted in her husband's play, *The Main Line* (1886), and taught makeup at the American Academy of Dramatic Arts, where he counted Cecil and William among his pupils and had himself studied under Belasco.[20] Acclaiming him as a "decorative artist and an electrical expert in stage lighting," *Moving Picture World* announced his move to Los Angeles in May 1914 in a piece titled "Getting Belasco Atmosphere."[21] Because Buckland's arrival at the West Coast studio coincided with the use of low-key lighting in campfire scenes in *The Virginian*, DeMille's attempt to establish his authorship was still problematic. But "Lasky lighting," also labeled "Rembrandt lighting," became the most distinctive, if not dramatic, aspect of the director's visual style before the First World War. Although Buckland served as art director until 1920 when set and costume design became decidedly more outré, DeMille in all likelihood proved himself to be once again a quick study. Scripts of the early feature films include details about the use of lighting effects, occasionally in the director's own handwriting. As he later recalled, cameramen were rated at the time according to "how clearly you could see under the table . . . how clearly you could see the back corner of the room—both corners. . . ." Undeniably, the filmmaker's rapid progression from flat, uniform lighting that flooded the entire set, to modeled lighting with highlight and shadows that could be attributed to naturalistic sources, to dramatic low-key lighting that was combined with color tinting were technical advances reinforcing his claim to authorship.[22] DeMille never ceased to acknowledge Buckland's contribution, however. Studio correspondence attests that he was personally involved in the art director's salary negotiations in the midst of the Famous Players–Lasky merger.[23] At the end of his decades-long career, he still observed: "Buckland is a man who has not been given credit that he deserves. . . . Belasco's productions were something nobody in the world could equal, and that was because of Buckland."[24]

At the time that Buckland abandoned the legitimate theater, the Lasky Company was still exploiting audience perception of stage and screen as intertexts by negotiating for the rights to Belasco's plays. *Moving Picture*

World touted an industry coup by announcing "the greatest tour de force of the season": "Lasky Gets Belasco Plays." According to Goldwyn, DeMille's family connections with Belasco were useful in outbidding Adolph Zukor's Famous Players in negotiations with the Broadway producer.[25] Given Belasco's stature, the significance of the Lasky Company acquiring the rights to his plays cannot be minimized. Belasco pontificated on the occasion: "The main feature of my agreement with Mr. Lasky and his company is their promise to put my plays on film in a manner befitting their success and reputation." Apparently reversing an earlier opinion regarding the cultural legitimacy of cinema, the producer shrewdly realized that motion picture rights would provide lucrative income after a stage play had completed its engagement and exhausted its stock company value. The transaction was worth one hundred thousand dollars.[26] For its part, the Lasky Company proved adept in exploiting the coup to attract middle-class patrons of the legitimate theater to its films. Ads in trade journals emphasized the intertextuality of stage and film productions in order to influence exhibiting practices and thereby audience reception. For example, an ad for DeMille's first Belasco adaptation, *Rose of the Rancho* (1914), set in California after the Mexican War, trumpeted "Jesse L. Lasky in association with David Belasco presents. . . ."

Such billing was not lost on DeMille, attempting to assert his own authorship, as he learned to model his persona after Belasco's. Although the director succeeded in dictating details about the display of his name when he achieved status as an author two years later, the marquee value of Broadway personalities was then unquestioned. Ads for *The Warrens of Virginia* thus featured Belasco as producer of the stage hit and William deMille as playwright. Underneath and in smaller letters, Cecil was identified as film director. But events in early film history, including the legitimation of cinema in relation to the stage and as a separate art form, developed very quickly. By 1916 the announcement of Lasky's acquisition of the rights to additional Belasco plays was buried at the bottom of a page in *Moving Picture World*. By 1918 *Photoplay* was contemptuous of Belasco's judgment that stage drama was superior to the screen and described "this greatest of American producers" as "speaking in ponderous generalizations of things concerning which he has, obviously, almost no knowledge."[27]

As filmmakers who relied upon intertexts to address educated middle-class audiences, DeMille and Lasky initially considered scriptwriting to be the key to success. During his first year in Los Angeles, DeMille wrote to Goldwyn, who dealt with distribution and exhibition in the company's

New York office: "I had always thought . . . that if the same technical and dramatic knowledge were applied to the scenario as to the play, the result would go far toward raising the standard of the photoplay." Similarly, he stated in an interview two years later, "If the scenario were written with the same care that is given to the writing of a drama, and were produced with . . . care and thought . . . , it would create an absolutely new clientele for motion pictures." When the West Coast studio was reorganized in 1915, Lasky announced, "We paid particular attention to the scenario department . . . [it] wholly controls the whole situation for the producer."[28] At the very least, DeMille must have been aware that his own assertion of authorship depended on his control of the scriptwriting process. A significant development occurred, therefore, when his brother, William, agreed late in the previous year to become the first head of the newly organized scenario department. The *New York Dramatic Mirror* reported his defection from the legitimate stage in September 1914: "Some surprise was caused [because] deMille . . . was one of the great playwrights of the decade and at the heyday of his success on the stage." Shortly after he arrived at the studio and was cast as an extra in *Rose of the Rancho*, William wrote to his wife about his new craft: "There is very much to be learnt about the structure of a scenario. . . . It is very tricky work and requires absolute concentration."[29] Assisted by former New Yorkers who had also abandoned the stage, namely Margaret Turnbull, a novelist and playwright with whom he had collaborated, and her brother, Hector Turnbull, a former drama critic of the *New York Tribune*, William quickly wrote several scripts. As part of a public relations effort to promote screenwriting, he even exploited his affiliation with his alma mater, Columbia University. The Lasky Company supported the institution's decision to establish a special course of lectures on filmmaking by announcing a scholarship for the student who wrote the most original scenario. With respect to film authorship, however, William quickly surmised, as did Lasky, that the role of the director was pivotal despite movie ads trumpeting Broadway names. Several months prior to the Lasky Company's merger with Famous Players, he stated, "really good directors in this game are worth almost any amount," and renounced writing in favor of directing. Although Lasky wrote to Goldwyn, "I have been concentrating on . . . directors and scenario writers," he also concluded, "the fate of a picture is so much in the hands of the director, even though the scenario department turns out first-rate scenarios."[30]

A bold move to consolidate feature film production for middle-class audiences, the merger—contemplated in 1915 but negotiated a year later—strained an understaffed scenario department but demonstrated the astuteness of focusing on screenplays to upgrade films. When DeMille wired that his scriptwriting methods were being undone in the midst of reorganization, Lasky, now headquartered in New York, countered that he was overwhelmed because Famous Players lacked not only a scenario department and a backlog of scripts, but positive reviews of recent releases. By contrast, the Lasky Company had been in a strong position to negotiate favorable terms for the merger. According to Lasky, "I always claimed we made better, if fewer, pictures than Famous Players in the early days." Indeed, DeMille had boastfully written to Goldwyn during his first year on the West Coast, "I can make Zukor productions for you in three weeks; in fact I will guarantee to turn you out a half a dozen 'Eagle's Mates' [a Famous Players film] weekly."[31] Under pressure to consolidate and streamline the newly formed corporation, Lasky, who assumed the role of vice-president under Zukor, named Hector Turnbull as head of a scenario department relocated in New York. Although the executive remained committed to producing high-quality films, he was impressed with Famous Players' cost-cutting practices, if not its organization, and quipped to DeMille, "my slogan is 'Dividends first and art second.' Or rather a blend of the two."[32]

As the Lasky Company and Famous Players demonstrated even before their well-publicized merger, the cultural legitimacy of feature films meant increased profit. And as cinema became increasingly recognized as an art form in its own right, DeMille began to assert his claim to film authorship. On this subject, Lasky sided with his director-general and explained to Goldwyn a year prior to the merger:

> Cecil showed me a copy of a letter he had written to you on publicity for himself. It seems that this has been in his mind for some months. . . . Cecil has proved his value to the firm in many ways and . . . there can be no question of his loyalty to us. That being the case, I think it a very good business move for us to build up his name as we are trying to build up Blanche Sweet's name. You know the public go to see a Griffith production, not because it may have a star in the cast, but because Griffith's name on it stands for so much. It seems to me that the time has come for us to do the same with Cecil's name. If we can accomplish this, we could let Cecil stage the plays that have no stars and his name in large type on the paper, advertising, etc., would undoubtedly in time take the plase of a star's. In a word, he is the biggest asset we have, so let's use it for all it is worth.[33]

As events unfolded, Lasky's strategy to build up DeMille's name as an auteur proved to be very profitable.

Critical Discourses

As Jesse L. Lasky recalled, perhaps with more nostalgia than accuracy, "feature pictures were established in 1914, [but] they didn't become respectable until late in 1915."[34] Discourse in trade journals supports his argument that cinema was not then widely recognized as an art form. When Metropolitan Opera soprano Geraldine Farrar starred in *Carmen*, an enthusiastic press acclaimed her sensational debut as a sign that motion pictures were becoming highbrow. Such events demonstrated that producers like the Lasky Company and Famous Players deployed the right strategy to establish multi-reel features as the industry standard to attract middle-class audiences. According to discourse in trade journals and fan magazines, however, as late as 1914 there was by no means unanimity on the subject of features, a term coined by *Motion Picture News* in the previous year. Captain Leslie T. Peacocke, who was affiliated with Universal Film Manufacturing Company and wrote *Photoplay*'s column on scriptwriting, cautioned that "all the companies are vieing [sic] to secure . . . leading attractions without taking into consideration whether the five and ten cent audience—who constitute the big patrons of the film drama and will always do so—will enthuse themselves over a play . . . or a book . . . of which they have never heard."[35] Asserting an opposite point of view in *Moving Picture World*, Jesse L. Lasky and Adolph Zukor disputed William Selig and Carl Laemmle on the desirability of features as against one- and two-reelers. Lasky argued:

> Features . . . have accomplished what the "one reel" subjects failed to attain in fifteen years . . . to interest the classes. . . . Fronts were changed, interiors rearranged, music improved, prices elevated, and advertising in the press resorted to. Features compelled recognition in the daily press. Regular reviewers . . . began reviewing feature photoplays from the same angle that the legitimate dramas are criticized. . . . The production of features have attracted [sic] a large number of men to the ranks of motion picture purveyors who could do naught else than dignify the industry.[36]

As Lasky recognized, feature films prompted critics to write reviews comparable to those of stage plays in newspapers and periodicals that influenced middle-class reception. The *New York Times*, for example, did not yet review films on a regular basis, as did trade papers and fan magazines, but it devoted space to adaptations starring celebrated artists like Geraldine Farrar. Discourse in trade journals was more consistent, but critics still valorized screen adaptations in terms of intertextual references to traditional art forms. Consequently, they too legitimated film according to the standards of genteel culture but in so doing diminished the authorial claim of filmmakers like DeMille. Critics, in other words, were still expressing uncertainty regarding the nature of film aesthetic during an important transitional period in the evolution of cinema. DeMille's first release, *The Squaw Man*, for example, was hailed as "one of the best visualizations of a stage play ever shown on screen." Yet the critic also asserted that the director should "realize the art of producing moving pictures is to be measured by its own canons alone." Another critic reacted to *Rose of the Rancho* with this comparison: "If the best stage plays can be picturized with such success then the picture even excels the play." Belasco's favorable response to the film, "This is better than the play," was widely publicized to validate the screen version. Significantly, the production of spectacles that surpassed those orchestrated on stage called attention to increased realism as a desirable characteristic distinguishing the new medium. Critics were thus impressed with "a real soda fountain" in *What's His Name*, "the ambushing and destruction of the supply train" in *The Warrens of Virginia*, and "picturesque settings" in *The Captive* (1915). Anticipating such reviews, DeMille had written to Goldwyn in 1914, "The scope of the photoplay is so much wider than that of the legitimate drama. In the first place we DO things instead of acting them. When a big effect is necessary, such as the burning of a ship, the blowing up of a mine, the wrecking of a train, we do not have to trick the effect with lights and scenery, we DO it."[37] As critical response became focused on the formal properties of a new mode of representation, film acquired greater currency as an art form. Within this context, the publication of Vachel Lindsay's *The Art of the Moving Picture* (1915), one of the first serious and extended essays on film aesthetic, is telling: the work asserted an independent status for cinema while discussing it with reference to traditional art forms like architecture and sculpture.[38]

DeMille's attempt to establish his credentials as an author when film had yet to achieve cultural legitimacy was initially compromised by his reputation for lighting effects. Given the fact that low-key lighting and color tinting on nitrate prints resulted in a pictorial mise-en-scène, critics referred to famous paintings as intertexts. Artwork such as chromolithographs had long since been commercialized for middle-class consumption, but paintings exhibited in museums still retained the aura of unique art objects. Critics thus simultaneously conferred and withheld authorship by focusing on DeMille's mise-en-scène. W. Stephen Bush, for example, claimed in *Moving Picture World* that the director's representation of a tenement district in *Kindling* (1914) was "as graphic as anything that ever came from the hands of Hogarth or Rembrandt." After viewing the *The Golden Chance* (1915), a Cinderella story based on an original screenplay, Bush exclaimed: "If the paintings in a Rembrandt gallery or a set of Titians or Tintorettos were to come to life . . . and transferred to the moving picture screen the effect could not have been more startling." Similarly, the *New York Dramatic News* praised "the masterly handling and lighting of Cecil deMille [*sic*]" in *Carmen* and noted that "the use of direct and only mildly suffused light in almost every picture emphasizes the figures and the play of facial muscles, and creates a quality akin to the tone of oil painting." DeMille himself maintained in a much-repeated anecdote that when Goldwyn objected to the shadowy effects of low-key lighting—most likely in scenes in *The Man from Home* or *The Warrens of Virginia*—he replied, "To Hell with it—tell them it's Rembrandt lighting." Since DeMille's claim to authorship had not yet been substantiated, credits of his early features signified his role as filmmaker with the phrase "picturized by" as opposed to "produced by" or "directed by." Aptly, an article in the *New York Dramatic Mirror* was titled "The Director as a Painter and the Players His Colors," a comparison that would cease to be accentuated when film became an independent art form.[39]

Although the intertextuality of cultural forms in genteel society served to dim as well as illuminate his achievement, DeMille exploited tenets regarding the sanctity of culture to assert his status as an author. Consistent with Protestant beliefs as well as Arnoldian concepts stressing human perfectibility, artists were then prompted to produce realistic representations that could be read as spiritual messages.[40] Belasco, not coincidentally, wore a clergyman's collar as part of his everyday dress and was dubbed an "apostle of art." As his heirs apparent in the cinema, the DeMille brothers reinterpreted the tradition of Victorian pictorialism so that it became an essential aspect of their mission as filmmakers. While still a playwright, William had claimed that "the primary essential of a play is that it shall teach a lesson." Cecil asserted that "to preach is to invite disaster, but . . . to be afraid to develop a message in the story is to miss a great possibility." Although the brothers shared a belief in the didactic function of art, they had serious ideological differences that would later become more apparent. William, a liberal, had married the daughter of single-tax reform advocate Henry George, and sympathized with the people against the "highbrows" and "uplifters"; he had even championed stage drama as "the art of the people as a whole" rather than "for a cultivated few."[41] Cecil was conservative and retained toward the public a stance of cultural stewardship that he shared with the elite classes of the Progressive Era.

Within the context of Progressive reform based on moral imperative, film critics too were proponents of the sanctity of culture and responded to DeMille's features in language saturated with didacticism. Such expressions accorded with the objectives of genteel reformers intent on assimilating immigrants and workers by emphasizing the value of education. Motion pictures were thus not just entertainment; they were "a titanic engine for popular education . . . [and] for the cultivation of the public mind." Accordingly, one critic waxed rhapsodic about film in relation to "the refining and intensifying of the emotions, the logic of civilization, and the development of the soul." Critics also used the rhetoric of uplift to describe the improving quality of feature film. A reviewer of *The Call of the North* proclaimed in *Moving Picture World* that the feature had reaffirmed his "faith in the approaching kingdom of quality." Similarly, *Photoplay* announced with awe and anticipation, "We stand at the threshold of the full-length screen play, as the living body of a higher and finer programme."[42] In sum, critics demonstrated that sacrosanct language associated with highbrow culture could be employed to legitimate the emergence of a popular mass medium. Although this practice was useful in securing for DeMille the status of a cultural custodian in his endeavor to establish authorship, ultimately the interpenetration of cultural forms contributed to a process of desacralization. The intertextuality of grand opera, stage melodrama, and feature film, in other words, signified that the elite would find the preservation of a cultural hierarchy unmanageable in a technological age.

Film: The New Democratic Art

Although film entrepreneurs initially exploited the intertextual relationship between feature film and traditional art forms, they were not shortsighted about the future of the industry. At the time he abandoned vaudeville for motion pictures, Jesse L. Lasky predicted, "Eventually we will have stories by authors of recognized standing and written expressly for the screen." The mode of production of early feature film was so fast-paced in response to market demand that filmmakers could not indefinitely rely on theatrical and literary sources for adaptations. DeMille therefore resorted to formulaic screenplays that not only gave him more stature as an author in his own right, but proved cheaper than negotiating for costly rights and better tailored to talent under contract. Studio emphasis on original scenarios also streamlined production because expensive delays attributed to scriptwriting problems, as Lasky complained to Goldwyn, meant that directors and stars had to be paid while awaiting rehearsals. Working at breakneck pace, DeMille doubled the number of his releases from seven in 1914 to thirteen in 1915, including three features, *The Captive, The Cheat,* and *The Golden Chance,* that were based on original screenplays. As director-general, moreover, he supervised the production of twenty-one features, including his own films, in 1914 and thirty-six in 1915.[43] Toward the end of 1915 and prior to the Famous Players–Lasky merger in June 1916, he began to include in his output original screenplays written by Jeanie Macpherson and Hector Turnbull. Macpherson, interestingly, had previously been employed under Oscar Apfel at the Edison Manufacturing Company and had written scenarios and directed films for Universal Film Manufacturing Company and Criterion Features.[44] After the merger, DeMille relied almost exclusively on Macpherson's scenarios, even though a general manager assumed his supervisory duties as director-general so that he could produce special features at a slower pace.

Undoubtedly, the extraordinary success of *The Cheat* and *The Golden Chance,* films based on original screenplays that DeMille simultaneously directed during a hectic production schedule, influenced his move away from adaptations. Critics responded with hyperbole even though they still compared film with the legitimate stage. The *Motion Picture News* critic, for example, referred to the theater when he claimed that "in staging 'The Cheat,' [DeMille's] genius reached a climax," but he also noted that the film "should mark a new era in lighting as applied to screen productions." Acknowledging film authorship, the *New York Dramatic Mirror* critic detected "the master hand of Cecil DeMille . . . throughout 'The Golden Chance'" and claimed the production could "be favorably compared to anything that either the stage or the screen has brought forth." As both Goldwyn and William deMille later recalled, critical acclaim for *The Cheat,* a sensational melodrama focused on an interracial relationship, elevated DeMille to the pantheon of early film directors.[45] After a series of successful features during a year when the names of Belasco, Farrar, and his brother, William, had been emblazoned above his own, Cecil was finally in a position to dictate that his name be "prominently displayed upon all motion pictures." When he signed a contract with Famous Players–Lasky shortly after the merger, he achieved recognition in the industry equivalent to that accorded luminaries of the legitimate stage and opera.[46] Fittingly, DeMille, hailed as "Creator of Artistic Productions Embodying High Box-Office Value," was the only director besides D. W. Griffith to be inducted into the *Motion Picture News* Hall of Fame in 1922.[47]

What was the significance of filmmakers like DeMille who came of age during the sacralization of culture and exploited a theatrical legacy to legitimate cinema and film authorship? Since motion pictures were an attraction for workers and immigrants in storefront nickelodeons before entrepreneurs sought legitimacy, middle-class film reception signified an important shift in patterns of cultural consumption. A number of social and cultural historians as well as film historians have debated whether early film attendance exemplifies a trickle-down or bottom-up model with respect to class and ethnic interaction in an urban environment. Were middle-class audiences patronizing nickelodeons at a much earlier date than has been assumed, as Russell Merritt and Robert C. Allen argue? Or was filmgoing a working-class diversion as late as 1914, as Roy Rosenzweig asserts, and thus evidence of a radical change in middle-class cultural practice? Steven J. Ross argues that filmgoing and to some extent filmmaking were mostly working-class modes of communication prior to the First World War. Significantly, Merritt and Allen do not distinguish between the upper and lower middle classes in their empirical studies, but Tom Gunning points out that by 1910, 25 percent of filmgoers were lower-middle-class salaried workers. Although Ben Singer affirms that nickelodeon audiences were mostly working-class, he included in their ranks a clerical class not to be confused with the middle class. Perhaps a distinction should be made between the "old" propertied and the "new" salaried middle classes in that the latter were pivotal in the rise of modern popular culture. Attention to ethnicity, as Singer suggests, would also be informative.

But were lower-class immigrant women indeed setting trends for middle-class women by patronizing commercialized amusement, as Kathy Peiss claims in arguing against the model of social control? Or were they, as Elizabeth Ewen contends, subject to the assimilative process of Americanization as represented on the screen? Were sociable immigrants translating Jürgen Habermas's concept of the public sphere into neighborhood nickelodeons, only to be textually constructed as spectators, as Miriam Hansen maintains? Or was the filmgoing experience of the working class, as Lizabeth Cohen asserts, significantly mediated by subcultures well into the 1920s? With respect to representational strategies and reading practices, were producers creating a mass audience by persuading the lower classes to join their "betters" in nickelodeons, as Janet Staiger argues, or were they in league with elite constituents, as William Uricchio and Roberta E. Pearson contend, to make films that could be read by the middle as well as working classes?[48]

The formation of producers like Famous Players and the Lasky Company, as well as distributors like Paramount, in my view, meant that entrepreneurs purposely developed a strategy to resituate cinema for "better" audiences during the years 1912–1915. Given the importance of cultural rituals and commodities to signify genteel status, industry leaders chose to upgrade production and exhibition practices to legitimate cinema and to enhance profit. Although filmgoing was most likely entertainment for the lower as opposed to upper middle class before World War I, the practice of showcasing features in downtown movie palaces overlapped and to some extent displaced a preexisting plebeian film culture. A reading of specific DeMille texts will show, moreover, that the representational strategy of feature films based on traditional cultural forms articulated genteel middle-class ideology to appeal to cultivated audiences. What appears ironic in retrospect is that filmmakers unwittingly contributed to the homogenization of culture that threatened the social identity of the very classes whom they were courting. Writers in trade journals did employ terms like "high-class" and "low-class" to differentiate clientele, but the eventual legitimation of film rendered such distinctions less meaningful. According to Douglas Gomery, by the mid-1920s approximately 50 percent of audiences in large urban centers were patronizing first- and second-run theaters.[49] The reception of cinema as entertainment that began to transcend established patterns of cultural consumption based on class and ethnicity thus proved to be a meaningful development.

The Lasky Company strategy to upgrade film in terms of intertextual readings indeed heightened contradictions that attenuated the sacrosanct status of genteel culture in an age of commercialized amusement. Distinctions between *highbrow* and *lowbrow*, for example, were difficult to sustain even in the legitimate theater, whose aura filmmakers sought for the cinema. Critical discourse on the Henry C. deMille–David Belasco domestic melodramas staged in fashionable theaters in the 1880s and 1890s was not always appreciative. As theatergoing became pervasive among genteel middle-class audiences demanding Broadway productions, critics expressed concern about such issues as style over substance. When William deMille's Civil War melodrama, *The Warrens of Virginia*, went on tour in 1908 after a successful run at the Belasco Theatre in New York, the *Cincinnati Inquirer* observed that it "proved more interesting as a production than as a drama." A few years later, *The Bookman* reacted to William's popular melodrama, *The Woman*, as "the best directed play Mr. Belasco ever yet produced" but "distinctly a well made play [that] expands no theme . . . of permanent importance to humanity."[50] When the new stagecraft displaced Victorian melodrama in the 1920s, Belasco was dismissed for stage plays that were more notable for pictorial realism than for literary merit.[51] Subject to the leveling impact of market conditions, the cultural consumption of the genteel classes, as shown by their taste in theatergoing, did not always adhere to Arnoldian standards of excellence.

Within this fluctuating context, the marketing of feature film adaptations further undermined cultural distinctions that were based on notions of excellence and buttressed by class and ethnic hierarchies. Fan magazines such as *Photoplay*, for example, published novelizations of motion pictures illustrated with stills that not only served as advertising but rendered film narrative as well as its intertexts more accessible. The May 1914 cover of the magazine read, "In This Issue: The Squaw Man. A Complete Novelette From the Feature Film." Adapted for the screen by DeMille, Edwin Milton Royle's stage play was subsequently novelized for fan magazine readers. At times, this circuitous practice led to novelizations of already existing novels. DeMille's *The Virginian* was "Novelized from the Film . . . Based on the Original Novel by Owen Wister [and the stage version by Kirk LaShelle]." Staff writers did not feel compelled to refrain from invention, as was the case when Bruce Westfall concluded his version of DeMille's *Rose of the Rancho*—adapted from the Belasco and Richard Walton Tully play—on a more conciliatory and less realistic note.[52] Aside from generating publicity, novelizations were probably useful to less educated audiences who were unfamiliar with the novel or stage version of convoluted plots such as DeMille's *The Call of the North*, a Western set in Canada that spanned two generations.[53] Yet narrative forms were undeniably diluted in the recycling process that screen adaptations set in motion. As more space in fan magazines was allocated to articles about movie stars, a sign of growing preoccupation with celebrities rather than narrative, a smaller percentage of pages was devoted to novelizations. Possibly, these recycled stories became redundant when film narration advanced to the point where an audience could follow complicated plot developments. As early fan magazine staples, however, novelizations illustrate the impact of filmmakers who, while claiming the aura of art for feature film, unwittingly collapsed distinctions between highbrow and lowbrow and paved the way for categories like middlebrow. The term *middlebrow*, which signified a decline of Arnoldian standards of excellence, was not coined until 1925, but the leveling impact of the market on cultural commodities had been in evidence for many decades. DeMille could not have exploited the genteel tradition so artfully if middle-class consumers had not already been seduced by stage plays and bestsellers whose titles would scarcely merit recognition today. As a description of class and ethnic distinctions in patterns of cultural consumption, the term *highbrow* has its uses as a label, but it was not necessarily synonymous with high art and could thus be reconfigured as middlebrow by the culture industry.[54]

Although the success of feature film ultimately contributed to the increasing homogenization of culture as an index of social status, could it then be argued that cinema succeeded mid–nineteenth-century theater as a new democratic art form?[55] Film reception, to be sure, was mediated by a number of variables including gender, class, ethnicity, religion, age group, and geographical region.[56] The significance of film as a revolutionary and powerful new medium with widespread appeal, however, was not lost on the filmmakers themselves. William deMille was quite prescient when he observed in 1915 that "for the first time in history a new art is being born that is more democratic than the drama." Indeed, his abandonment of a prestigious stage career can in some measure be attributed to his liberal politics and to his vision regarding the future of cinema. Asserting a similar viewpoint, *Photoplay* observed, "films . . . are a basic amusement, recreation and instruction for the entire world— for the highbrow and for the fellow whose cowlick grows into his eyebrows."[57] Given the context of turbulent class and ethnic relations in the early twentieth century, this industry development was not inconsiderable. Despite the conclusion of a trade journal survey that the building of picture palaces had not diminished the importance of small houses as the "bread and butter" of the business, the existence of first-run theaters in major cities signified not only the increasing cultural legitimacy of film but its broad appeal.[58] Certainly, the newly built or renovated movie palaces had seating arrangements, as in nineteenth-century theaters partitioned into boxes, gallery, and balcony, that reinforced social distinctions. Specific showtimes meant less accessibility than continuous screenings at nickelodeons. Notwithstanding the preference of workers and immigrants for neighborhood venues, "high-class" theaters proved more accessible for them than other forms of middle-class culture. Granted, programs offered a selection of orchestral and vocal music that appealed to more educated listeners, but feature film, newsreels, educational footage, and comedies were hardly inaccessible to a younger generation of working-class and ethnic groups. As Richard Koszarski has pointed out, the diverse components of a balanced program at first-run theaters had more in common with vaudeville, initially a working-class and ethnic diversion, than with the legitimate theater.[59] Whether exhibited in movie palaces or neighborhood houses, feature film ultimately represented a form of expression that merged art and entertainment to exert an appeal transcending social barriers. What resulted was a shared cultural experience based to a significant extent on representations of genteel values that would become pervasive, even as the cultural distinctiveness of the middle class, especially its lower rungs, became tenuous in an age of mass culture. A contextualized reading of DeMille's early feature film adaptations therefore demonstrates how middle-class cultural practice became the basis for a redefinition of cinema as a democratic art form.

NOTES

I am grateful to James V. D'Arc at Brigham Young University; Jan-Christopher Horak (now in Los Angeles), Paolo Cherchi Usai, Edward E. Stratmann, and Becky Simmons at George Eastman House; and Ned Comstock at the University of Southern California for helping me with my research. I owe a special debt of gratitude to the late James Card, who showed me DeMille's films on so many occasions, and his colleague, the late George Pratt, for encouraging my research in silent film when there was little interest in the subject.

1. William deMille to Cecil B. DeMille, 3 September 1913, and William deMille to David Belasco, 25 July 1911, William deMille Papers, New York Public Library, Manuscripts and Archives Division; William deMille, *Hollywood Saga* (New York: E. P. Dutton & Co., 1939), 18. William, unlike Cecil, signed his last name with a lower case d.

2. Adolph Zukor, "Famous Players in Famous Plays," *Moving Picture World*, July 11, 1914, 186.

3. See A. Nicholas Vardac, *Stage to Screen: Theatrical Origins of Early Film: David Garrick to D. W. Griffith* (Cambridge, Mass.: Harvard University Press, 1949; New York: DaCapo, 1987); Rick Altman, "Dickens, Griffith, and Film Theory Today," *South Atlantic Quarterly* 88 (Spring 1988): 321–59. See also Tom Gunning, *D. W. Griffith and the Origins of American Narrative Film* (Urbana: University of Illinois Press, 1991); Gunning, "Weaving a Narrative: Style and Economic Background in Griffith's Biograph Films," *Quarterly Review of Film Studies* 6 (Winter 1981): 11–26. Charles Musser contests Gunning's argument regarding the industry's attempt to woo the middle class in "The Nickelodeon Era

Begins: Establishing the Framework for Hollywood's Mode of Representation," *Framework* 22/23 (Autumn 1983): 4–11. See also Musser, *The Emergence of Cinema: The American Screen to 1907* (New York: Charles Scribner's Sons, 1990); Musser with Carol Nelson, *High-Class Moving Pictures: Lyman H. Howe and the Forgotten Era of Traveling Exhibition, 1880–1920* (Princeton, N.J.: Princeton University Press, 1991). On the class composition of early film audiences, see Janet Staiger, *Interpreting Films: Studies in the Historical Reception of American Cinema* (Princeton, N.J.: Princeton University Press, 1992), chap. 5; Miriam Hansen, *Babel and Babylon: Spectatorship and Silent Cinema* (Cambridge, Mass.: Harvard University Press, 1991); Judith Mayne, "Immigrants and Spectators," *Wide Angle* 5:2: 32–40; Mayne, *Private Novels, Public Films* (Athens: University of Georgia Press, 1988); Charlie Keil, "Reframing the Italian: Questions of Audience Address in Early Cinema," *Journal of Film and Video* 42 (Spring 1990): 36–48; William Uricchio and Roberta E. Pearson, "'Films of Quality,' 'High Art Films' and 'Films de Luxe': Intertextuality and Reading Positions in the Vitagraph Films," *Journal of Film and Video* 41 (Winter 1989): 15–31; Uricchio and Pearson, *Reframing Culture: The Case of the Vitagraph Quality Films* (Princeton, N.J.: Princeton University Press, 1993); Roberta Pearson, "Cultivated Folks and the Better Classes: Class Conflict and Representation in Early American Film," *Journal of Popular Film and Television* 15 (Fall 1987): 120–28; Douglas Gomery, "Movie Audiences, Urban Geography, and the History of the American Film," *Velvet Light Trap* 19 (1982): 23–29; Robert C. Allen, "Motion Picture Exhibition in Manhattan, 1906–1912: Beyond the Nickelodeon," *Cinema Journal* 17 (Spring 1979): 2–15; reprinted in John L. Fell, ed., *Film Before Griffith* (Berkeley: University of California Press, 1983), 144–52; Allen, *Vaudeville and Film 1895–1915: A Study in Media Interaction* (New York: Arno Press, 1980); Russell Merritt, "Nickelodeon Theaters 1905–1914: Building an Audience for the Movies," in Tino Balio, ed., *The American Film Industry* (Madison: University of Wisconsin Press, 1975), 59–82; Garth S. Jowett, "The First Motion Picture Audiences," in John L. Fell, ed., *Film Before Griffith*, 196–206; Ben Singer, "Manhattan Nickelodeons: New Data on Audiences and Exhibitors," *Cinema Journal* 34 (Spring 1995): 5–35.

4. Jesse L. Lasky with Cecil B. DeMille, Agreement, October 16, 1913, DeMille Archives, Brigham Young University (hereafter cited as DMA, BYU).

5. Lawrence W. Levine, *Highbrow/Lowbrow: The Emergence of Cultural Hierarchy in America* (Cambridge, Mass.: Harvard University Press, 1988), 86, 23, 76, parts 1 and 2. Levine's argument is anticipated by Neil Harris (see note 6 below) and David Grimsted, *Melodrama Unveiled: American Theater and Culture, 1800–1850* (Chicago: University of Chicago Press, 1960; Berkeley: University of California Press, 1987, with an introduction by Levine). See also Paul DiMaggio, "Cultural Entrepreneurship in Nineteenth-Century Boston: The Creation of an Organizational Base for High Culture in America," *Media, Culture and Society* 4 (January 1982): 33–50.

6. Neil Harris, "Four Stages of Cultural Growth: The American City," in Arthur Mann, Neil Harris, and Sam Bass Warner, Jr., *History and Role of the City in American Life* (Indianapolis: Indiana Historical Society, 1972), 25–49; reprinted in Harris, *Cultural Excursions: Marketing Appetites and Cultural Tastes in Modern America* (Chicago: University of Chicago Press, 1990), 12–28. See also Dale A. Somers, "The Leisure Revolution: Recreation in the American City, 1820–1920," *Journal of Popular Culture* 5 (Summer 1971): 125–45.

7. Levine, *Highbrow/Lowbrow*, 76, part 3; Daniel Czitrom, *Media and the American Mind* (Chapel Hill: University of North Carolina Press, 1982), chap. 2; Joan Shelley Rubin, *The Making of Middlebrow Culture* (Chapel Hill: University of North Carolina Press, 1992), chap. 1; John S. Gilkeson, Jr., *Middle-Class Providence, 1820–1940* (Princeton, N.J.: Princeton University Press, 1986), chap. 6; Levine has been criticized for not taking into account the pervasive influence of Protestantism on American culture. See David D. Hall, "A World Turned Upside Down?" *Reviews in American History* (March 1990): 11–13.

8. Levine, *Highbrow/Lowbrow,* 221–22, part 3; John Higham, *Strangers in the Land: Patterns of American Nativism 1860–1925* (New Brunswick, N.J.: Rutgers University Press, 1955), 113–57. See also Barbara Miller Solomon, *Ancestors and Immigrants: A Changing New England Tradition* (Cambridge, Mass.: Harvard University Press, 1956; Boston: Northeastern University Press, 1989); David H. Bennett, *The Party of Fear: From Nativist Movements to the New Right in American History* (Chapel Hill: University of North Carolina Press, 1988).

9. See Robert Sklar, *Movie-Made America: A Cultural History of American Movies* (New York: Random House, 1975). Sklar argues that his work is still relevant in "Oh! Althusser!: Historiography and the Rise of Cinema Studies," *Radical History Review* 41 (Spring 1988): 10–35, reprinted in Sklar and Charles Musser, eds., *Resisting Images: Essays on Cinema and History* (Philadelphia: Temple University Press, 1990), 12–35. Donald Crafton and Janet Staiger disagree on early cinema audiences in a special issue of *Iris* (Summer 1990): 1, 24. See also Lary May, *Screening Out the Past: The Birth of Mass Culture and the Motion Picture Industry* (New York: Oxford University Press, 1980); Garth Jowett, *Film: The Democratic Art* (Boston: Little, Brown, 1976); Roy Rosenzweig, *Eight Hours for What We Will: Workers and Leisure in an Industrial City, 1870–1920* (Cambridge: Cambridge University Press, 1983); Francis G. Couvares, *The Remaking of Pittsburgh* (Albany: State University of New York Press, 1984); Elizabeth Ewen, *Immigrant Women in the Land of Dollars: Life and Culture on the Lower East Side 1890–1925* (New York: Monthly Review Press, 1985); Kathy Peiss, *Cheap Amusements: Working Women and Leisure in Turn-of-the-Century New York* (Philadelphia: Temple University Press, 1986). For an exchange between Sklar and May, see *American Historical Review* 86 (October 1981): 945–46; and 87 (June 1982): 913–15. Among other issues, they disagree about the argument in *Screening Out the Past* that the film industry was the "handmaiden of Progressivism." Rosenzweig and Couvares argue that far from exerting control over mass communications, upper- and middle-class reformers were displaced by the leisure industry. See also Nancy J. Rosenbloom, "Between Reform and Regulation: The Struggle over Film Censorship in Progressive America, 1909–1922," *Film History* 1 (1987): 307–25, and "Progressive Reform, Censorship, and the Motion Picture Industry, 1909–1917," in Ronald Edsforth and Larry Bennett, eds., *Popular Culture and Political Change in Modern America* (Albany: State University of New York Press, 1991), 41–60. On the issue of Progressivism, see Richard L. McCormick's assertion, "we cannot avoid the concept of progressivism—or even a progressive movement—because . . . after 1910, the terms were deeply embedded in the language of reformers," in his *Party Period and Public Policy: American Politics from the Age of Jackson to the Progressive Era* (New York: Oxford University Press, 1986), 269. See also Peter G. Filene, "An Obituary for the Progressive Movement," *American Quarterly* 22 (Spring 1970): 20–34; David M. Kennedy, "The Progressive Era," *The Historian* 37 (1975): 453–68; Daniel T. Rogers, "In Search of Progressivism," *Reviews in American History* 10 (December 1982): 113–32. Standard works on the Progressive Era include Richard Hofstadter, *The Age of Reform: From Bryan to F.D.R.* (New York: Alfred A. Knopf, 1955); Robert Wiebe, *The Search for Order 1877–1920* (New York: Hill & Wang, 1967).

10. See Deborah Anne Federhen, Bradley C. Brooks, Lynn A. Brocklebank, Kenneth L. Ames, and E. Richard McKinstry, *Accumulation and Display: Mass Marketing Household Goods in America, 1880–1920* (Wilmington, Del.: Union Press, 1986).

11. "Lasky and DeMille Enter Picture Field," *Motion Picture News,* December 20, 1913, 15.

12. Interview with Adolph Zukor, April 3, 1957, in Executives, Adolph Zukor folder, Personal: Autobiography files, DMA, BYU. Because box and folder numbers have been rearranged since I completed most of my research, I have not included that information. See James V. D'Arc, ed., *The Register of the Cecil B. DeMille Archives* (Provo, Utah: Brigham Young University, 1991). As for citations of interviews with DeMille, these ses-

sions were tape-recorded for an autobiography prepared by Art Arthur and Donald Hayne and published posthumously. Unlike the publication, the interviews provide more insight into the director's personality. Unfortunately, the transcripts were cut up and filed according to topics and therefore do not exist in their entirety. See James V. D'Arc, "'So Let It Be Written . . .': The Creation of Cecil B. DeMille's Autobiography," *Literature/Film Quarterly* 14 (1986): 1–9.

13. K. Owen, "The Kick-In Prophets," *Photoplay*, October 1915, in Cecil B. DeMille scrapbook, Robinson Locke Collection, Library and Museum of the Performing Arts, New York Public Library at Lincoln Center (hereafter cited as RLC, LMPA).

14. On auteurism, see John Caughie, ed., *Theories of Authorship* (London: Routledge & Kegan Paul, 1981); David Bordwell, *Making Meaning: Inference and Rhetoric in the Interpretation of Cinema* (Cambridge, Mass.: Harvard University Press, 1989), 151–65, passim; Roland Barthes, "The Death of an Author," in *Image-Music-Text*, trans. Stephen Heath (New York: Hill & Wang. 1977), 142–48; Michel Foucault, "What Is an Author?" in Donald F. Bouchard, ed., *Language, Counter-Memory, Practice*, trans. Donald F. Bouchard and Sherry Simon (Ithaca: Cornell University Press, 1977), 113–38; Andrew Sarris, *The American Cinema: Directors and Directions, 1929–1968* (New York: E. P. Dutton, 1968). Sarris ranks DeMille as a metteur en scène, as do French critics, rather than an auteur. See Jacques Second, "Les Livres," *Positif* 167 (March 1975): 86–87.

15. K. Owen, "Dustin Farnum," *Photoplay*, July 1915, 123; Johnson Briscoe, "Photoplays vs Personality: How the Identity of the Players is Fast Becoming Known," *Photoplay*, March 1914, 39.

16. "Lasky Films Coming Oscar Apfel to Direct Company Leaving for Pacific Coast Soon," *New York Dramatic Mirror*, December 10, 1913, 27; "Organize Lasky Forces," *NYDM*, December 17, 1913, 26; Robert Grau, *The Theatre of Science* (New York: Benjamin Blom, 1914), 165–66.

17. David Bordwell, Janet Staiger, and Kristin Thompson differentiate between cross-cutting and parallel editing in *The Classical Hollywood Cinema: Film Style and Mode of Production to 1960* (New York: Columbia University Press, 1985), 48. Eileen Bowser gives a history of editing terms in *The Transformation of Cinema 1907–1915* (New York: Charles Scribner's Sons, 1990), 58–59.

18. "The Squaw Man," *MPW*, February 28, 1914, 1068; "The Squaw Man," *NYDM*, February 25, 1914, 37; Kenneth MacGowan, *Behind the Screen: The History and Techniques of the Motion Picture* (New York: Delacorte Press, 1965), 163. The photo by J. A. Ramsey is reproduced in Paolo Cherchi Usai and Lorenzo Codelli, eds., *The DeMille Legacy* (Pordenone: Edizioni Biblioteca dell'Immagine, 1991), 36–37. According to James V. D'Arc, studio correspondence in the DeMille Archives attests that Apfel was highly valued in 1914 but posed unspecified "problems" in 1915.

19. Interview with DeMille, April 25, 1957, in Biography folder, Personal: Autobiography files, DMA, BYU; Beatrice DeMille, "The DeMille Family in Motion Pictures," *NYDM*, August 4, 1917, 4.

20. *Feet of Clay* folder, Personal: Autobiography files, DMA, BYU.

21. "Getting Belasco Atmosphere," *MPW*, May 30, 1914, 1271. Detailed descriptions of the staging of Belasco plays are in A. Nicholas Vardac, *Stage to Screen*; Lise-Lone Marker, *David Belasco: Naturalism in the American Theatre* (Princeton, N.J.: Princeton University Press, 1975). Significantly, Belasco does not acknowledge Buckland, who had been his pupil at the Lyceum Theatre School of Acting, later the American Academy of Dramatic Arts, either in his own writing, *The Theatre through Its Stage Door* (New York: Benjamin Blom, 1919), or in William Winter's two-volume biography, *The Life of David Belasco* (1918; reprint, Fairport: Books for Libraries Press, 1970).

22. Script of *The Cheat*, University of Southern California, Cinema-TV Library; Interview with DeMille, June 5, 1957, in Lighting folder, Personal: Autobiography files, DMA,

BYU. See Rudolf Arnheim, *Film as Art* (Berkeley: University of California Press, 1957), 65–73; Peter Baxter, "On the History and Ideology of Film Lighting," *Screen* 16 (Autumn 1975): 96–97; Bordwell, Staiger, and Thompson, *The Classical Hollywood Cinema,* 224–25; Lea Jacobs, "Lasky Lighting," in Cherchi Usai and Codelli, eds., *The DeMille Legacy,* 250–61. For a discussion of color tinting and toning, see Paolo Cherchi Usai, "The Color of Nitrate," *Image* 34 (Spring/Summer 1991): 29–38. Fittingly, when DeMille was made an honorary member of the Society of Motion Picture Art Directors, he claimed that his contribution lay in securing Buckland's talent for film production. (Wilfred Buckland folder, Personal: Autobiography files, DMA, BYU.)

23. DeMille to Lasky, June 7, 1916, in Jesse Lasky 1916 folder; DeMille to Arthur S. Friend, October 28, 1916, in Arthur S. Friend 1916 folder, Lasky Co./Famous Players-Lasky, DMA, BYU.

24. Interview with DeMille, April 25, 1957, in Biography folder, Personal: Autobiography files, DMA, BYU.

25. "Lasky Gets Belasco Plays," *MPW,* June 6, 1914, 1412; "Lasky's First Year," *MPW,* January 9, 1915, 674; Interview with DeMille, April 25, 1957, in Biography folder, Personal: Autobiography files, DMA, BYU.

26. "A New Outlet for Genius," *NYDM,* February 17, 1915, 23; *The Autobiography of Cecil B. DeMille,* ed. Donald Hayne (Englewood Cliffs, N.J.: Prentice-Hall, 1959), 106.

27. See cover, *MPN,* February 20, 1915; "More Belasco Plays by Lasky," *MPW,* March 25, 1916, 2035; "Close-Ups," *Photoplay,* July 1918, 75.

28. DeMille to Goldfish, July 23, 1914, DMA, BYU (Although Goldfish had not yet changed his name, I refer to him in the text as Goldwyn, as he was known for most of his career.); "Men Who Owe Success to the Movies," *Los Angeles Examiner,* July 2, 1916, in Cecil B. DeMille scrapbook, RLC, LMPA; "Lasky Views the Future," *MPW,* March 27. 1915, 1911.

29. "William C. DeMille with Lasky," *NYDM,* September 30, 1914, 25; William deMille to Anna deMille, October 16, 1914, William deMille cage file, LMPA.

30. "Lasky Scholarship for College Scenario Course," *MPN,* November 6, 1915, 76; "Lasky Company Offers Scholarship to Columbia Students," *MPW,* October 30, 1915, 765; William deMille to Anna deMille, October 16, 1914, William deMille cage file, LMPA; Lasky to Goldfish, October 11, 1915, and October 2, 1915, DMA, BYU. Although William deMille wrote satisfactory scripts, apparently he was not an able administrator. Lasky wrote to Goldfish, "We are preparing to let Billy direct . . . and if he doesn't make us a first class picture, we will put him back to writing but not to head the Department." Later, he stated more bluntly, "William was useless as head of the Scenario Department. " (Lasky to Goldfish, October 11, 1915, and October 25, 1915, DMA, BYU.)

31. DeMille to Arthur S. Friend, September 13, 1916, in Arthur S. Friend 1916 folder; Lasky to DeMille, September 14, 1916, in Jesse Lasky 1916 folder, Lasky Co./Famous Players-Lasky, DMA, BYU; Julian Johnson wrote in "The Shadow Stage" (*Photoplay,* December 1916, 83), "for months this fine studio . . . has sent out the dullest, most conventional plays." Johnson's observation supports Lasky's contention, "The real reason why Famous Players finally gave in to coming in with us on an even 50–50 basis was because they finally realized that they were in a hole regarding scenarios, stories and productions and could not keep up pace" (Lasky to DeMille, June 27, 1916, in Jesse Lasky 1916 folder, Lasky Co./Famous Players-Lasky, DMA, BYU); Jesse L. Lasky, *I Blow My Own Horn* (London: Victor Gallanez, 1957), 102; DeMille to Goldfish, September 17, 1914, DMA, BYU.

32. "Lasky Makes Radical Move," *NYDM,* July 1, 1916, 46; Lasky to DeMille, July 21, 1916, in Jesse Lasky 1916 folder, Lasky Co./Famous Players-Lasky, DMA, BYU.

33. Lasky to Goldfish, July 6, 1915, DMA, BYU.

34. Jesse L. Lasky, *I Blow My Own Horn,* 116.

35. "Feature Film," *MPN*, October 25, 1913,17; Leslie T. Peacocke, "The Practical Side of Scenario Writing," *Photoplay*, May 1914, 132.

36. Jesse L. Lasky, "Accomplishments of the Feature," *MPW*, July 11, 1914, 214. Garth Jowett argues in *Film: The Democratic Art* that "the development of film criticism, and the prominence given to film journalism of all types, was a major factor in the expansion of the industry by attracting a class of patrons curious to see this 'new art'" (98). See also Myron O. Lounsbury, *The Origins of American Film Criticism 1909–1939* (New York: Arno Press, 1973).

37. "The Squaw Man," *MPW*, February 28, 1914, 1068; William A. Johnston, "The Rose of the Rancho," *MPN*, November 28, 1914, 41; "What's His Name," *MPN*, November 7, 1914, 39; "Feature Films of the Week," *NYDM*, February 24, 1915, 29; "The Captive," *MPW*, May 1, 1915, 743; DeMille to Goldfish, July 23, 1914, DMA, BYU.

38. Vachel Lindsay, *The Art of the Moving Picture* (New York: Liveright, 1915). See Nick Browne, "Orientalism as an Ideological Form: American Film Theory in the Silent Period," *Wide Angle* 11 (October 1989): 23–31.

39. W. Stephen Bush, "Kindling," *MPW*, July 24, 1915, 655; "The Golden Chance," *MPW*, January 8, 1916, 255; *New York Dramatic News*, November 6, 1915, in Geraldine Farrar scrapbook, RLC, LMPA; Interview with DeMille, June 5, 1957, in Lighting folder; Interview with DeMille, July 3, 1957, in *The Warrens of Virginia* folder, Personal: Autobiography files, DMA, BYU; Margaret I. MacDonald, "The Director as a Painter and the Players His Colors," *NYDM*, January 14, 1914, 50.

40. Robert M. Crunden, *Ministers of Reform: The Progressives' Achievement in American Civilization, 1889–1920* (New York: Basic Books, 1972), chap. 4; James Lincoln Collier, *The Rise of Selfishness in America* (New York: Oxford University Press, 1991), chap. 2.

41. *Boston Transcript*, December 28, 1912; William deMille, "Speech before the Drama League at the Plymouth Theater," unidentified clipping; "You Can't Uplift the Drama," *New York Sun*, October 28, 1911, in William deMille scrapbook, RLC, LMPA; "The Heart and Soul of Motion Pictures," *NYDM*, June 12, 1920, in Cecil B. DeMille scrapbook, RLC, LMPA.

42. "Moving Pictures a Social Force," *MPN*, September 6, 1913, 15; MacDonald, "The Director as a Painter and the Players His Colors," 50; "Call of the North," *MPW*, August 22, 1914, 1080; "Close-Ups," *Photoplay*, June 1916, 63–64.

43. "Jesse L. Lasky in Pictures," *MPW*, January 3, 1914, 35; Lasky to Goldfish, January 14, 1915, DMA, BYU; Kenneth MacGowan, *Behind the Screen*, 166; Lasky, *I Blow My Own Horn*, 112. Interestingly, Lasky wrote to Goldwyn, "We have just decided to take Hector Turnbull off all writing entirely as his scenarios are not proving satisfactory, and instead, we are going to have him supply original ideas so that we will have plenty to choose from when we want plays for the other writers to prepare." (Lasky to Goldfish, October 19, 1915, DMA, BYU.)

44. Barbara Beach, "The Literary Dynamo," *Motion Picture Magazine*, July 1921, 54–55, 81.

45. William Ressman Andrews, "The Cheat," *MPN*, December 25, 1915, 127; "The Golden Chance," *NYDM*, January 29, 1915, 50; William deMille, *Hollywood Saga*, 139; Samuel Goldwyn, *Behind the Screen* (New York: George H. Doran, 1939), 82; Interview with DeMille, July 23, 1957, in *The Cheat, Chimmie Fadden, Chimmie Fadden Out West* folder, Personal: Autobiography files, DMA, BYU. According to DeMille, "Up to this time, foreign receipts would be $10,000 or $4,000—that sort of thing. . . . *The Cheat* did $41,000 foreign."

46. Cecil B. DeMille with Famous Players-Lasky Corporation, Cecil B. DeMille cage file, LMPA.

47. "The Motion Picture News Hall of Fame," *MPN*, December 30, 1922, 32. Also inducted were Adolph Zukor, Samuel Rothapfel, Mary Pickford, Charles Chaplin, Douglas Fairbanks, George Eastman, Thomas Edison, John D. Williams, Will Hays, and Carl Laemmle.

48. Staiger, *Interpreting Films*, chap. 5; Rosenzweig, *Eight Hours for What We Will*, chap. 8; Ewen, *Immigrant Women in the Land of Dollars*, chap. 12; Peiss, *Cheap Amusements*, chap. 6; Hansen, *Babel and Babylon*, chap. 2; Lizabeth Cohen, *Making a New Deal: Industrial Workers in Chicago, 1919–1939* (Cambridge: Cambridge University Press, 1990), chap. 3; Gunning, *D. W. Griffith and the Origins of American Narrative*, 256–57. On working-class cinema, see Kay Sloan, *The Loud Silents: Origins of the Social Problem Film* (Urbana: University of Illinois Press, 1988); Steven J. Ross, "Struggles for the Screen: Workers, Radicals, and the Political Uses of Film," *American Historical Review* 96 (April 1991): 336–67; Ross, "Cinema and Class Conflict: Labor, Capital, the State and American Silent Film," in Robert Sklar and Charles Musser, eds., *Resisting Images*, 68–107; Ross, *Working-Class Hollywood: Silent Film and the Shaping of Class in America* (Princeton, N.J.: Princeton University Press, 1998); Singer, "Manhattan Nickelodeons." See also Sumiko Higashi, "Dialogue: Manhattan's Nickelodeons," Robert C. Allen, "Manhattan Myopia; or, Oh! Iowa!" and Ben Singer, "New York, Just Like I Pictured It . . . ," *Cinema Journal* 35 (Spring 1996): 72–128. On modes of production and representation in relation to class, see note 3 above.

49. Douglas Gomery, "The Picture Palace: Economic Sense or Hollywood Nonsense?" *Quarterly Review of Film Studies* 3 (Winter 1978): 24–25. See also Gomery, *Shared Pleasures: A History of Movie Presentation in the United States* (Madison: University of Wisconsin Press, 1992), part 1.

50. *Cincinnati Inquirer*, December 6, 1908; *The Bookman*, 1911, in William deMille scrapbook, RLC, LMPA.

51. See Lise-Lone Marker, *David Belasco*, Introduction.

52. *Photoplay*, May 1918, 20–39; November 1914, 55–75; January 1915, 39–56.

53. Charles Musser challenges A. Nicholas Vardac's argument that stage melodrama could easily be adapted without dialogue for the screen in "The Nickelodeon Era Begins," 6.

54. See Rubin, *The Making of Middlebrow Culture*; Janice Radway, "The Scandal of the Middlebrow: The Book-of-the-Month Club, Class Fracture, and Cultural Authority," *South Atlantic Quarterly* 89 (Fall 1990): 703–36. See also Rubin, "Between Culture and Consumption: Mediations of the Middlebrow," in Richard Wightman Fox and T. J. Jackson Lears, eds., *The Power of Culture: Critical Essays in American History* (Chicago: University of Chicago Press, 1993): 163–94. Radway differentiates her study from Rubin's by asserting that middlebrow culture was "a separate aesthetic and ideological production constructed by a particular fraction of the middle class."

55. See Jowett's discussion of the rise of the star system, features, and movie palaces in *Film: The Democratic Art*, chap. 3; Richard deCordova, *Picture Personalities: The Emergence of the Star System in America* (Urbana: University of Illinois Press, 1990).

56. See Rosenzweig, *Eight Hours for What We Will*, chap. 8; Couvares, *The Remaking of Pittsburgh*, chap. 8; Ewen, *Immigrant Women in the Land of Dollars*, chap. 12; Peiss, *Cheap Amusements*, chap. 6; Gilkeson, Jr., *Middle-Class Providence*, chap. 6. See also note 3 above.

57. "William DeMille Talks on the Drama," *MPW*, October 9, 1915, 258; "Close-Ups," *Photoplay*, August 1915, 121.

58. L. C. Moon, "Statistics of the Motion Picture Industry," *MPN*, December 16, 1922, 3024. Exhibition statistics during the period 1916–1922 were considered relatively unchanged.

59. See Richard Koszarski, *An Evening's Entertainment: The Age of the Silent Feature Picture, 1915–1928* (New York: Charles Scribner's Sons, 1990).

Pearl Bowser
Louise Spence

Writing Himself into History: Oscar Micheaux

Oscar Micheaux (1884–1951) did not make it into Andrew Sarris's 1968 pantheon of great American film directors. But to many African Americans, he was a hero. Micheaux both provoked and capitalized on that reputation, using elements of his own life story to construct the legendary "Oscar Micheaux." In a filmmaking career that spanned thirty years, Micheaux made nearly forty movies, with more than half of his total output produced in the first decade (1918–1929).[1] His personal vision, the narrative and business strategies he chose to articulate that vision, and the historical and cultural context of his work intertwine in a dialectical relation to one another and tell us much about the construct "Oscar Micheaux." The three silent films now extant (*Within Our Gates* [1920]; *The Symbol of the Unconquered* [1920]; and *Body and Soul* [1925]), together with his novels, promotional materials, and correspondence, illuminate the degree to which Micheaux used his "biographical legend" (his socially constructed identity, political point of view, and status as African American entrepreneur) and authorial discourses within and among his texts to promote and shape the reception of his works.[2] Writing himself into history, Micheaux made expressive use of selected actual and imaginary events from his life in his films and novels. This strategy also gave credibility to his role as an entrepreneur and pioneer. During this first decade, Micheaux developed the public persona of an aggressive and successful businessman and a controversial and confident maverick producer. This image sustained him for the next twenty years, although little of his creative work after his first sound picture, *The Exile* (1931), would seem to justify it.[3] However, there were many contradictions in

From *Writing Himself into History: Oscar Micheaux, His Silent Films, and His Audiences.* © 2000 by Pearl Bowser and Louise Spence. Reprinted by permission of the authors and Rutgers University Press.

his struggles for power and autonomy, and in the complex psychological dynamic of being both entrepreneurial and oppositional at the same time.

The son of former slaves, Oscar Micheaux was the product of a generation of African American migrants searching for ". . . the freedom of life and limb, the freedom to work and think, the freedom to love and aspire."[4] The first of his seven novels, *The Conquest: The Story of a Negro Pioneer* (1913), written on the plains of South Dakota, tells of venturing forth from his home in southern Illinois in 1901, at the age of seventeen, in pursuit of a career. Heading north to Chicago, he supported himself at odd jobs: shining shoes, bailing water in a coal mine, laboring in a factory, the stockyards, and as a Pullman porter. While working as a porter, Micheaux was able to save enough money to set up an agrarian enterprise, a homestead on the Rosebud Reservation in South Dakota.[5] There, he taught himself the rudiments of Great Plains agriculture and, bent on disproving the widely-held belief that "the Negro," when faced with hardships of homesteading, would opt for the "ease and comfort" of the city, he worked hard to demonstrate to his white neighbors that he was an honest, hardworking man determined to succeed.[6]

After eight years homesteading, Micheaux became an author, publishing and marketing his own books. In 1918 an advertisement in *The Chicago Defender* for his semi-autobiographical third novel, *The Homesteader*, caught the attention of George P. Johnson, general booking manager of the Lincoln Motion Picture Company of Los Angeles, an African American concern which had by then already released three films. Johnson wrote Micheaux inquiring into the film rights to the book.[7] There followed a rapid exchange of correspondence between the two. While Johnson tried to convince Micheaux that he had more expertise in "the picture game" and promised to mold the book "into a first-class feature," Micheaux probed for information from the Lincoln Company, just as he had approached learning to farm by inquiring from others.[8] At the same time he asserted rather grandiosely that his 500-page novel warranted a big picture, at least six reels, not the Johnsons' usual two- or three-reel product. Micheaux was also apparently convinced that, far from being a detriment to profitability as Johnson feared,[9] the controversial nature of such themes as interracial marriage would be a very good selling device and should be exploited: "Nothing would make more people as anxious to see a picture than a litho reading: SHALL THE RACES INTERMARRY?"[10]

With no movie experience at all, Micheaux ultimately decided to produce *The Homesteader* himself, incorporating under the name of the

Micheaux Book and Film Company. Full of energy, enthusiasm, and optimism, he was able to convince many small investors in Iowa, Illinois, South Dakota, and Nebraska to buy shares in his newly incorporated company to make a Negro feature photoplay. Bragging to Lincoln that he was able to raise $5,000 in less than two weeks,[11] Micheaux went on to produce an eight-reeler, the longest African American film at that time. He advertised it as "Oscar Micheaux's Mammoth Photoplay," premiered it in Chicago's Eighth Regiment Armory on February 20, 1919, and declared that it was "destined to mark a new epoch in the achievements of the Darker Races."[12] The program included a patriotic short on the homecoming of "the 'Black Devils' who sent the Kaiser into oblivion," as well as a musical selection from "Aida" by the tenor George R. Garner Jr., and the Byron Brothers Symphony Orchestra playing music written by Dave Peyton.

His first ad for the film, a half page in the *Chicago Defender*, included his own photo along with those of the main performers and solicited support: "Every Race man and woman should cast aside their skepticism regarding the Negro's ability as a motion picture star, and go and see, not only for the absorbing interest obtaining herein, but as an appreciation of those finer arts which no race can ignore and hope to obtain a higher plane of thought and action." Such promotional material tells us a bit about the persona with which Micheaux confronted the world.

With the release of his first picture, Micheaux joined the growing number of small companies producing Black-cast films for African American audiences. By the end of 1920, he had moved to New York (still maintaining an office in Chicago), and had four features in circulation. In his silent films based on his own novels, his original scripts, and his adaptations of stories by C. W. Chesnutt, T. S. Stribling, Henry Francis Downing, and others, Micheaux endeavored to represent African American life as he saw it (his moral vision of the world) and to raise his audience's consciousness about social injustice. These films were known then as Race pictures, a term of pride that identified them as products generated by and for the community. Although "the community" may never have been as homogeneous as the discourses of the time implied, Race consciousness and racial identification were cohesive and binding forces and these movies were an articulation of self that challenged the dominant culture's ordering of reality.

An examination of Micheaux's films, letters, ads, and press coverage suggests that, in his silent movies, he persistently chose themes that were explosive in their time. By addressing such contemporary social issues as rape, concubinage, miscegenation, peonage, and lynching, he created a textured and expressive response to the social crises that circumscribed American Negro life. *Within Our Gates* (1920), for example, strips away the anonymity of the mob, exposing its members as ordinary townsfolk: men, women, and even children who participate in hunting down and lynching a Black family. *The Symbol of the Unconquered* (1920) reveals the economic underpinnings of the Ku Klux Klan. In *The Gunsaulus Mystery* (1921), a reworking of the Leo M. Frank case, a Black man is wrongfully accused in the murder of a white woman.[13] Promotion for *The Dungeon* (1922) touted the film as dealing with the then-pending Dyer Anti-Lynching Bill, and *The Brute* (1920) condemned racketeering and the abuse of women. Crossing the color line is the central theme of *The House Behind the Cedars* (1925); *Body and Soul* (1925) confronts hypocrisy and duplicity in the church; and racially restrictive real estate covenants are challenged in *Birthright* (1924).

As a Black filmmaker, Micheaux was constantly in conflict with the ruling hierarchy. His films generated heated debate and were subject to censorship by official censor boards, community groups, and individuals such as local sheriffs and theater owners.[14] But Micheaux was first and foremost a businessman. An assertive and enterprising salesman, he promoted himself to censor boards the same way he promoted himself to theater owners. In the letters that accompanied his applications for a license, he often tried to cajole the boards to move favorably on his submission and to impress them with the importance of his business. His letterhead during this period listed all the films he had in distribution and announced the Micheaux Film Corporation as "Producers and Distributors of High Class Negro Feature Photoplays."

Micheaux strove—with a sense of daring, optimism, and resolve—in a field filled with many imponderables. He pursued areas and opportunities considered closed to Negroes and was determined to succeed. Part of what intrigues us about Micheaux today is that, in spite of a less-than-privileged position and without the protections of post–New Deal and Civil Rights movement entitlements, he stood up to institutional barriers. He struggled not only for the advancement of the Race, but for changes within the system to make it more equitable. Like the "bruised speculator," Thomas W. Lawson, whose book, *Frenzied Finance*, Micheaux praised in his first novel, Micheaux wanted to reform the system to make it work for him.[15]

Although our research suggests that there was a social distinction between Micheaux and the intellectuals of the Harlem Renaissance—

Micheaux and his popular melodramas were either ignored or not taken seriously—he apparently felt a strong kinship with these artists. Sharing their belief that the Negro would gain acceptance once reasonable men saw that they were men of culture, strivers, and activists, he envisioned himself among those who worked for a better understanding between the races. He saw himself as progressive, an "active citizen" who embraced Booker T. Washington's ideal of pulling oneself up by one's own bootstraps as a concrete policy for "the uplift of the Negro" (what we would now call a pro-active stance). Micheaux contrasted this to what he saw as a more "reactionary" stance and criticized that "class of the negro race that desires ease, privilege, freedom, position, and luxury without any great material effort on their part to acquire it. . . ."[16]

Rather than holding on to "the time-worn cry of 'no opportunity,'" he urged his people to accept personal responsibility. For Micheaux, placing the blame on discrimination robbed individuals of the impetus, inspiration, and motivation to better themselves. This idealization of the individual was compatible not only with Washington's political philosophy, but also with Micheaux's use of melodrama. That is, his melodramas gave structure to the aspirations of the individual. His use of the genre's moral tableaux and moral certainties reiterated the ideals of the Protestant ethic: a faith in work, duty, and the redemption of the just and virtuous. In a telling note to C. W. Chesnutt, Micheaux suggested that the screenplay for his adaptation of *The House Behind the Cedars* make the blacksmith Frank more striving—in order to make Rena's affection for him more believable. "I would make the man Frank more intelligent at least towards the end of the story permitting him to study and improve himself, for using the language as he does in the story, he would not in anyway be obvious as a lover or that the girl could have more than passing respect for him."[17] Frank's self-improvement and industry elevate him from a minor role in the novel to a more exemplary status in the film, and render him a model hero, amazingly like Micheaux's own biographical legend. Rather than claiming to represent the political and social aspirations of the Negro, by necessity speaking for the majority, as many of the Black intelligentsia did, Micheaux felt that the majority needed models, heroes, to mold public opinion and for the elevation of public sentiment. In *The Homesteader*, the pioneer proposes that his people needed examples, "and such he was glad he had become."[18] Mildred Latham, the love interest of the homesteader, author, and itinerant book peddler in *The Forged Note*, admires the hero as "a Negro pioneer . . . [who would] blaze the way for others."[19]

The frontier, for Micheaux, was the mythic space of moral drama and the site of golden opportunities (seemingly free of the social arrangements and racial antagonisms of the rural South and the urban metropolis), where the characteristic model of economic expansion is entrepreneurship. His first novel, *The Conquest,* set in Gregory County, South Dakota, had celebrated enterprising individuals: homesteaders, merchants, bankers, and real estate dealers involved in commercial clubs, land booms, and speculation about the route of the railroad.

Convinced of the truthfulness of his own experience, Micheaux saw himself as a role model and as an instructive voice from within the Black community. In his desire to serve as an example for others, Micheaux highlighted certain aspects of his life, made artistic use of his personal history, and dramatized salient motifs. The hero of *The Symbol of the Unconquered,* Hugh Van Allen, a man of the frontier, self-willed and self-motivated, is a clear articulation of Oscar Micheaux's "biographical legend." Accumulating wealth through hard work and self-denial, he is almost a metaphor for the spirit of individualism. Other heroes not only embodied characteristics Micheaux saw in himself, but also undertook ennobling adventures that illuminate the ability of the individual to overcome adversities and achieve estimable accomplishments.[20] With such stories, Micheaux created a public persona that continues to exert influence today, even though many of his films are lost and forgotten. The construct "Oscar Micheaux" still speaks to us about racial identity, and the challenges of both inter- and intra-group differences and conflicts.[21]

However, Micheaux's racial uplift and impulse toward autonomous responsibility challenged white definitions of race without actually changing the terms. Some of his contemporaries—Sterling Brown, Langston Hughes, and Zora Neale Hurston, for example—questioned those terms, demanding new definitions of Race from within Black America. They saw themselves as reclaiming images of blackness, an attempt, as Alain Locke put it, to build Americanism on Race values.[22] Like them, Micheaux spoke as a Negro; the "blackness" of the author is a strong presence. He shared their optimism in spite of failed promises. But because of his sense of personal responsibility and uplift, he envisioned himself as an instructive voice and an empowering interpreter of Black life for the community. He took the position early in his career that a strong story and "accurate" depiction of Black life was what the public wanted. After only a year in the film business, he surmised that "the appreciation my people have shown my maiden efforts convince me that they want Racial photoplays depicting Racial life, and to that task I have consecrated my mind and efforts."[23]

––––––––

Micheaux saw his audience in the growing urban Black communities and in smaller towns in the South. Those populations were hungry for success stories and eager to see themselves in identifiable roles. In the beginning of his film career, Micheaux fought tenaciously to gain a foothold in those markets, aggressively selling the racial themes in his films. Although there were networks of picture houses catering to African American audiences in the cities, he formulated a distribution and exhibition strategy to create demand in smaller towns, offering to mail (without charge) heralds, imprinted with the theater name, address, and dates the films were to play, to every resident in the local directory. Describing his speciality as "Negro features," Micheaux promised to "work-up the interest" in the community by pursuing bookings "in all the worth while [*sic*] towns in [the] territory and then advertise the picture conspicuously in the daily papers. . . ."[24] It appears from the exhibition dates of the initial run of *The Homesteader* that this strategy was successful in the South.[25]

This bold newcomer was laying the cornerstone for a career. By launching *The Homesteader* in the *Chicago Defender*, with two-thirds of its circulation outside of Chicago, he was creating a mystique across the country around the exhibition of his movie.[26] Such tactics enabled the novice not only to attract new southern sites and notify patrons of specific show dates, but also to impress theater owners and potential investors in Chicago and other centers of capital. With his very first film, Micheaux presented himself as if he were an experienced distributor, confident and professional.[27]

Within a year and a half of premiering his first movie, Micheaux had three feature films in distribution, establishing his company as the top producing Black house in the country. A year later, in 1921, with five feature-length pictures produced, Micheaux's competitive instincts pushed him to describe his Chicago-based company in a stock offering as founded in 1913 (the year of his first novel), predating the competing Lincoln Motion Picture Company's 1916 founding by three years!

Micheaux saw his life as a parable, as living proof of what could be accomplished through hard work and industry. To himself at least, he now appeared as a "self-help hero" on two fronts: his success as a filmmaker and novelist established him as an exemplar businessman, and the success of his autobiographical films and novels refreshed and popularized his reputation as a pioneering African American homesteader. At the heart of this seemingly egocentric discourse was a call, implicit or explicit, for the transformation of the system of values that undermined self-confidence, opportunity, and the possibility of accomplishment.

Oscar Micheaux's films and novels were acts of recollection and imagination, creations and re-creations shaped by his personal experience and the desire to construct an image of himself for his audience. "[T]hat which any writer has been more closely associated with, are the things he can best portray," Micheaux wrote in the "publisher's" note to the reader in *The Homesteader.* "Oscar Micheaux has written largely along the lines he has lived, and, naturally of what he best knows." Suspended between autobiography and commerce, memory and dreams, his stories, though often personal, were not unique; they were woven with threads of commonality and communality. He spoke from his living history and from the specific realities of his time, pointed references to what lay beneath or beyond the particular.

However, the decision to work in the autobiographical mode—a form of personal and collective self-fashioning—may have been partially an economic decision. Whereas there were only a handful of commercially published African American novels in 1913, there had been a tradition of financially successful first-person narratives in early Negro literature.[28] Writing himself over and over again, Micheaux continued with variations on a successful formula—ebullient new tellings of a proven success. This pattern of recurrence and repetition, in which each telling is both familiar and new, was not uncommon in African American expressive culture, where retellings were often valued for their spontaneous inventiveness; by putting a new interpretation on a known story or tune, one left one's own stamp on the material.

———

As the management of his career demonstrates, Oscar Micheaux refused to dwell upon the depredations of racism or white America's moral and social corruption. He was committed to optimism and the uplifting of the Race, and believed in the work ethic and in the importance of the strength of character. But none of this precluded him from picturing scenes of tragic and frightening oppression in his films. There are contradictory, even multiple, Micheauxes even within the legend he built for himself.

The Micheaux writing from Gregory, South Dakota, in an article headlined "WHERE THE NEGRO FAILS," instructed his reader not to seek advice from "the average colored man around Chicago or . . . his brother porters or waiters. . . . Ask the president of the Saint Paul [rail]road or the president of the First National Bank or any other great man and see what they say."[29] But three years later, in a chapter of *The Conquest* also entitled, "Where the Negro Fails," Micheaux named muckrakers—Ida M. Tarbell, Ray Standard Baker, and Thomas W. Lawson—not the captains of industry, as worthy authorities.[30]

There is the Micheaux who was remembered by his sister-in-law and her husband as being a perfectionist and by one of his leading ladies as exacting;[31] upon the completion of his first scenario, he pronounced that he wanted to make his film "in every detail so absolutely perfect that the people in leaving the theatre will be compelled to say: 'My, but that was a wonderful picture.'"[32] And there is also the Micheaux who compromised his "perfection" when business called for it: the Micheaux who edited footage, without reshooting, in *The Symbol of the Unconquered*, even though the too-wide shot revealed that the rain hoses had hit only part of the barn. There is Micheaux-the-producer who praised *The Brute* as being "in a class by itself," but went on to note, "It has some faults—none of us have as much money to make the best picture we might think up, as fine as it should be in technical detail. . . ."[33] And there is the Micheaux who wrote to Charles W. Chesnutt expressing admiration for his novel *The House Behind the Cedars*, assuring the author it would be filmed "with the utmost care and the finest possible skill" but suggesting that it would be "much more profitable from a financial point of view" if the heroine did not die in the end.[34]

These multiple personas reveal much about how Oscar Micheaux worked. Because of the constraints confronting his filmmaking practice—financial, commercial, and political—he was constantly trying to maneuver within restricted circumstances. In *Symbol of the Unconquered*, for example, there are spectacular nighttime shots of the Klan's ride, shot with the natural light from their torches. Could those have been taken by the same camera operator who shot the awkwardly framed and lit woman running out of the barn at night? Some of Micheaux's aesthetics were certainly determined by his brisk production schedule (single takes, little time for rehearsals) and the limitations of his budget. But much might also have been driven by his own personal philosophy. In *The Conquest*, he writes that when he finally established a decent bank account, rather than inviting frivolity, he "put everything foolish and impractical entirely out of my mind, and economy, modesty and frugality became fixed habits of my life" (42). Perhaps he was also limited, even impatient, as a director. He seems to acknowledge his limitations in an appreciative letter about the performances in *The Brute*: "[T]he acting is so fine. To the Lafayette players I owe this. They were able to carry out my direction as fine as I knew how to give it to them."[35]

And then there was Micheaux's reluctance to delegate: he did everything himself. Certainly, this was partly because he lacked money to hire others, but he also seems to have wanted total control over his filmmaking enterprise, from script to advertising and distribution. Because of this mode of operation, in the late twenties he was still producing a handmade product in a period of increasing rationalized production in the rest of the film industry.

In the early 1940s, Oscar Micheaux left filmmaking behind temporarily and returned to writing, publishing, and selling his novels. Although these new works concerned Nazi spies and Communists rather than homesteaders, Micheaux once again inserted his own biographical legend into the plots. Sidney Wyeth, his surrogate in the novel *The Forged Note* and the film *The Gunsaulus Mystery*, appears again as the bookseller, writer, and former motion picture producer in two of Micheaux's 1940s fictions, *The Story of Dorothy Stanfield* and *The Case of Mrs. Wingate*.[36] A character in *The Story of Dorothy Stanfield* praises Wyeth for making photoplays "true to Negro life" and explains why this Micheaux-like figure gave up filmmaking. Suggesting it was difficult to make a profit with only a few hundred houses catering to the "colored trade," the character also tells of difficulty raising money and dealing with the partners that higher budgets necessitated (197–200). "Except for pictures made years ago, and which the theatres for colored people here in Memphis have played over and over again until, to me, they have long since become monotonous, we never see any Negro pictures in Memphis any more" (197).

The book also includes a character called Frank Knight, "A Negro author who married a white woman," a thinly veiled allusion to Richard Wright. Three characters compare Knight to Sidney Wyeth. First they praise Wyeth's *The Homesteader*, a "corking good story," singling out the book's discussion of Booker T. Washington, who "insisted our people actually do something and not just getting an education—then talking about it" (72). Though one character thinks Knight's books, *Nature's Child* and *Black Narcissus*, "very interesting," these works are ultimately found wanting. "I don't altogether like his pattern, but I suppose that it was, to some degree, laid out by his publishers," the character states. "Sidney

Wyeth seems to be the only Negro engaged in writing fiction, who is free and independent in what he writes. . . . He is about the only Negro author who writes about us colored people as we are living and thinking today; about the only writer who puts the love and the romance of our lives in his stories" (73). Questioning how white readers liked Knight's fiction, one character comments, "[I]t is so easy for white people to picture a Negro as unfortunate and hard up. It seems to be the condition they expect to find the Negro submerged in—poverty and misery" (81). Another character notes that publishers and the reviewers "have the race couched in a groove and seek to keep him in that groove as much as they can" (p. 74).

Micheaux's fifteen-page comparison of Wyeth with Knight points to the envy he must have felt over Richard Wright's success and the disappointment he must have experienced with his own lack of recognition and status. Interviewed in the *New York Amsterdam News* in the mid-1940s, Micheaux claimed to have made a good living, selling over 125,000 books during his thirty year career.[37] But these numbers paled compared to Wright's success. *Native Son*'s Book-of-the-Month Club selection and high sales (more than 200,000 copies in less than three weeks)[38] had become a symbol of what Micheaux had been unable to achieve after more than thirty years as a self-published writer.

Whether piqued by falling sales and/or the lack of critical attention to his novels, or merely once again promoting the controversial aspects of his work, Micheaux included a publisher's preface to *The Story of Dorothy Stanfield*, in which he claimed that his previous novel, *The Case of Mrs. Wingate*, had been ignored because he "dared reverse the old order, and recited in his book the case, based on fact, of a wealthy and aristocratic, but passionate, white girl who fell in love with a Negro youth. . . ." He went on to claim that in the past few years "especially since the rise of Communism in America, there has been an increased amount of race-mixing, mostly between white women and colored men. . . ." Further, "the publisher" asserts that "Race-mixing is not the theme of Mr. Micheaux's novels by any means, notwithstanding that here and there and now and then it happens to occupy a part in the development of his plots. The practice, as stated, is going on all over the North and is the subject of conversation and debate among Negroes the country over. So why does the great American press condemn Mr. Micheaux's books just because he chooses the facts to some degree and they exist? This is democracy and 'freedom of speech'—with a penalty!" Proud of writing commercial books for a popular market, Micheaux then lamented the lack of literary respect they were accorded.

But if he was combative, Micheaux was not dispirited: in the spring of 1947, seeing that his book business was declining, he began making movies again after a seven-year hiatus. Despite severe arthritis, he set to work once more on a "big picture," his last.[39] *The Betrayal* (1948), a three-hour epic, dealt with many of the potentially contentious themes of the more inflammatory early films.[40] Adapted from his 1943 novel, *The Wind from Nowhere, The Betrayal* reworked *The Homesteader* story, again recalling a past from which Micheaux was by then many years removed. Reasserting his biographical legend, he returned to his first majestic concerns: his life had become his life's work.[41] Instead of attacking discrimination directly, as Richard Wright, for example, had, Micheaux was once again constructing an enabling fiction in which good is beneficently rewarded. A Washingtonian morality continued to drive his stories to the end.

The world did not always conform to Micheaux's heroic image of himself. His work, like that of others, was inevitably constrained by the symbolic and material resources at his disposal; and, as an African American engaged in a capital-intensive culture industry, he faced special challenges. If he invented himself in opposition to some of his contemporaries, his lofty ambitions and high-minded ideals were sometimes in conflict with his own nature as well. Yet despite obstacles and contradictions, Micheaux managed to craft an authorial persona that sustained him over a long professional career. The rediscovery of his work in the 1990s testifies to the success of that endeavor and to the potency of the myth he created.

NOTES

1. Micheaux's work has aroused considerable critical interest during the last decade. Among the most notable of these new assessments is J. Ronald Green's *Straight Lick: The Cinema of Oscar Micheaux* (Bloomington: Indiana University Press, 2000), and *Oscar Micheaux and His Circle*, edited by Pearl Bowser, Jane Gaines and Charles Musser (Bloomington: Indiana University Press, 2001). The latter volume contains an exhaustive filmography and bibliography.

2. The term "biographical legend" is Boris Tomasevskij's [Tomashevsky]. He writes: "Thus the biography that is useful for the literary historian is not the author's curriculum vitae or the investigator's account of his life. What the literary historian really needs is the biographical legend created by the author himself." See "Literature and Biography" in *Readings in Russian Poetics: Formalist and Structuralist Views*, Ladislav Matejka and Krystyna Pomorska, eds. (Ann Arbor: University of Michigan Press, 1978), 55.

3. A previous film, *Daughter of the Congo*, 1930, was billed by Micheaux as a "talking, singing and dancing" picture; however, there was only one short sound sequence (*New York Age*, 4/5/30).

4. *The Souls of Black Folk*, in *W.E.B. Du Bois Writings*, Nathan Huggins, ed. (New York: The Library of America, 1986), 370.

5. *The Conquest*, (Lincoln, Neb.: The Woodruff Press, 1913), 47. Richard Slotkin (in *The Fatal Environment: The Myth of the Frontier in the Age of Industrialization, 1800–1890* [New York: Atheneum, 1985], 284–85) suggests that the Homestead legislation that divided Indian lands into homestead-type allotments was planned as both a safety valve for urban discontent and a way to integrate Native Americans into "civilized society" by making them into yeoman farmers. However, "unlike homesteading in the well-watered and forested Middle West, plains farming required considerable investment of capital and a larger scale of operations to make it profitable. . . . Indeed, the greatest beneficiaries of the Homestead legislation were railroad, banking, and landholding corporations; and thirty years after the first Homestead Act, land ownership in the Great Plains states was being steadily consolidated in fewer and fewer hands." Micheaux himself seldom mentions the Native American population. He seems to have shared the same willful self-deception that held the popular imagination of most of the rest of the non-Native population.

6. *The Conquest*, 145.

7. 5/7/18, George P. Johnson Negro Film Collection, Department of Special Collections, Charles E. Young Research Library, University of California, Los Angeles. Lincoln was founded in 1916 and incorporated in 1917.

8. See, for example, letters 5/13/18, 5/15/18, 5/31/18, and 6/25/18, George P. Johnson Collection, UCLA.

9. Johnson's brother and founder of the company, the actor Noble M. Johnson, had reviewed the novel and proposed that parts of it—the romance between the Black homesteader and his white neighbor, most likely—were too controversial for them to deal with, adding, "It is a little too advanced on certain subjects for us yet and unless we would change [it] so decidedly that it would hardly be recognizable, we could not expect much support from white houses." (Noble Johnson to George Johnson, no date [this letter seems to be the end of May, 1918, immediately before George Johnson's 5/31/18 letter to Micheaux] George P. Johnson Collection, UCLA.)

10. In a letter from Micheaux to the Lincoln Motion Picture Company, June 25, 1918, George P. Johnson Collection, UCLA; capitalization and punctuation thus in original. Micheaux certainly was cognizant of the public attention brought to the interracial marriage of the champion boxer Jack Johnson and the government's attempt to legally entrap him.

11. Oscar Micheaux to Clarence A. Brooks, 8/13/18, George P. Johnson Collection, UCLA. Most of the stock was sold in the Midwest. The offering budgeted $15,000 for the total cost of the film, including four prints, overhead, and advertising lithos. Interestingly, this was minimum amount suggested for a feature in 1917 articles in the fan magazine *Motion Picture Classic* and the trade paper *The Dramatic Mirror*. See Frederick James Smith's "The Cost of a Five-reel Photoplay," (*The Dramatic Mirror*, 7/7/17) and Jay Edwards's "Hustling for the 'Movie Fan'" (*Motion Picture Classic*, July 1917).

12. *The Chicago Defender*, 2/22/19.

13. Frank, a Jewish man convicted of the rape and murder of a young white woman, was lynched by a mob in Marietta, Georgia, in 1915.

14. For instance, one southern police official ordered a Race theater to discontinue showing *Within Our Gates* because, in his estimation, the lynching scenes would incite a riot. (Letter to Frank T. Monney, Superintendent of Police, from Theodore A. Ray, Captain, Special to the Superintendent, March 19, 1920, George P. Johnson Collection, UCLA). The Virginia State Board of Motion Picture Censors rejected the full version of *The House Behind the Cedars* for "presenting the grievances of the negro in very unpleasant terms and even touching on dangerous ground, inter-marriage between the races" (2/4/30, Commonwealth of Virginia, Department of Law, Division of Motion Picture Censorship, list of films rejected in toto since August 1, 1922, Virginia State Library and Archives, Richmond). In his 1925 review of *The House Behind the Cedars*, the board's chair, Evan Chesterman, wrote that

the film "contravenes the spirit of the recently enacted anti-miscegination law which has put Virginia in the forefront as a pioneer in legislation aimed to preserve the integrity of the white race." In liberal New York State the state censor board forced Micheaux to cut four of the nine reels of *Body and Soul* in order to show the film.

Birthright, in particular, faced daunting censorship challenges. When Micheaux presented the film to the Maryland State Board of Motion Picture Censors, the board demanded twenty-three eliminations. Even though the film was based on a popular novel (*Birthright* [New York: The Century Company, 1922]) by T. S. Stribling, a white southerner, the board found objectionable scenes and intertitles in all but two of the ten reels. They were particularly offended by suggestions of miscegenation, the questioning of white authority, and the depiction of racist attitudes of whites in the everyday interactions between the races. (The Black press noted how closely the film followed the book. See, for example, *New York Age,* 1/19/24: "In adapting the story for the screen, Mr. Micheaux followed the book very closely, even using in the [intertitles] the identical language contained therein"; in a similar vein, D. Ireland Thomas wrote in the *Chicago Defender,* "Mr. Micheaux is not the author of *Birthright*. He is not responsible for the bad language used in the production. He filmed the production as the author wrote it" [10/24/24].) When Micheaux showed *Birthright* in Baltimore without making all the cuts, the print was confiscated. (Maryland State Board of Motion Picture Censors, List of Eliminated Films, Week ending January 26, 1924; letter, Micheaux to Virginia State Board of Censors, 10/14/24, both, Virginia Division of Motion Picture Censorship, Virginia State Library and Archives.) In Virginia, he deliberately ignored the jurisdiction of the State Board of Censors and affixed a bogus seal from another picture on a print of *Birthright*. The movie played at the Attucks Theatre in Norfolk, the Idle Hour in Petersburg, the Dixie in Newport News (and perhaps others) before the censor board found out. This set off a flurry of activity around the state with the board corresponding with mayors, chiefs of police, and theater owners, as well as a network of informants, to prevent future screenings. ("Correspondence Regarding Controversial Pictures, 1924–1965," Virginia Division of Motion Picture Censorship, Virginia State Library and Archives.) Although the board had not examined the film, they sent letters saying that *Birthright* was "a photoplay released by a negro concern which touches most offensively on the relations existing between whites and blacks." (See, for example, letter from E. R. Chesterman, Virginia State Board of Censors, to C. C. Collmus, Jr. of Norfolk, 2/28/24, Virginia Division of Motion Picture Censorship, Virginia State Library and Archives.) Micheaux made a sound version of the film in 1939.

15. The apt description of Lawson as a "bruised speculator" is Richard Hofstadter's in *The Age of Reform* (New York: Vintage Books, 1955, 195). Micheaux praised Lawson's 1906 book in *The Conquest,* 142.

16. *The Conquest,* 250.

17. Letter, Oscar Micheaux to C. W. Chesnutt, 1/18/21, Charles W. Chesnutt papers, Western Reserve Historical Society, Cleveland, Ohio; the extant version of the sound remake, *Veiled Aristocrats,* suggests that Micheaux, in the sound version at least, did make the changes in the character.

18. 147.

19. (Lincoln, Neb.: Western Book Supply Company, 1915), 48.

20. The central character of his film, *The Millionaire* (1927), for example, is a soldier of fortune, "a man who as a youth possessing great initiative and definite objectives, hies himself far from the haunts of his race" to the pampas of South America, the "wild, billowy plains of The Argentine," and returns to the community as a rich man (clipping, the *Chicago Bee,* n.d., courtesy Grace Smith). In his autobiographical sketch on the flyleaf of one edition of his 1917 novel *The Forged Note,* Micheaux describes himself as "Young, courageous, persistent in a contention that the Negro did not put forward the effort he could and should,

from an industrial point of view, for his ultimate betterment . . ." (edition in the Schomburg Center for Research in Black Culture, New York City).

21. See, for example, the article by Garland L. Thompson on the Commentary page of the April 13, 1991 *Baltimore Sun* discussing *New Jack City* and *The Five Heartbeats* in the context of Micheaux's career, and Carl Franklin's homage to Micheaux in *Devil in a Blue Dress* (1995). There was also a lively debate on Micheaux's life and films during a panel discussion on "Mainstreaming Independent Film" at the February 1990 annual conference of the College Art Association among filmmakers Isaac Julien and Arthur Rogbodiyan [Arthur Jafa], and *City Sun* critic Armond White.

22. *The New Negro: An Interpretation.* (New York: A. and C. Boni, 1925), 12.

23. Quoted in the *Chicago Defender*, 1/31/20.

24. Micheaux Book and Film Co., Inc., open letter to exhibitors, March 1919, George P. Johnson Collection, UCLA.

25. On a personal trip, Micheaux was able to book what he advertised as a "Great Southern Tour" in May, June, and July of 1919, with a week in New Orleans and one- to three-day runs in Louisville, Kentucky; Pensacola, Florida; Nashville, Chattanooga, and Memphis, Tennessee; Florence, Sheffield, Decatur, Birmingham, Bessemer, Mobile, and Montgomery, Alabama; Shreveport, Alexandria, Monroe, and Baton Rouge, Louisiana; Spartanburg, Columbia, and Greenville, S.C. ; Macon and Atlanta, Georgia; Reidsville and Durham, N.C. He advertised the tour in the *Chicago Defender* by calling it the "longest picture engagement in the history of the South" (the *Chicago Defender*, 5/31/19).

26. Besides enjoying a wide readership in Chicago, the *Defender* was influential in the South, distributed along the route of the Illinois Central Railroad System and other lines passing through the nation's rail hub, with railroad personnel often acting as publicists and distributors of the paper. See James R. Grossman, *Land of Hope: Chicago, Black Southerners, and the Great Migration* (Chicago: University of Chicago Press, 1989), 66–81.

27. Micheaux promoted the "uniqueness" of *The Homesteader* by announcing in the ads that "Negro Productions such as this are restricted . . . to Negro Theaters and cannot be booked through regular exchanges on the usual basis" and insisting that the film would never be shown for less than a twenty-five cent admission price. On this tour, the Micheaux Book and Film Company received a percentage of the ticket price while building a market and charting new territories for Race movies. After only a little more than six months of distributing films in the South, in the first three months of 1920, he was able to book one- and two-day runs in twenty-six sites in North and South Carolina, and Georgia alone for *Within Our Gates.* (For a list of venues and dates, see Bowser, Gaines, and Musser, *Oscar Micheaux and His Circle*, 234–35.) While the film netted $150 in a one-day rental in Altanta, the firm only took in $35.90 for two days in Sandersville (ledger, African Diaspora Images, Brooklyn, New York). Later that year, five of the nine prints of *The Brute* were "working" in the South two months after the film's debut. (Letter Swan Micheaux, General Manager, Micheaux Film Corporation to George P. Johnson 10/27/20, George P. Johnson Collection, UCLA.)

28. The best known of these, *The Autobiography of an Ex-Colored Man*, was not revealed as fiction until 1927. See Donald C. Goellnicht, "Passing as Autobiography: James Weldon Johnson's *The Autobiography of an Ex-Coloured Man*," *African American Review* 30:1 (Spring 1996): 18.

29. The *Chicago Defender*, 3/19/10.

30. 142–43.

31. Fred and Blanche Crayton, Oscar Micheaux's brother-in-law and sister-in-law, interviewed by Pearl Bowser, 8/10/75, Chicago; Edna Mae Harris, interview, 1/8/91, for the film *Midnight Ramble: Oscar Micheaux and the Story of Race Movies* (Bester Cram and Pearl Bowser, 1994).

32. Letter, Micheaux to Clarence A. Brooks, 9/13/18, George P. Johnson Collection, UCLA.

33. Letter, Micheaux to George P. Johnson, 8/14/20, George P. Johnson Collection, UCLA.

34. 1/18/21, Charles W. Chesnutt papers, Western Reserve Historical Society, Cleveland, Ohio.

35. Letter, Micheaux to George P. Johnson, 8/14/20, George P. Johnson Collection, UCLA. The Layfayette Players advertised as being in *The Brute* were Evelyn Preer, A. B. De Comathiere, Susie Sutton, Lawrence Chenault, and Alice Gorgas.

36. *The Case of Mrs. Wingate* (New York: Book Supply Company, 1945); *The Story of Dorothy Stanfield* (New York: Book Supply Company, 1946).

37. Quoted in Henry T. Sampson, *Blacks in Black and White: A Source Book on Black Films*, 2d ed. (Metuchen, N.J.: Scarecrow Press, 1995), 166.

38. Michel Fabre, *The Unfinished Quest of Richard Wright* (New York: William Morrow, 1973), 180.

39. Described as such in a letter from Mrs. Oscar Micheaux (Alice B. Russell) to Micheaux's sister, Ethel, January 7, 1948, quoted in Richard Grupenhoff's "The Rediscovery of Oscar Micheaux, Black Film Pioneer," *Journal of Film and Video* 40:1 (Winter 1988).

40. The film's premiere in New York City ran 183 minutes, cut down from 195 minutes (*Variety*, 6/30/48).

41. "Your next book should be an autobiography," Deborah, the love interest, tells the hero, "Martin Eden, young Negro man of Conquest, who built an agricultural empire in the Dakota wilderness." (*The Betrayal*, dialogue sheet, New York State Archives, Albany, New York).

David E. James

The Filmmaker as Poet:
Stan Brakhage

Despite a continuing abstract, plastic tradition, the postwar American avant-garde film was most commonly understood in the fifties and sixties through analogies with poetry. From the arguments made by Maya Deren at the Cinema 16 symposium on "Poetry and the Film" in 1953 through the early taxonomies of Jonas Mekas and P. Adams Sitney, the virtual congruency of the "experimental film" with the "film poem" bespoke their ancestry in Symbolism and French Surrealism.[1] When in 1957 Hans Richter argued a distinction between "the entertainment film as 'novel'" and "the exploration into the realm of mood, the lyrical sensation as 'poetry,'" and expressed a desire to "call all experimental films 'film poetry,'"[2] he was voicing a set of terminological equivalences that had been commonplace for a decade in the reception of experimental films made by Maya Deren, Kenneth Anger, Curtis Harrington, Ian Hugo, Willard Maas, Gregory Markopoulos, Sidney Peterson, and Stan Brakhage.

At the Cinema 16 symposium, for example, Parker Tyler noted two groups of "poetical expression": "the shorter films that concentrate on poetry as a visual medium . . . a surrealist poetry of the image," such as *Blood of a Poet, Andalusian Dog,* and *Lot in Sodom;* and the films that develop "poetry as a visual-verbal medium," including those of Jean Vigo, Peterson, Maas, Hugo, and Sergei Eisenstein.[3] Maya Deren, her own work already influential, attempted a more restrictive distinction, arguing that the "poetic construct arises from the fact, if you will, that it is a 'vertical' investigation of a situation, in that it probes the ramifications of the moment," as distinct from the "horizontal" construction of drama.[4] When challenged, she reformulated her distinction between vertical and horizontal as one between lyric and narrative, and argued that the specificity of film poetry lay in the metaphoric elaboration of discrete incidents rather than the continuously unfolding linear action of the feature film.

Recalling formalist models of how poetic language makes itself visible against a background of automatized, standard prose by foregrounding the devices of its own production, such binaries also had evaluative capacities. Privileging metaphor over metonymy and paradigm over syntagm, they justified the poetic film's density and intensity, its difficulty and its cavalier unconcern with filmic illusion. All of these were taken as a function of a lyric expressivity that marked it as a purer art and elevated it over commercial narrative drama. The argument was idealist, both in asserting a trans-historical essence of poetry and in phrasing that essence in formal terms, and consequently Deren and her successors reproduced the poetics dominant at the time, the high modernist moment of Romanticism. References to T. S. Eliot and Ezra Pound punctuated the symposium and subsequent theorizing, with Pound's concepts of Imagism and Vorticism used to facilitate comprehension of the nonnarrative organization of diegetically disarticulate images.

Stan Brakhage's singular assertion of the primacy of vision—his commitment to letting "the *prima materia* of film, the Visual, constitute its own 'story'"[5]—produced one of the most rigorously coherent filmic essentialisms. Nonetheless, he fits comfortably into this general field, and it supplies the terms of his formal accomplishment. There are parallels between his fragmented screen space and the visual field of abstract expressionism that also locate him in the post–Len Lye painterly tradition, and he found models of composition in music from Bach to Messiaen and Cage; but he has been especially responsive to contemporary poets. Gertrude Stein, Ezra Pound, Charles Olson, Louis Zukofsky, Robert Duncan, Robert Creeley, Robert Kelly, Edward Dorn, and Michael McClure all featured prominently in his attention, and all except Stein and Pound figured in his life. The formal qualities of his prolific writing and talking, by and large also those of his films, are recognizably the formal qualities of modernist poetry. His use of repetitions, puns, and other tropes to destabilize language, even within the frame of the syllable, is clearly in the post-Stein tradition. He has designated parts of his work in literary terms, and his magnum opus was to have been *The Book of the Film*. His major exegete defined the phases of his work as "lyrical" and "mythopoeic,"[6] terms drawn from poetics. And initially Brakhage understood his filmmaking as the material form of his activity as a poet: "Like Jean Cocteau, I was a poet who also made films."[7] Despite the almost complete exclusion of verbal language from his films, these metaphors tie his work to a conception of the self and its negotiation in cultural practice whose prototypical manifestation occurred at the inauguration of the modern period in the response of poets to the industrial revolution.

The English Romantic poets conceptualized the individual's imagination as the mediator between consciousness and nature, and also the location of all aesthetic, spiritual, and social values. Registering the social changes of late eighteenth-century industrialization and especially marking a shift from the overt didacticism and ethical orientation of Neoclassic poetics, this apotheosis of the imagination that set the paradigms of modernism into play also framed the alienation of the modern poet. Displaced from a praxis within a corroborative community environment, whether of the village, the church, or the court, poets now had to confront the reification of their art as it took the form of one more commodity in a competitive marketplace. Compounded by the difficulty of sustaining utopian republican aspirations after the failure of revolutionary movements throughout Europe, this social dislocation led poets to scrutinize their consciousness and to elevate the drama of that scrutiny into an end in itself, the essential function of art. Where any general social effectiveness could be envisioned, it was supposed to follow from the renovation of the individual imagination in the experience of poetry.

Variously dressed, this projection supplied the liberal tradition its critical posture against the dehumanization of capitalism and the industrialization of consciousness. By the twentieth century, the presupposition of the primacy of the imagination and the individual creative act had been so thoroughly internalized that it appeared the natural condition of art; its invisibility as ideology set the stage for a theology of art as expanded consciousness that delegitimized concern with the conditions of its material production and social uses. Reaching its apogee in the confessional investigation of private neurosis, the intense inwardness of most postwar American poetry documents sensibility adrift without recourse to a public language or certainty of an audience, the former having seeped away in the jargons of politics and advertising and the latter almost entirely conditioned by the communication and entertainment industries.

The analogy between the Romantic poet and the avant-garde filmmaker first becomes fully visible in the formal elaboration of "poetics in the field of the visual"[8] by Brakhage and others. These formal parallels between poetry and experimental film reflect a more fundamental similarity in their respective social dislocations. In the modern world, *poetry* designates a preferred medium, but it also implies a mode of social marginality or exclusion. It bespeaks a cultural practice that, in being economically insignificant, remains economically unincorporated and so retains the possibility of cultural resistance. For poets in both words and film, the hyperbolic invocations of ultimate value that arc from Shelley's celebration of the poet as "the happiest, the best, the wisest and the most illustrious of men" compensate for an institutional and social neglect. But the void of functionlessness they confront, so palpably dissimilar from the context of artists in other mediums, may still be the space of negation. This possibility informs Brakhage's radical reaction, his attempt to bring film into the tradition of cultural practices whose supersession is summarized by the capitalist commodity cinema: Hollywood.

Before the forties no sustained tradition of filmmaking in the United States existed to provide an independent filmmaker who understood his or her work as Art—as an end sufficient to itself rather than as a means of entry into the studio industry—with a model of production methods and a theory of his or her social role.[9] Both were supplied by Maya Deren; her installation of the filmmaker as a *poet* had, then, both theoretical and practical components. It involved the conceptualization of the film artist as an individual author, a Romantic creator—a conceptualization made possible by manufacturing a tradition of such out of previous film history; and it necessitated a working organization, a mode of production and distribution, alternative to the technology, labor practices, and institutional centrality of Hollywood.

Following Deren's lead, Brakhage's innovations in none of these respects was entirely unique or original; rather, his singular importance derives from the extremes to which he pushed in each area and from the integrity with which he maintained their interdetermination. Anchored ideologically and aesthetically at the center of Romantic idealism, he reproduced it in an interdependent array of film styles, a mode of film production, and a projection of the film artist's social function. In his domestic, artisanal production, he materialized a theory of film as an entirely personal activity, erupting like Romantic poetry from a spring that is at once biological and quasi-divine. All of these aspects of his career are essentially homologous, each the others' precondition and effect, and the practice he developed was so totalized that it was virtually seamless. Each aspect of his intervention, from the style of the films to their international ramifications, articulates the others. This, the reticulated, autotelic integrity of his aesthetic, is the condition of Brakhage's singular achievement; it also predetermines his limitations.

Three years after his first film, *Interim* (1952), Brakhage's work seemed "to be the best expression of all the virtues and sins of the American film poem today."[10] Like the film poems of his predecessors, Deren, Anger, Markopoulos, and Harrington, Brakhage's early films retarded narrative action by metaphoric interpolations that elaborate character and mood. Accompanied by spatial distortions of the visual field, such temporal aberrations were cued by a dominant structural motif, derived from the surrealists and expressionists (though also common in the contemporaneous film noir), the use of a distressed protagonist whose subjective experience the visual field more or less closely reproduced. The increasing congruence of the protagonist's vision with the filmmaker's in these "trance" films,[11] soon allowed Brakhage his crucial shift to an entirely first-person camera, and it encouraged his understanding of filmic subjectivity in general. The discovery that film could accommodate authorial psychodrama made it possible for him to reread film history for his own purposes. Prefiguring the *politique des auteurs*, but in terms derived from surrealism, he discovered an avant-garde tradition of personal films made by obsessive individual stylists supposedly uninfluenced by their historical contexts—primarily the prewar classic European directors, and then the postwar American independents.

The organization of such a lineage eventually supplied a justifying vector for Brakhage's work on two levels. First, it allowed him to understand his own use of the medium for interior investigation as properly traditional. Hence Brakhage would inevitably understand the history of cinema as the refraction of the lives of its avatars, and his book *Film Biographies* would show the canonical directors using the medium to come to grips with psychic trauma. Their narratives all engage not a historical situation or a social function, but rather some kind of demon, usually of a psychosexual origin: Méliès as a magician trying to find a heroine who will restore his psyche, which was shattered by prenatal trauma; Griffith fulfilling his destiny to right all wrongs under the mental guidance of his sister, Mattie; Dreyer searching out "the demon-of-himself"; and even Eisenstein fighting the animal that had ravaged his personal being in the womb.[12] Second, it allowed Brakhage to claim the authority of a tradition of film practices, however dissimilar from those of the contemporary commercial cinema, as the matrix of his own style.

My big problem has been, all these years, that no one has recognized that I (and all my contemporaries) are working in a lineal tradition of

Méliès Griffith, Dreyer, Eisenstein, and all the other classically accepted film makers. . . . I took my first cues for fast cuts from Eisenstein, and I took my first sense of parallel cutting from Griffith, and I took my first sense of the individual frame life of a film from Méliès, and so on.[13]

Brakhage's reading of this tradition completely elided methods of production, except insofar as studio mechanisms or other bureaucratic controls were seen to inhibit the creative genius of the filmmaker. The tradition could, then, supply a lineage for his own stylistic practice and intended use of the medium, but not a model of how a contemporary filmmaker, similarly seeking to chart the depths of his own psyche, could organize the necessary social and technical resources. None of the directors he considered worked inside the studio system proper, and not since RKO's difficulty with Orson Welles and the financial failure of *Citizen Kane* had any American studio allowed the degree of authorial power he envisaged. Though independents in the late fifties considered varying degrees of affiliation with and aspiration toward the industry, after the early sixties the Underground accepted an uneasy coexistence with Hollywood.

Brakhage adopted this position. He understood Hollywood not as a competitor or threat, but as an entirely separate enterprise, except insofar as the hegemonic system was taken as coextensive with the medium per se. A co-founder of the Film-Makers' Cooperative in 1962 and a member of the selection committee of Anthology Film Archives, he participated actively in the Underground cinema, as well as in the peripheral support systems of museums, colleges, and film societies, and he depended financially on independent distribution. However, his relationship with the alternative cinema was always checkered, ruptured again and again by personal quarrels and policy disagreements. These altercations became especially violent with the politicization of the counterculture in the late sixties, when he withdrew his films from the Coop for a period and resigned from the Archives. Brakhage was prominent and even notorious in the Underground; *Desistfilm* was "the first important beatnik film with the air of a spontaneous Happening,"[14] and by the mid-sixties his style was virtually a synecdoche for the counterculture at large. But in almost as many ways as he embodied the Underground, he rejected it.

Brakhage's social and aesthetic distance from the bohemian Underground jelled when almost simultaneously he discovered his mature filmic mode and began a family. After the winter of 1959, when the family moved to a nineteenth-century log cabin in the Rockies behind Boulder, he was at once geographically and culturally remote from the bohemian enclaves in which his art had developed. He did, of course, maintain personal connections with other Underground filmmakers and with his audience, invigorating them by his frequent presentations of new work and eventually by his teaching, and his necessary recourse to film stock and laboratories also ensured his connections with the corporate state. But otherwise it was in isolation from mass society that he discovered his life's work. His importance for the modern cinema is inseparable from his removal from it. In the blankest rejection of the history of the medium, he made home movies his essential practice of film.

Prefiguring a decade when such rustications would acquire increasing cultural authority, Brakhage's retreat to the Colorado wilderness imitated a primary Romantic strategy: Thoreau's, of course, but more appositely Wordsworth's removal to Grasmere, 150 years before, with the social microcosm of his sister, Dorothy, and the poet Coleridge. Defeated by the modern world, he there discovered the restorative trinity of nature, the domestic circle, and art itself. Similarly defeated, in the mountains Brakhage felt most free from the anxieties of history and urban life, free to recreate the Wordsworthian paradigm in the cycles of nature. This ideal of an anti-technological, organically human, domestic cinema, entirely separate from rather than oppositional to Hollywood, circumscribed Brakhage's life and art and the peculiarly integral relation between them. If the move and the marriage did not solve the traumas of his youth—the idiotoxic illness, the search for a community of artists, and the sexual hunger that fuels *Desistfilm, Reflections on Black,* and the other melodramas of the fifties—they did provide a relatively stable social situation and a vocabulary of human relationships in which these traumas could be investigated.

Inevitably, then, Brakhage's perception of his wife, children, or pets in their mountain home preoccupy his art. They are the vehicle, or rather the instances, of his most fundamental concerns: "birth, sex, death, and the search for God."[15] As it does in respect to the attainment of first-person vision, *Anticipation of the Night* (1958) marks this transition, even though Brakhage's expectation of his own death was almost fulfilled in the near suicide that it took to finish it. Its shooting coincided with the breakup of Brakhage's previous engagement and his meeting with Jane Collum, and he edited it during the first month of their marriage. The subsequent films of 1959–1961 represent Brakhage's attempt to engage the primary events of natural life: birth, in the films about the birth of their first and third children, *Window Water Baby Moving* and *Thigh Line Lyre Triangular;* sex, in the erotic films of the newlyweds, like *Wedlock House: An Intercourse;* and death, in *Sirius Remembered* and *The Dead.* All the concerns of these films and the stylistic innovations developed in them culminate in the cosmic reach of *Dog Star Man* (1961–1964). In this film, the rhyming superimposition of the medical and astronomical imagery figures a projection of the biological onto the metaphysical that also includes everything visible in between.

In these and subsequent films, Brakhage used the medium to attend to what he saw in his daily life, and to document the crises of biological cycles rather than to fabricate fictions of history—"sharing a sight" rather than "showing sights."[16] But his fundamental innovation was in the sphere of production: he rejected the alienated labor of an industrial career in which work in film could at best have financed a life outside it. When his project was understood simply as style or subject matter, as films separate from the cinema they implied, it was inevitably misread, most egregiously, of course, as pornography. By becoming an amateur, one who, according to a favorite pun that he derived from Maya Deren, did it for love, not money, he made filmmaking the agency of his being. Bridging the aesthetic and the existential, film became coextensive with his life, simultaneously his vocation and avocation, his work and play, his joy and terror—as integral as breathing.

The films about birth, sex, and death have a cinematic significance even beyond their status as meditations on the biological processes of life: the domestication of cinema allowed its radical incorporation into life's most crucial transactions. If in telling its own story the visual tells all others, the exchange of vision between people becomes the means of social interaction; and so film—a means of seeing—becomes not just an instrument of personal documentation, or yet simply the means by which a subjectivity may be documented, but also the vehicle of a relationship's practice. The sign of intimacy becomes the medium of intimacy; the intercourse of sight is the site of intercourse.

On occasion, then, Brakhage and his wife photographed each other at moments of heightened psychic and physical interaction—quarreling, for example, in what became *Wedlock House: An Intercourse:*

> As we began passing the camera back and forth, the quarrel was pitched onto a visual level. . . . Her images came out of such a quality that they could actually cut back and forth with mine. She too grabbed the light as I had done and began taking up the same form of paint-

ing—in my image with moving light source, she automatically grasped what my style was on a feeling level, and went right on with her version of it. This was the first time we were both photographing; I photographing her, she me, but in relation to the form that was springing out of me. We got glimpses of each other, in flashes of moving light, as if emerging out of long hallways in sheer darkness. All the quarrels we were having at that time became pitched on that visual level.[17]

The couple also photographed each other during lovemaking and parturition, creating the films of the first years of their marriage in which the mutual recording of family life is transformed into a means of negotiating family life, of articulating and understanding it.

The performative collaboration of these films tends to decline after Jane's substantial role in the photography of *Dog Star Man*, but the urgency of psychological and visual interdependence it reflects sustains Brakhage's entire oeuvre, necessitating a working process "pitched between" himself and Jane.[18] Eventually that source encompasses the entire family.

"By Brakhage" should be understood to mean "by way of Stan and Jane Brakhage," as it does in all my films since marriage. It is coming to mean: "by way of Stan and Jane and all the children Brakhage" because all the discoveries which used to pass only thru the instrument of myself are coming to pass thru the sensibilities of those I love. . . . Ultimately "by Brakhage" will come to be superfluous and understood as what it now ultimately is: by way of everything.[19]

There are to be sure elements of disingenuousness in such claims, and doubtless the interactive family cinema was more an aspiration than a fully achieved practice. Brakhage retained at least conscious control over the films that proceed from it, and, as in home movies in general at that time, the family patriarch generally operated the camera himself. But his constant deflection of authority from himself to the family unit in which he constituted himself, his constant reference to Jane's role in the films, and his insistence on his absolute psychic obligation to her represent a domestic premonition of a radical reorganization of the roles of producer and consumer in a genuinely social cinema.

Beyond such heuristic value however, Brakhage's innovations remind us that in his restaging of the Romantic confrontation between the individual consciousness and its surroundings, the affirmation of the self is always preliminary to escape from it. Inhabiting all the realms of

Brakhage's cinema is a tension between individuation and its transcendence, between self-consciousness and antiself-consciousness. This tension produces the paradoxical conjunction of an increasingly aggressive idiosyncratic style and a rejection of individual imaginative creativity in a mode of filmmaking that becomes essentially documentary. That shift is demonstrated in Brakhage's own understanding of his endeavor, as the following remarks from 1963 and from 1972 respectively make clear:

> OF NECESSITY I BECOME INSTRUMENT FOR THE PASSAGE OF INNER VISION, THRU ALL MY SENSIBILITIES, INTO ITS EXTERNAL FORM. My most active part in this process is to increase all my sensibilities (so that all films arise out of some total area of being or full life) AND, at the given moment of possible creation to act only out of necessity. In other words, I am principally concerned with revelation.[20]

> I am the most thorough documentary film maker in the world because I document the act of seeing as well as everything that the light brings me. . . . I have added nothing. I've just been trying to see and make a place for my seeing in the world at large.[21]

Emphasizing existential attentiveness to biological urgency as the motor of composition, the first passage reveals a development from his previous preoccupation with his own ego as representatively human and thus potentially the access to "universal concerns."[22] But it also contains residual notions of art as the realization or externalization of a process other than itself, with the artist a conduit for an activity whose origin is hidden so far behind the specific moment of composition that it dissolves into the divine. Brakhage continues to invoke this unknowable source, frequently designating it as "the Muses." But progressively those Muses are discovered in the perceptual organs themselves, and in their physiological reaction to light. The consequent "immanentism" may be understood as the postmodernist moment in Romantic poetics; and Brakhage found it in "objectism," Charles Olson's critique of "the individual as ego."

A Romantic anti-hellenism, Objectism was Olson's answer to the Aristotelian dualisms, especially the polarization of consciousness and the external world which, he believed, form the prison of Western discourse. According to Olson, we are alienated from the real by a false epistemology, entrapped in an Euclidean space that informs the very structures of language; the sensuous present of our contact with the world is constantly deferred by generalized logical classification. The reintegration of humanity as continuous with reality rather than discrete from it requires circumvention of that historically and socially conditioned consciousness and the grammar of its language. Thus the polemical center of objectism entails "the getting rid of the lyrical interference of the individual as ego, of the 'subject' and his soul," on the grounds that it is a presumption interposed between humanity and the rest of nature.[23]

The identification of perception with creation in Olson's mutually dependent aesthetic and epistemology implies a situation of the self in respect to nature and a corresponding stylistic practice, both of which may be defined by Charles Altieri's distinction between two Romantic poetic modes. The symbolist, modernist tradition of Yeats, Eliot, and Stevens derives from Coleridge's representation of "the mind's dialectical pursuit of an ideal unity," while the postmodernist, immanentist mode that culminates in Olson, Robert Duncan, and Gary Snyder is the essentially Wordsworthian "discovery and the disclosure of numinous relationships within nature [rather than] the creation of containing and structuring forms."[24] This latter mode may have recourse to historical or philosophical paradigms (as it did for both Wordsworth and Olson), but its primary imperative is the dynamic experience of what is phenomenally present, the engagement of consciousness by nature when they most illuminate each other.

Ideally the immanentist mode foregoes "any ideas or preconceptions from outside the poem,"[25] especially large mental structures that satisfy the desolate modern ego. Instead it attempts to eliminate that ego in direct contact between consciousness and nature. By rejecting the intending role of the humanist ego and of ideas that *refer* to reality rather than *embody* it, the poet is presumably allowed to go beyond the imagination to unmediated perception, to that place where consciousness and nature are in direct contact. Seeking not to describe but to enact, poetry becomes an articulation of that contact as well as the means to it. So in a successful poem, "ONE PERCEPTION MUST IMMEDIATELY AND DIRECTLY LEAD TO A FURTHER PERCEPTION." Form is then organic, a function of content discovered in the experience of creation: "FORM IS NEVER MORE THAN AN EXTENSION OF CONTENT."[26] Finally, since the ego is bypassed, the significant drama is displaced into the body. As both the source and agent of perception—the site of what Olson called *proprioception*—the body produces the biological imperative in the form of the breath, which Olson posits as the unit of composition.

Olson supplied Brakhage with a theoretical infrastructure and vocabulary for what the filmmaker had already discovered as his essential concern, the regeneration of the visual discourse of the West as it was articulated filmicly. The two-dimensional representation of three-dimensional space by the codes of Renaissance perspective and the representation of linear causality by the codes of narrative drama—both ideologically overdetermined grammars of vision—had to be destroyed and reconstructed in an immanentist way. To do so, Brakhage proposed attention to vision in as intense, extensive, and complete a way as possible. Since sight was the sense par excellence in which inside met outside, physical met psychological, it was the ideal site of proprioception; and since film was capable of recording the continuous present of the encounter between them, it was the ideal objectist medium.

The feasibility of an objectist cinema became clear when Brakhage abandoned the acted dramatic film; this move allowed him to jettison both the structure of narrative and, more importantly, the normative frame of objective vision that contained the heightened perception of the trance protagonists. *Anticipation of the Night* is usually taken as marking this transition. In this liminal work, the extremely rapid camera movement, the use of the full range of aperture and focus, the scintillating visual arpeggios, and other tropes that were to constitute Brakhage's mature style are first comprehensively articulated. *Anticipation of the Night* inaugurated Brakhage's attempt to regain an originary, prelapsarian vision; the Wordsworthian loss lived in the passage from infancy to adulthood is seen to recapitulate the debasement of the phylogenic acculturation of the West as a whole. Brakhage thinks of this debasement both in terms of the fall of unmediated visual perception into the categories of verbal language and, historically, in terms of the degenerate materialism of post-Renaissance optics.

> Imagine an eye unruled by man-made laws of perspective, an eye unprejudiced by compositional logic, an eye which does not respond to the name of everything but which must know each object encountered in life through an adventure of perception. How many colors are there in a field of grass to the crawling baby unaware of "Green"? How many rainbows can create light for the untutored eye? How aware of variations in heat waves can that eye be? Imagine a world alive with incomprehensible objects and shimmering, with an endless variety of movement and innumerable gradations of color. Imagine a world before "the beginning was the word."[27]

This famous manifesto is parallel to Olson's meta-project of replacing "the Classic-representational by the *primitive abstract*,"[28] and it supplies the basis for Brakhage's use of the body as an epistemological instrument.

The attempt to circumvent the cultural coding of received visual languages produces the coherence of his theory and practice during the sixties. The overwhelming visual presence and energy of Brakhage's work in this period derives from several factors: he rejects sound as the vehicle of verbal categories as well as a detraction from the visual; and he is totally involved in the shooting process at a physical level, positing the camera as both an extension of the eye and a material-specific medium for the collection of light. All these strategies manifest his insistence that the film must generate itself out of the immediate present of perception.

Brakhage's project is thus to return to continuity what previous filmmaking, in its reproduction of Western ontology, has distinguished as three separate realms: the phenomenal world; the optical apparatuses, both mechanical and biological; and the work of the brain-memory (imagination, "close-eye vision," hypnagogic and eidetic imagery, and dream). In the integration of these realms, the dualisms that sustain almost all other uses of film—the dualisms of subject and object, of physiological and psychological, of perception and creation, and of vision and its instruments—are subsumed in a single gestalt. Once Brakhage had committed himself to first-person vision, the documentary mode was open to him. The bridging of the *I* and the *eye* in the interacting physiology and psychology of perception, and the mediation of subjectivity and objectivity via light and the apparatus form the matrix of his oeuvre. The titles of some of his most magisterial achievements—*The Art of Vision, The Riddle of Lumen, The Act of Seeing with One's Own Eyes,* and *The Text of Light*—attest to the priority and fecundity of this major preoccupation, but also to the variety of contexts in which it was deployed.

Attention to different areas within the general matrix produce the different subgeneric divisions of Brakhage's work and the different phases of his career. The first-person perception of the major mode—the epic spectacle of his family life which begins with the lovemaking and childbirth films of the early 1960s and continues for the next fifteen years—itself subtends various collateral forms. The autobiography of perception is variously displaced in considerations of specific topics but also in other modalities such as film letters. The pursuit of lost vision is a recurring project, though the films in which this is undertaken always involve the perception of material objects in which traces of the past are supposed to have been preserved. Thus the reconstruction of prenatal vision and children's vision in the *Scenes from Under Childhood* series includes the perception of children—how children look, in both senses. The more strictly autobiographical project of *Sincerity* and its cognate *Duplicity,* in which

Brakhage attempts to rediscover his own childhood and adolescence, entails the camera's scrutiny of old photographs, as if their appearance preserved sight itself. Other films are more critically oriented to the apparatus and to film-specific sights that can be generated by editing or other material work on the filmstrip. Such techniques are supposed either to simulate or stimulate optical effects otherwise unavailable or to have some metaphoric relationship to them. In the most elaborate of the hand-painted films—*The Horseman, The Woman and The Moth,* example—the drama of the filmmaker's interaction with the materials of the film's construction is supposed optically to recapitulate hypnagogic vision.

At other moments within this strategic oscillation between "the light *of* Nature" and "the Nature of Light,"[29] Brakhage is most interested in the peculiarities of his own eyesight. He explores both phosphenes and other forms of closed-eye vision and the open-eyed perception of, for example, the streaks of light in the sky before rain or the glow with which certain objects present themselves to him. At his most extreme, he hypostatizes light itself as an ontological absolute, invoking at such times Pound's reference to Erigena's dictum, "Omnia quae sunt, Lumina sunt" (All things that are, are lights), and thus produces his "purest" films. In them, the literal or symbolic reference of the imagery is subsumed in the sensual play of light. Even in these films, however, reflexive metaphors for the apparatus or the politics of vision appear: locks, windows, screens, and the like in the ethereal precision of *The Riddle of Lumen,* for example. Even apparently intractable works that antedate the mature mode often turn out, like *Reflections on Black,* to be narrative premonitions of it, or self-negating narratives, like *Blue Moses,* that finally reauthorize the dominant mode. Even an anomaly as remarkable as *Mothlight,* which circumvents the photographic process entirely, returns allegorically to the matrix. By displacing Brakhage's own vision into that of the moth— "what a moth might see from birth to death if black were white and white were black"[30]—it conjoins two extremes in the perceptual continuum, material nature and the light of the projector, on the materiality of the filmstrip and the retina of the spectator's eye.

Purely visual relationships—continuities or contrasts of shape, color, movement, and light—discovered in those portions of the profilmic that achieve registration in the filmic supply the main basis of Brakhage's editing. In addition, the integration of the three spheres of subject, object, and apparatus is articulated by visual analogies or metaphorical relations among the profilmic, the filmic, and Brakhage's psychophysiology. Some examples of these rhymes follow:

- between profilmic and filmic: the vertical green grass and the green scratches on the emulsion in *Prelude;* the sexual energy and the red edge-flares in *Cat's Cradle;* the baby's face and the "visual cramps" of the splice bars[31] in *Dog Star Man, Part II.*
- between filmic and subjective: the grain of the emulsion, especially of 8mm, as equivalent to closed-eye vision ("this grain field in 8 mm is like *seeing* yourself *seeing*"[32]); the solid red frames and the soft focus shots indicating prenatal and children's vision in *Scenes from Under Child-hood.*
- between profilmic and subjective: the locks and doors imprisoning the child in *The Weir-Falcon Saga* as symbols of Brakhage's entrapment in adult vision.

The articulation of relations across the different realms of the filmic supplies Brakhage with his dominant shooting and editing strategies. Consequently, rhymes among body, filmic material and apparatus, and phenomenal field are so omnipresent, so insistently foregrounded, that they usurp the priority of the literal or iconographic thrust of any represented material. As the profilmic is claimed either as evidence of the behavior of light or as metaphors for vision itself, light becomes the medium of exchange in the two-way passage between the inner and outer worlds. Affirming that the site of his creative activity is the sight of the camera eye, Brakhage translates the overall project of postmodernist poetry into cinema.

NOTES

1. See, respectively, for example, "Poetry and the Film: A Symposium," *Film Culture Reader,* ed. P. Adams Sitney (New York: Praeger, 1970); Jonas Mekas, "The Experimental Film in America," *Film Culture* 3 (May–June 1955), 15–20; and P. Adams Sitney, *Visionary Film: The American Avant-Garde,* 2d ed. (New York: Oxford University Press, 1979).

2. "Hans Richter on the Nature of Film Poetry," *Film Culture* 11 (1957), 6.

3. "Poetry and the Film," 172.

4. Ibid., 174.

5. Robert Kelly, cited in Stan Brakhage, *Metaphors on Vision* (New York: Film Culture, 1963), 82.

6. Sitney, *Visionary Film.*

7. *Brakhage Scrapbook: Collected Writings 1964–80* (New Paltz: Documentext, 1982), 113.

8. *The Avant-Garde Film: A Reader of Theory and Criticism* (New York: New York University Press, 1978), 87.

9. Though scattered and isolated earlier artisanal projects did exist, including, for example, those of Robert Florey, Watson and Webber, and Mary Ellen Bute, and the very differently conceived achievements of the Workers Film and Photo Leagues.

10. Jonas Mekas, "The Experimental Film in America," 17.

11. The term "trance film" was coined by P. Adams Sitney in respect to Maya Deren's *Meshes of the Afternoon* (1943), in which "'the heroine undertakes an interior quest. She encounters objects and sights as if they were capable of revealing the erotic mystery of the self" (*Visionary Film*, 11). It specifies the structure of what became the dominant genre of American experimental film in the 1950s and early 1960s.

12. *Film Biographies* (Turtle Island, Calif.: Berkeley, 1977).

13. *Brakhage Scrapbook*, 179.

14. Parker Tyler, *Underground Film: A Critical History* (New York: Grove Press, 1969), 26.

15. *Metaphors on Vision*, 25.

16. *Brakhage Scrapbook*, 187.

17. *Metaphors on Vision*, 6.

18. Ibid., 12.

19. Ibid., 2.

20. Ibid., 77.

21. *Brakhage Scrapbook*, 188.

22. *Metaphors on Vision*, 23.

23. Charles Olson, *Selected Writings* (New York: New Directions, 1966), 24.

24. Charles Altieri, *Enlarging the Temple: New Directions in American Poetry During the 1960s* (Lewisburg: Bucknell University Press, 1979), 17.

25. Olson, *Selected Writings*, 20.

26. Ibid., 16.

27. *Metaphors on Vision*, 23.

28. Olson, *Selected Writings*, 28.

29. *Brakhage Scrapbook*, 74.

30. Ibid., 246.

31. Ibid., 64.

32. Ibid., 481.

Selected Bibliography

The following titles are grouped into three sections. Section I features significant discussions of general issues surrounding authorship, which scholars working in the areas of media studies may wish to draw on for theoretical models, historical contexts, or interdisciplinary comparisons. Section II covers scholarship that treats general questions of authorship in the fields of film and television. Section III represents a selection of work on specific filmmakers that also advances arguments about the nature of authorship per se.

Because of the vast number of works that have relevance to the topic of authorship, I have chosen to list a large selection of titles rather than to single out and annotate a lesser number. Only works in English are included. In the case of anthologies on the subject, I have not specified the titles of individual articles within them, except for a few seminal essays by Barthes, Foucault, Sarris and others, which are cited in their original English-language sources, even though they also appear in anthologies. In the case of essays later incorporated into books by the same author, only the book is cited. Researchers wishing further guidance may consult the general introduction to this volume, where I have attempted to provide a brief gloss on the range of material available.

I. General Studies of Authorship

Alpers, Svetlana. *Rembrandt's Enterprise: The Studio and the Market* (Chicago: University of Chicago Press, 1988).

Barthes, Roland. "The Death of the Author." In *Image-Music-Text*, ed. and trans. Stephen Heath (New York: Hill & Wang, 1977), 142–48.

Benjamin, Walter. "The Author as Producer." In *Reflections*, ed. and trans. Peter Demetz (New York: Harcourt, Brace, Jovanovich, 1978), 220–38.

Birotti, Maurice, and Nicola Miller, eds. *What Is an Author?* (Manchester: Manchester University Press, 1993).

Bloom, Harold. *The Anxiety of Influence: A Theory of Poetry* (New York: Oxford University Press, 1978).

Bourdieu, Pierre. *The Field of Cultural Production*, ed. and trans. Randal Johnson (New York: Columbia University Press, 1993).

Brecht, Bertolt. *Brecht on Theatre: The Development of an Aesthetic*, ed. and trans. John Willett (New York: Hill and Wang, 1994; originally published 1957).

Burke, Seán, ed. *Authorship: From Plato to the Postmodern* (Edinburgh: Edinburgh University Press, 1995).

———. *The Death and Return of the Author: Criticism and Subjectivity in Barthes, Foucault and Derrida* (Edinburgh: Edinburgh University Press, 1992).

Chartier, Roger. "Figures of the Author." In *The Order of Books*, trans. Lydia G. Cochrane (Stanford, Calif.: Stanford University Press, 1994), 25–60.

Chinoy, Helen Krich. "The Emergence of the Director." In *Directors on Directing: A Source Book for the Modern Theater*, ed. Toby Cole and Helen Krich Chinoy (New York: MacMillan, 1963), 1–78.

Coombe, Rosemary J. *The Cultural Life of Intellectual Properties: Authorship, Appropriation and the Law* (Durham, N.C.: Duke University Press, 1998).

Ede, Lisa, and Andrea Lunsford. "Collaboration and Concepts of Authorship," *PMLA* 116:2 (March 2001): 354–69.

Edelman, Bernard. *Ownership of the Image: Elements in a Marxist Theory of Law* (London: Routledge & Kegan Paul, 1979).

Feyerabend, Paul. "Creativity: A Dangerous Myth," *Critical Inquiry* 13 (Summer 1987): 700–11.

Foucault, Michel. "What Is an Author?" In *Language, Counter-Memory, Practice*, ed. Donald F. Bouchard, trans. Donald F. Bouchard and Sherry Simon (Ithaca, N.Y.: Cornell University Press, 1977), 113–38.

Genette, Gerard. "The Name of the Author." In *Paratexts: Thresholds of Interpretation*, trans. Jane E. Lewin (New York: Cambridge University Press, 1997; originally published 1987).

Hesse, Carla. "Enlightenment Epistomology and the Laws of Authorship in Revolutionary France," *Representations* 30 (1990): 109–37.

Hughes, Justin. "The Personality Interest of Artists and Inventors in Intellectual Property," *Cardozo Arts and Entertainment Journal* 16:1 (1998): 81–182.

Inge, M. Thomas. "Collaboration and Concepts of Authorship," *PMLA* 116:3 (May 2001): 623–31.

Jaszi, Peter, and Martha Woodmansee. "The Ethical Reaches of Authorship," *South Atlantic Quarterly* 95:4 (Fall 1996): 947–78.

Kamuf, Peggy. *Signature Pieces: On the Institution of Authorship* (Ithaca, N.Y.: Cornell University Press, 1988).

Knapp, Steven, and Walter Benn Michaels. "Against Theory," *Critical Inquiry* 8 (Summer 1982): 723–42.

Leonard, James A., et al. *Authority and Textuality: Current Views of Collaborative Writing* (West Cornwall: Locust Hill, 1994).

Lunsford, Andrea A., and Lisa Ede. *Singular Texts/ Plural Authors: Perspectives on Collaborative Writing* (Carbondale: Southern Illinois University Press, 1990).

Masten, Jeffrey. *Textual Intercourse: Collaboration, Authorship, and Sexualities in Renaissance Drama* (New York: Cambridge University Press, 1997).

Meltzer, François. *Hot Property: The Stakes and Claims of Literary Originality* (Chicago: University of Chicago Press, 1993).

Miller, Jacqueline T. *Poetic License: Authority and Authorship in Medieval and Renaissance Contexts* (New York: Oxford University Press, 1986).

Miller, Nancy K. "Changing the Subject: Authorship, Writing and the Reader." In *Feminist Studies/ Critical Studies*, ed. Teresa de Lauretis (Bloomington: Indiana University Press, 1986), 102–20.

Nesbit, Molly. "What Was an Author?" *Yale French Studies* 73 (1987): 229–57.

Newberry, Michael. *Figuring Authorship in Antebellum America* (Stanford, Calif.: Stanford University Press, 1997).

North, Michael. "Authorship and Autography," *PMLA* 116:5 (October 2001): 1377–85.

Park, Clara Claiborne. "Author! Author! Reconstructing Roland Barthes," *Hudson Review* 43 (1990): 377–98.

Pease, Donald. "Author." In *Critical Terms for Literary Study*, ed. Frank Lentricchia and Thomas McLaughlin (Chicago: University of Chicago Press, 1990), 105–20.

Rodden, John. "Appraising Famous Men: Mediating Biography and Society." In *The Politics of Literary Reputation: The Making and Claiming of "St. George" Orwell* (New York: Oxford University Press, 1989), 3–14.

Rose, Mark. *Authors and Owners: The Invention of Copyright* (Cambridge, Mass.: Harvard University Press, 1993).

Saunders, David. *Authorship and Copyright* (New York: Routledge, 1992).

Saunders, David, and Ian Hunter. "Lessons from the 'Literatory': How to Historicize Authorship," *Critical Inquiry* 17:3 (1991), 479–509.

Sherman, Brad, and Alain Strowel, eds. *Of Authors and Origins: Essays on Copyright Law* (New York: Oxford University Press, 1994).

Simion, Eugene. *The Return of the Author*, trans. James W. Newcomb and Lidia Vianu (Evanston, Ill.: Northwestern University Press, 1996).

Stillinger, Jack. *Multiple Authorship and the Myth of the Solitary Genius* (New York: Oxford University Press, 1992).

Tomashevsky, Boris. "Literature and Biography." In *Readings in Russian Poetics*, ed. Ladislav Matejka and Krystyna Pomorska (Cambridge, Mass.: MIT Press, 1971), 47–55.

Trimbur, John. "Agency and the Death of the Author: A Partial Defence of Postmodernism," *JAC* 20 (2000): 283–98.

Walker, Cheryl. "Feminist Literary Criticism and the Author." *Critical Inquiry* 16.3 (Spring 1990): 551–71.

Weimann, Robert. "Text, Author-Function and Society: Towards a Sociology of Representation and Appropriation in Modern Narrative." In *Literary Theory Today*, ed. Peter Collier and Helga Geyer-Ryan (Ithaca, N.Y.: Cornell University Press, 1990), 91–106.

Wolff, Janet. "The Death of the Author." In *The Social Production of Art*, 2d ed. (New York: New York University Press, 1993), 117–43.

Woodmansee, Martha. *The Author, Art, and the Market: Rereading the History of Aesthetics* (New York: Columbia University Press, 1994).

Woodmansee, Martha, and Peter Jaszi, eds. *The Construction of Authorship: Textual Appropriation in Law and Literature* (Durham, N.C.: Duke University Press, 1994).

II. Theoretical Analyses of Authorship in Cinema and Television

Andrew, Dudley. "The Unauthorized Auteur Today." In *Film Theory Goes to the Movies*, ed. Ava Preacher Collins, Jim Collins, and Hillary Radner (New York: Routledge, 1993), 77–85. Rpt. in *Film and Theory*, ed. Robert Stam and Toby Miller (Malden, Mass.: Blackwell, 2000), 20–30.

Astruc, Alexandre. "The Birth of a New Avant-Garde: La Caméra-Styló." In *The New Wave*, ed. Peter Graham (London: Secker and Warburg, 1968; originally published 1948), 17–23.

Bazin, André. "La Politique des Auteurs," trans. Peter Graham. In *The New Wave*, ed. Peter Graham (Garden City, N.Y.: Doubleday, 1968; originally published in French in 1957), 137–56.

Bordwell, David, Janet Staiger, and Kristin Thompson. *The Classical Hollywood Cinema: Film Style and Mode of Production to 1960* (New York: Columbia University Press, 1985).

Branigan, Edward. "Diegesis and Authorship in Film," *Iris* 7 (1986): 37–54.

Browne, Nick. *Cahiers du Cinéma: The 1970s* (Cambridge, Mass.: Harvard University Press, 1990).

Carringer, Robert. "Collaboration and Concepts of Authorship," *PMLA* 116:2 (March 2001): 370–79.

Caughie, John, ed. *Theories of Authorship* (London: British Film Institute, 1981).

Clayton, Sue, and Jonathan Curling. "On Authorship," *Screen* 2:1 (Spring 1979): 35–61.

Cook, David. "Auteur Cinema and the 'Film Generation' in Hollywood." In *The New American Cinema*, ed. Jon Lewis (Durham, N.C.: Duke University Press, 1998), 11–37.

Cook, Pam, Noel King, and Toby Miller. "Authorship." In *The Cinema Book*, 2d ed., ed. Pam Cook and Mieke Bernink (London: British Film Institute, 1999), 235–319.

Corliss, Richard. "Introduction: Notes on a Screenwriters' Theory, 1973." In *Talking Pictures: Screenwriters in the American Cinema* (New York: Penguin, 1975), xvii–xxvii.

Crofts, Stephen. "Authorship and Hollywood." *Wide Angle* 5:3 (1983): 16–22. Rev. and rpt. in *The Oxford Guide to Film Studies*, ed. John Hill and Pamela Church Gibson (New York: Oxford University Press, 1998), 310–24.

Darke, Chris. "Why *Cahiers* Still Matters," *Film Comment* 37:5 (September/October 2001): 37.

Dougherty, Jay. "Not a Spike Lee Joint? Issues in the Authorship of Motion Pictures Under U.S. Copyright Law," *UCLA Law Review* 49 (2001): 225–334.

Doty, Alexander. "Whose Text Is It, Anyway?: Queer Cultures, Queer *Auteurs*, and Queer Authorship." In *Making Things Perfectly Queer: Interpreting Mass Culture* (Minneapolis: University of Minnesota Press, 1993), 17–38.

Dyer, Richard. "Believing in Fairies: The Author and the Homosexual." In *inside/out*, ed. Diana Fuss (New York: Routledge, 1991), 185–201.

Film Criticism 19:3 (Spring 1995). Special Issue on Film Authorship.

Film History 7:4 (1995). Special Issue on "Auteurism Revisited."

Fine, Richard. *Hollywood and the Profession of Authorship, 1928–1940* (Ann Arbor, Mich.: UMI Research Press, 1985).

Fischer, Lucy. *Shot/Countershot: Film Tradition and Women's Cinema* (Princeton, N.J.: Princeton University Press, 1989).

Flitterman-Lewis, Sandy. "To Desire Differently: Feminism and the French Cinema." In *Film and Theory*, ed. Robert Stam and Toby Miller (Malden, Mass.: Blackwell, 2000), 16–19.

Forbes, Elliot, and David Pierce. "Who Owns the Movies?" *Film Comment* 30:6 (1994): 43–50.

Gaines, Jane. "The Portrait of Oscar Wilde: Photography 'Surprises' the Law." In *Contested Cutlure: The Image, the Voice, and the Law* (Chapel Hill, N.C.: University of North Carolina Press, 1991), 42–83.

Grant, Catherine. "www.auteur.com?" *Screen* 41:1 (Spring 2000): 101–108.

Heath, Stephen. "Comment on 'The Idea of Authorship,'" *Screen* 14:3 (Autumn 1973).

Hess, John. "La Politique des Auteurs, Part 1," *Jump/Cut* 1 (May/June 1974): 19–22.

———. "La Politique des Auteurs, Part 2," *Jump/Cut* 2 (July/August 1974): 20–22.

Hillier, Jim, ed. *Cahiers du Cinéma: The 1950s: Neo-Realism, Hollywood, New Wave* (Cambridge, Mass.: Harvard University Press, 1985).

———. *Cahiers du Cinéma: The 1960s: New Wave, New Cinema, Reevaluating Hollywood* (Cambridge, Mass.: Harvard University Press, 1986).

Kehr, Dave. "*Cahiers du Cinéma,*" *Film Comment* 37.5 (September/October 2001): 30–36.

Lapsley, Robert, and Michael Westlake. "Authorship." In *Film Theory: An Introduction* (Manchester: Manchester University Press, 1988), 105–28.

Levy, Emmanuel. *Citizen Sarris, American Film Critic: Essays in Honor of Andrew Sarris* (Lanham, Md.: Scarecrow Press, 2001).

Litwak, Mark. *Reel Power: The Struggle for Influence and Success in the New Hollywood* (New York: William Morrow, 1986).

Maule, Rosanna. "De-Authoring the Auteur: Postmodern Politics of Interpellation in Contemporary European Cinema." In *Postmodernism in the Cinema,* ed. Cristina Degli-Esposti (New York: Oxford University Press, 1998), 113–30.

Maltby, Richard. "The Multiple Logics of Hollywood Cinema" and "Theories after Poststructuralism." In *Hollywood Cinema* (Cambridge, Mass.: Blackwell, 1995), 30–35, 434–40.

Mayne, Judith. "Female Authorship Reconsidered." In *The Woman at the Keyhole: Feminism and Women's Cinema* (Bloomington: Indiana University Press, 1990), 89–123.

———. "Lesbian Looks: Dorothy Arzner and Female Authorship." In *Feminism and Film,* ed. E. Ann Kaplan (New York: Oxford University Press, 2000), 159–80.

Murray, Janet. "Agency." In *Hamlet on the Holodeck: The Future of Narrative in Cyberspace* (Cambridge, Mass.: MIT Press, 1997), 126–53.

Naremore, James. "Authorship and the Cultural Politics of Film Criticism," *Film Quarterly* 44:1 (1980): 14–22.

Neale, Steve. "Art Cinema as Institution," *Screen* 27:1 (1981): 11–39.

Newcomb, Horace, and Robert S. Alley. "The Television Producer: An Introduction." In *The Producer's Medium: Conversations with Creators of American TV* (New York: Oxford University Press, 1983), 3–45.

Perkins, V. F. "Direction and Authorship." In *Film as Film* (Middlesex, Eng.: Penguin Books, 1972), 158–86.

———. "Film Authorship: The Premature Burial," *CineAction* 21/22 (1990): 57–64.

Polan, Dana. "Auteur Desire." In *Screening the Past,* uploaded March 1, 2001. www.latrobe.edu.au/screeningthepast/firstrelease/fr0301/dpfr12a.htm.

Porter, Vincent. "Film Copyright, Film Culture," *Screen* 19:1 (1978): 90–108.

Powdermaker, Hortense. *Hollywood: The Dream Factory: An Anthropologist Looks at Moviemakers* (Boston: Little, Brown and Company, 1950).

Rosenbaum, Jonathan. "Guilty by Omission," *Film Comment* 27:5 (September/October 1991): 42–45.

Rosten, Leo. *Hollywood: The Movie Colony, the Movie Makers* (New York: Harcourt, Brace, 1941).

Salokannel, Marjut. *Ownership of Rights in Audiovisual Productions: A Comparative Study* (London: Kluwer Law International, 1997).

Sarris, Andrew. "Notes on the *Auteur* Theory in 1962,"*Film Culture* 27 (1962/63): 1–8. Rpt. in Sarris, *The American Cinema: Directors and Direction 1929-1968* (New York: Dutton, 1968; rpt. Chicago: University of Chicago Press, 1985); rpt. in *Film Theory and Criticism*, ed. Gerald Mast and Marshall Cohen (New York: Oxford University Press, 1985), 527–40.

———. "Toward a Theory of Film History." In *Interviews with Film Directors*, ed. Andrew Sarris (New York: Avon, 1967).

Saxton, Christine. "The Collective Voice as Cultural Voice," *Cinema Journal* 26:1 (Fall 1986), 19–30.

Solanas, Fernando, and Octavio Getino. "Towards a Third Cinema: Notes and Experiences for the Development of a Cinema of Liberation in the Third World." In *The New Latin-American Cinema*, vol. I, ed. Michael T. Martin (Detroit, Mich.: Wayne State University Press, 1997), 33–58.

Solman, Greg. "Uncertain Glory," *Film Comment* 29: 3 (May–June 1993): 19–27 [on directors' cut editions].

Staiger, Janet. "Blueprints for Feature Films: Hollywood's Continuity Scripts." In *The American Film Industry*, ed. Tino Balio (Madison: University of Wisconsin Press, 1985), 173–92.

———. " 'Tame' Authors and the Corporate Laboratory: Stories, Writers and Scenarios in Hollywood," *Quarterly Review of Film Studies* 8:4 (Fall 1983): 33–45.

Stam, Robert. "The Cult of the Auteur," "The Americanization of Auteur Theory," and "Interrogating Authorship and Genre." In *Film Theory: An Introduction* (New York: Blackwell, 2000), 83–92, 123–130.

Stoddart, Helen. "Auteurism and Film Authorship." In *Approaches to Popular Film*, ed. Joanne Hollins and Mark Jancovich (Manchester: Manchester University Press, 1995), 37–58.

Thompson, Robert J., and Gary Burns, eds. *Making Television: Authorship and the Production Process* (New York: Praeger, 1990).

Trasker, Yvonne. "Authorship and Contemporary Film Culture," In *Fifty Contemporary Filmmakers*, ed. Yvonne Trasker (New York: Routledge, 2002), 1–5.

Truffaut, François. "A Certain Tendency in the French Cinema." *Cahiers du Cinéma in English* I (1966): 30–40. Rpt. in *Movies and Methods*, vol I, ed. Bill Nichols (Berkeley: University of California Press, 1976); rpt. in *The Film Studies Reader*, ed. Joanna Hollins, Peter Hutchings, and Mark Jancovich (London: Arnold, 2000), 58–63.

Wexman, Virginia Wright. "Film as Art and Filmmakers as Artists: 100 Years," *Arachné* 2:2 (1995): 265–78.

Wide Angle 6:1. Special Issue on Film Authorship.

Wollen, Peter. "The Auteur Theory." In *Signs and Meaning in the Cinema* (Bloomington: Indiana University Press, 1972), 74–115.

III. Case Studies

Bach, Steven. *Final Cut: Art, Money, and Ego in the Making of* Heaven's Gate, *the Film That Sank United Artists,* updated ed. (New York: Newmarket Press, 1999).

Bellour, Raymond. "Hitchcock, the Enunciator," trans. Bertrand Augst and Hilary Radner, *Camera Obscura* 2 (Fall 1977): 66–91.

Bordwell, David. "An Author and His Legend." In *Carl-Theodor Dreyer* (Berkeley: University of California Press, 1981), 9–24.

———. "A Filmmaker's Legend." In *Ozu: The Poetics of Cinema* (Princeton, N.J.: Princeton University Press, 1988), 5–7.

Braddock, Jeremy, and Stephen Hock, eds. *Directed by Allen Smithee* (Minneapolis: University of Minnesota Press, 2001).

Brewster, Ben. "Brecht and the Film Industry," *Screen* 16:4 (Winter 1975–1976): 16–29.

———. "Notes on the Text *Young Mr. Lincoln* by the Editors of *Cahiers du Cinéma,*" *Screen* 17:1 (Spring 1976).

Bruno, Giuliana. "Anatomy of an Analysis: The Authorial Noir." In *Streetwalking on a Ruined Map: Cultural Theory and the City Films of Elvira Notari* (Princeton, N.J.: Princeton University Press, 1993), 233–40.

Budd, Michael. "Authorship as a Commodity: The Art Cinema and *The Cabinet of Dr. Caligari,*" *Wide Angle* 6:1 (1984): 12–19.

Cahiers du Cinéma editors. "John Ford's *Young Mr. Lincoln,*" trans. Helen Lackner and Diana Matias, *Screen* 13:3 (Autumn, 1972): 5–44. Rpt. in *Movies and Methods,* vol. I, ed. Bill Nichols (Berkeley: University of California Press, 1976), 493–528; rpt. in *Film Theory and Criticism,* 3d ed., ed. Gerald Mast and Marshall Cohen (New York: Oxford University Press, 1985; originally published 1970), 695–740.

Carringer, Robert. *The Making of* Citzen Kane (Berkeley: University of California Press, 1996).

Coward, Rosalind. "Dennis Potter and the Question of the Television Author." *Film and Theory: An Anthology,* ed. Robert Stam and Toby Miller (Malden, Mass.: Blackwell, 2000), 7–15.

Elsaesser, Thomas. "The Old, the Young and the New: Commerce, Art Cinema and *Autorenfilm*" and "The Author in the Film: Self Expression as Self-Representation." In *New German Cinema: A History* (New Brunswick, N.J.: Rutgers University Press, 1989), 36–116.

———. *Fassbinder's Germany: History, Identity, Subject* (Amsterdam: Amsterdam University Press, 1996).

Erb, Cynthia. "A Showman's Dream: The Production and Release of *King Kong.*" In *Tracking* King Kong: *A Hollywood Icon in World Culture* (Detroit, Mich.: Wayne State University Press, 1998), 31–64.

Harmetz, Aljean. *The Making of* The Wizard of Oz: *Movies, Magic and Studio Power in the Prime of MGM* (New York: Hyperion, 1998).

———. *On the Road to Tara: The Making of* Gone With the Wind (New York: Harry N. Abrams, 1996).

———. *"Round Up the Usual Suspects": The Making of* Casablanca (New York: Hyperion Books, 1993).

Jewell, Richard. "Orson Welles and the Studio System: The RKO Context." In *Perspectives on* Citizen Kane, ed. Ronald Gottesmann (Boston: G. K. Hall, 1995).

Kapsis, Robert. E. *Hitchcock: The Making of a Reputation* (Chicago: University of Chicago Press, 1992).

Kerr, Paul. "My Name Is Joseph H. Lewis," *Screen* 24:4–5 (July–October 1983): 48–67. Rpt. in *The Studio System*, ed. Janet Staiger (New Brunswick, N.J.: Rutgers University Press, 1994), 50–73.

Klawans, Stuart. "The Politics of Authorship." *Film Follies: The Cinema Out of Order* (New York: Cassell, 1999), 41–68 [on Erich von Stroheim].

Klinger, Barbara. *Melodrama and Meaning: History, Culture and the Films of Douglas Sirk* (Bloomington: Indiana University Press, 1994).

Koszarski, Richard. *The Man You Loved to Hate: Erich Von Stroheim and Hollywood* (New York: Oxford University Press, 1983).

Langer, Mark. "*Tabu:* The Making of a Film," *Cinema Journal* 24:3 (Spring 1985): 42–64.

Mayne, Judith. *Directed by Dorothy Arzner* (Bloomington: Indiana University Press, 1994).

Modleski, Tania. "Hitchcock, Feminism, and the Patriarchal Unconscious." In *The Women Who Knew Too Much: Hitchcock and Feminist Theory* (New York: Methuen, 1988), 5–15.

Medhurst, Andy. "That Special Thrill: *Brief Encounter,* Homosexuality and Authorship," *Screen* 32:2 (1991): 197–208.

Musser, Charles. *Before the Nickelodeon: Edwin S. Porter and the Edison Manufacturing Company* (Berkeley: University of California Press, 1991).

Naremore, James. *The Films of Vincente Minnelli* (New York: Cambridge University Press, 1993).

Nowell-Smith, Geoffrey. *Visconti* (London: Secker and Warburg, 1967).

Polan, Dana. "Rethinking Authorship." In *Jane Campion* (Bloomington: Indiana University Press, 2002).

Rogin, Michael. "'The Sword Became a Flashing Vision': D. W. Griffith's *Birth of a Nation,*" *Representations* 9 (Winter 1985): 150–195.

Rothenberg, Randall. "Yesterday's Boob Tube Is Today's High Art," *New York Times,* October 17, 1990, Sec. H. 1, 39.

Rothman, William. "Postscript." In *Hitchcock: The Murderous Gaze* (Cambridge, Mass.: Harvard University Press, 1982).

Self, Robert. "Robert Altman and the Theory of Authorship," *Cinema Journal* 25:1 (Fall, 1985): 2–10.

Sklar, Robert, and Vito Zagarrio, eds. *Frank Capra: Authorship and the Studio System* (Philadelphia: Temple University Press, 1998).

Studlar, Gaylyn, and David Desser, eds. *Reflections in a Male Eye: John Huston and the American Experience* (Washington, DC.: Smithsonian Press, 1993).

Wood, Robin. "The Question of Authorship." In *Hitchcock's Films Revisited* (New York: Columbia University Press, 1989), 1–27.

Wyatt, Justin. "Economic Constraints/Economic Opportunities: Robert Altman as Auteur," *The Velvet Light Trap* 38 (Fall 1996): 51–67.

Yacowar, Maurice. *The Films of Paul Morrissey* (New York: Cambridge University Press, 1993).

Contributors

David Bordwell is Jacques Ledoux Professor of Film Studies at the University of Wisconsin-Madison. He has written several books on film history and theory, most recently *Planet Hong Kong: Popular Cinema and the Art of Entertainment* (2000).

Pearl Bowser is founder and director of African Diaspora Images, a collection of historical and contemporary African-American and African films and memorabilia. She is coauthor, with Louise Spence, of *Writing Himself into History: Oscar Micheaux, His Silent Films, and His Audiences* (2000).

Timothy Corrigan is Professor of English and Film Studies at Temple University. His books include *Film and Literature: An Introduction and Reader* (1998), *A Cinema without Walls: Movies and Culture after Vietnam* (1991), *Writing about Film* (2000), and *New German Film: The Displaced Image* (1994).

Marvin D'Lugo is Professor of Spanish and Screen Studies at Clark University. He is author of two books on Spanish cinema: *The Films of Carlos Saura: The Practice of Seeing* (1991) and *Guide to the Cinema of Spain* (1997). He has written extensively on Spanish and Latin American film topics and is currently working on a book-length study of Spanish-language international co-productions.

Tom Gunning is a Professor in the Art Department and the Acting Chair of the Cinema and Media Committee at the University of Chicago. Author of *D. W. Griffith and the Origins of American Narrative Film* (1991), and the recently published *The Films of Fritz Lang: Allegories of Modernity and Vision* (2000), he has written numerous essays on early and international silent cinema, and on the development of later American cinema, in terms of Hollywood genres and directors as well as avant garde film.

Sumiko Higashi is professor emerita in the Department of History at SUNY Brockport. She is the author of *Cecil B. DeMille and American Culture: The Silent Era* (1994) and numerous works on women in American silent film, silent film history, and the historical film.

David E. James teaches at the University of Southern California. His most recent book is *Power Misses: Essays Across (Un)Popular Culture* (1996).

Colin MacCabe teaches English and Film at Pittsburgh and Exeter Universities. He previously taught at the universities of Cambridge and Strathclyde and between 1985 and 1998 he worked at the British Film Institute first as Head of Production and then as Head of Research. His most recent book was *The Eloquence of the Vulgar* (1999).

Judith Mayne is Professor of French and Women's Studies at Ohio State University. She is the author of several books in film studies, including *Framed: Lesbians, Feminists and Media Culture* (2000) and *Directed by Dorothy Arzner* (1994).

Chon A. Noriega is Professor in the UCLA Department of Film, Television, and Digital Media and Associate Director of the UCLA Chicano Studies Research Center. He is author of *Shot in America: Television, the State, and the Rise of Chicano Cinema* (2000). He is also editor of eight books on Latino media, performance and visual art and is editor of *Aztlan: A Journal of Chicano Studies*.

Marjut Salokannel has worked as a lawyer for the Finnish government and has acted as a counsel in the film industry. She has held various academic positions since 1987 in the University of Helsinki and the Academy of Finland. She has written extensively on copyright questions relating to audiovisual rights and new media, including the book *Ownership of Rights in Audiovisual Production* (1997). She is currently the Director of an Academy of Finland research project on redefining the boundaries of intellectual property rights.

Andrew Sarris is Professor of film at Columbia University. Among his many books and articles is *The American Cinema: Directors and Directions, 1929–1968* (1968).

Tom Schatz is Professor and Chair of the Radio-Television-Film Department at the University of Texas. His books include *Hollywood Genres* (1981), *The Genius of the System* (1996), and *Boom and Bust: American Cinema in the 1940s* (1997).

Kaja Silverman is professor of Rhetoric at the University of California, Berkeley. Among her most recent books are *World Spectators (Cultural Memory in the Present)* (2000) and *Male Subjectivity at the Margins* (1992).

Louise Spence teaches Media Studies at Sacred Heart University. Coauthor (with Pearl Bowser) of *Writing Himself into History: Oscar Micheaux, His Silent Films, and His Audiences* (2000), she has also published articles in numerous academic journals and has contributed to several anthologies.

Virginia Wright Wexman teaches film and media studies at the University of Illinois at Chicago, where she is Professor of English. The author of numerous books and articles, including *Creating the Couple: Love, Marriage and Hollywood Performance* (1993), she is currently working on a history of the Directors Guild of America.

Index